Gandhi in the Twenty First Cent

Anshuman Behera · Shailesh Nayak
Editors

Gandhi in the Twenty First Century

Ideas and Relevance

NIAS

Springer

Editors
Anshuman Behera
National Institute of Advanced Studies
Bengaluru, Karnataka, India

Shailesh Nayak
National Institute of Advanced Studies
Bengaluru, Karnataka, India

ISBN 978-981-16-8478-4   ISBN 978-981-16-8476-0 (eBook)
https://doi.org/10.1007/978-981-16-8476-0

© National Institute of Advanced Studies 2022
This work is subject to copyright. All rights are solely and exclusively licensed by the Publisher, whether the whole or part of the material is concerned, specifically the rights of translation, reprinting, reuse of illustrations, recitation, broadcasting, reproduction on microfilms or in any other physical way, and transmission or information storage and retrieval, electronic adaptation, computer software, or by similar or dissimilar methodology now known or hereafter developed.
The use of general descriptive names, registered names, trademarks, service marks, etc. in this publication does not imply, even in the absence of a specific statement, that such names are exempt from the relevant protective laws and regulations and therefore free for general use.
The publisher, the authors and the editors are safe to assume that the advice and information in this book are believed to be true and accurate at the date of publication. Neither the publisher nor the authors or the editors give a warranty, expressed or implied, with respect to the material contained herein or for any errors or omissions that may have been made. The publisher remains neutral with regard to jurisdictional claims in published maps and institutional affiliations.

This Springer imprint is published by the registered company Springer Nature Singapore Pte Ltd.
The registered company address is: 152 Beach Road, #21-01/04 Gateway East, Singapore 189721, Singapore

Acknowledgements

The idea of this book was conceived following a conference on 'Gandhi @ 150: Ideas and Relevance to Contemporary Societal Challenges' which was organised at National Institute of Advanced Studies (NIAS) in September 2019. The intense discussions on Gandhi during the conference guided us to pick up the theme of revisiting Gandhi's ideas and their relevance in twenty-first century. In the process of completion of this project, we have received support from several people. We would like to thank the NIAS community for wholeheartedly participating in the conference and subsequently discussing and debating their ideas with us whenever we approached them. We owe gratitude to Shri Subramaniam Ramadorai, the Chairman of NIAS Council, for his support in terms of supporting this book project and sharing his critical insights on the relevance of Gandhi's vision on trusteeship in the contemporary period. We also remember the contribution of Prof. Lajwanti Chattani in this book project. Unfortunately, she could not contribute her paper which she read during conference because of her ill health. We thank her for her constant support in the completion of this project. We would also like to thank all the contributors of this volume for patiently responding to our reminders and request during this unprecedented trying times. Without their support this book would not have been a possibility. The comments and suggestions we received from the anonymous reviewers on the book have had a substantial role in shaping the book better. We thank the reviewers for their comments and suggestions. Last, but certainly not the least, we thank Ms. Satvinder Kaur, Senior Editor, Humanities and Social Sciences, Springer India, for her constant support and patience in guiding and helping us in the entire process of finalising the volume.

Contents

Part I Introduction

1 Gandhi in the Twenty-First Century: Ideas and Relevance 3
   Anshuman Behera and Shailesh Nayak

Part II Democracy, Development and Swaraj

2 Gandhi, Oceanic Circle, and Participatory Democracy 19
   Arun Kumar Patnaik

3 Sustainable Development Goals in Gandhi's Thought
   Perspective 37
   Sudarshan Iyengar

4 The Great *Tapasvi*: The Ethics of Gandhi's Politics *Swabhava,
   Ramrajya, Satyagraha, Tapasya* 57
   Bindu Puri

5 Governance and Public Policy in India: Gandhian Perspective 67
   Chetan Singai

Part III Science, Values and Education

6 Making of a Man: A Reading of Gandhi's Philosophy in 21st
   Century 81
   Ranjan K. Panda

7 Between Fact and Value: Locating Gandhian Science 97
   Subhasis Sahoo

8 Education for Un-Alienated Life: Gandhian Principles 113
   Satyabrata Kar

Part IV Environment and Public Health

9 Resolving Environmental Crises: A Gandhian Approach 133
   Nibedita Priyadarshini Jena

10 Mahatma Gandhi's Insights on Air Pollution and Clean Air 147
   S. N. Sahu

11 Mahatma Gandhi and Public Health in India 161
   Rajni Kant

Part V Conflict Resolution and Peace

12 Peaceful Resolution of Violent Conflicts in India: The
   Gandhian Way 175
   Anshuman Behera

13 Gandhi's *Satya*: Truth Entails Peace 189
   Venkata Rayudu Posina

14 Dissent and Protest Movements in India: Revisiting Gandhi's
   Ideas of Peaceful Protest 199
   Ambikesh Kumar Tripathi

15 Mahatma Gandhi: Architect of Non-violent Conflict
   Resolution 211
   Pascal Alan Nazareth

About the Editors

Anshuman Behera is Associate Professor in Conflict Resolution and Peace Research Programme at NIAS, Bengaluru. He earned a Doctorate Degree in Political Science, University of Hyderabad, Telengana. He has co-edited a book on 'Reasoning Indian Politics' published by Routledge in 2018 and co-authored a book on 'Militant Groups in South Asia' published by Pentagon Press and IDSA in 2014. His research interests include social–political conflicts and conflict resolution, political processes in South Asia and political theory.

Shailesh Nayak is Director of National Institute of Advanced Studies, Bengaluru, and Chancellor of TERI Institute of Advanced Studies, New Delhi. He obtained his Ph.D. degree in Geology from the M.S University of Baroda in 1980. Being Former Secretary, Ministry of Earth Sciences, and Chair, Earth System Science Organisation (ESSO) during 2008–2015, he had set up the state-of-the-art tsunami warning system for the Indian Ocean and developed marine services. He was conferred the ISC Vikram Sarabhai Memorial Award—2012.

Abbreviations

AIHB	All India Handicrafts Board
AISA	All India Spinners Association
AIVIA	All India Village Industries Association
CAA	Citizenship Amendment Act
CAPART	Council for Advancement of People's Action and Rural Technology
CPI	Maoist-Communist Party of India-Maoist
CWMG	Collected Works of Mahatma Gandhi
DPSP	Directive Principles of State Policy
GDP	Gross Domestic Production
GS	Gandhian Science
HDC	Handicraft Development Corporation
IIT	Indian Institute of Technology
INA	Indian National Army
J&K	Jammu and Kashmir
JNU	Jawaharlal Nehru University
KVIC	Khadi and Village Industries Commission
LDC	Less developed countries
MNREGA	Mahatma Gandhi Rural Employment Guarantee Act
NEP	National Education Policy
NPM	New Public Management
NRC	National Register of Citizens
OBC	Other Backward Caste
PSM	People's Science Movements
PWG	People's War Group
RTE	Right to Education
S&T	Science and technology
SASS	Swaraj, Antyodaya, Sarvodaya and Satyagraha
SBM	Swachh Bharat Mission
SDG	Sustainable Development Goals
ST	Scheduled Tribe
UNDP	United Nations Development Program

UNESCO	United Nations Educational, Scientific and Cultural Organization
UNICEF	United Nations Children's Fund
UN	United Nations
WHO	World Health Organization

Part I
Introduction

Chapter 1
Gandhi in the Twenty-First Century: Ideas and Relevance

Anshuman Behera and Shailesh Nayak

Abstract This is an introductory chapter of this edited volume. This chapter reflects on the relevance of Gandhian ideas in dealing with the contemporary societal challenges. Departing from a body of literature that confines Gandhi and his ideas to a specific time, this chapter holds the view that Gandhian ideas transcend time. Accordingly, the chapter stresses on the critical need for revisiting Gandhi's ideas keeping in mind the challenges that the society is witnessing. To blur the distinction between Gandhi as a philosopher, an activist, and a freedom fighter, this chapter highlights the surplus element in Gandhi in his multiple personality and roles. The first part of the chapter reasons with the need for and importance of revisiting and engaging with Gandhi's ideas. And the second part briefly explains the fourteen critical themes pertaining to Gandhi's ideas around which the book has been compiled.

Keywords Gandhi · Relevance of Gandhi's ideas · Surplus philosopher · Ramraj · Bhoodaan · Gramdaan

Introduction

One of the greatest leaders of his people and of humankind, Mahatma Gandhi was a pacifist who brought social and political change. He lived during the ages of fascist leaders, communist dictators, and the colonial masters. However, his ideas and philosophies concerning the issues of *Swaraj* (freedom and self-rule), empowerment of the lower strata of the social order and women, communal harmony amongst socially divided identities, and the struggle against racial discrimination offered a contrary and the most acceptable socio-political development. It also helped to liberate millions of people in the Asian, African, and American nations. In the Indian

A. Behera (✉) · S. Nayak
National Institute of Advanced Studies, Indian Institute of Science Campus, Bengaluru, Karnataka, India
e-mail: anshumanbehera@nias.res.in

S. Nayak
e-mail: shailesh@nias.res.in

context, the most important contribution of Gandhi, unlike that of other freedom fighters, is his ability to link the social, political, economic, and cultural issues and discriminations with the larger frame of India's freedom struggle against the British colonial rule. Gandhi's ideas of seeking freedom from the imperial rule make him one of the towering anti-imperial thinkers. His ideas of independence of humankind are state-centric and explicitly political, very much rooted in socio-cultural bases. Gandhi is mostly remembered as the Father of the Nation, rightly so for transforming India from a colony of the British to a nation. His contributions on strengthening and ensuring the autonomy of the 'village republic' in aspects such as economic self-reliance, empowerment of the women, struggle against the social evils of untouchability, and bridging the gaps amongst the religious communities have had substantial and critical implications on Indian society. Gandhi's ideas and philosophies continue to offer solutions to most of the socio-political challenges that humankind witnesses, but at the same time a re-engagement with his ideas with the contemporary issues could open up fresh perspectives. In line with the commemoration of Gandhi's 150th birth anniversary across the globe, the major objective of this book is to revisit his ideas on two significant counts: first, the question about the relevance of degree of Gandhi's ideas in the twenty-first century, when the humankind is witnessing rapid changes in every sphere of their lives; and second, the question of whether his ideas offer potential solutions to the multiple challenges faced by human society in the twenty-first century.

Gandhi in the Twenty-First Century

Any discussion on Mahatma Gandhi invariably begins, rightfully so, with a certain sense of reverence for his personality and ideas. For a person who patiently believed and followed non-violence, truth, and non-possession, amongst many other noble principles, to fight against the mighty British empire, age-old practices of untouchability and apartheid, and the very popular western-centric modernisation, such reverences are not completely unnatural. Ideally, Mahatma Gandhi, as one of the most revered personalities, should not be diluted with his position as a philosopher, a political activist, a politician, and moreover, a social reformer. Accordingly, in this book the focus is more on Gandhi's ideas and philosophies than on his personality. In its attempt to engage with Gandhi's ideas, the book also explores its relevance in the recent times and in that process, it becomes necessary to juxtapose his ideas with the contemporary challenges. There could be a question here as to why Gandhi and his ideas. As rightly put by Arjun Appadurai on Gandhi, 'no modern leader was as fully a product of his times as committed to changing what these times could be and become' (Appadurai, 2011). Most of Gandhi's ideas on many matters concerning humankind have transcended time. They were constructive in the past, and they seem to be so in the present and, as many believe, they will have same bearing in the future as well. On the relevance of Gandhi, Jayaprakash Narayan, one of the greatest socio-political reformers of India once said: 'As long as there is violence which threatens the very future of humanity, the relevance of Gandhi would continue. He will remain relevant till the danger of total annihilation of humanity is removed' (1969). Similarly, to many other, Mahatma Gandhi's ideas were ahead of his time. General Douglas McArthur opines the same and said: 'In the evolution of civilisation if it is to survive, all men cannot fail eventually to adopt his belief that the process of mass application of force to resolve continuous issues is fundamentally wrong but contains within itself the germs of self-destruction' (McArthur as cited in Pyarelal, 1958). McArthur was referring to the importance of Gandhi's ideas of non-violence for the survivability and sustainability of the human civilisation.

The relevance of Gandhi's ideas can be better articulated through formulating specific questions on contemporary societal challenges and juxtaposing it with those challenges. In this connection, Terchek (1986) writes: 'Plato is important today not because we want to construct the small polity he envisioned in The Republic, but because we want to know what he had to say about justice. By the same token, Rousseau's simple society is not what attracts the modern reader to The Social Contract, but rather a concern about legitimacy and civic virtue. In a similar vein, Gandhi needs to be read with the intention of finding what he wanted to accomplish rather than concentrating on some of his suggested institutional solutions.' This book also deals with various aspects of Gandhi other than exploring the relevance of his ideas in resolving these challenges.

A major way the scholars have engaged with Gandhi is as a philosopher and a political theorist. This position is debated though. In some scholars' view, Gandhi is not being acknowledged as a political thinker or a philosopher on par with Plato or Karl Marx (Srivastava, 1968). The logic behind rejecting Gandhi as a philosopher is that unlike Plato or Marx, Gandhi hardly propounded theories and concepts of politics, and so he is not considered as a political theorist. A contrary position to this claim holds the view that Gandhi's ideas are deeply rooted in abstract epistemologies that make him a philosopher. Bilgrami (2003) argues: 'about specific political strategies in specific contexts flowed from ideas that were very remote from politics; instead, they flowed from and were integrated to the most abstract epistemological and methodological commitments.' Arne Naees, a leading Gandhian scholar states: 'Gandhi needs help to enter the history of philosophy and his philosophy has to be extracted from action and speech' (Galtung, 2011). In other words, Gandhi's socio-political actions have deep philosophical foundations. Scholars have observed that in the present scenario there is a subtle but very important shift in Indian politics from philosopher politicians to politicians seeking philosophy from others (Pani & Behera, 2018). In that context, Gandhi would place his philosophy first and actions later. Nonetheless, there could be two important factors that highlight his actions overshadowing the philosophical foundations of his ideas. Firstly, the popular expectation is to situate him as a great man of spirituality and uniqueness; secondly, the intellectuals' interest is to locate him as a nationalist leader with a strikingly effective method of non-violent political actions (Bilgrami, 2002). Moreover, as Bilgrami argues, a sentimental perception of him as a *Mahatma* (a great soul) has substantially outshone the scope of exploring Gandhi as a political thinker. As suggested by Arne Naees, there is a need to extract philosophy from Gandhi's actions. This is evident from the fact that his ideas, which are morphed often into slogans, have strong philosophical and conceptual foundations. For instance, Gandhi's idea of non-violence offers critical conceptual foundation, and it should not be confined to the usage of mere political actions. The very concept of non-violence, unlike that of violence, hardly has any classification, and it is practised for social and political causes without any condition. Similarly, the idea of *Satyagraha* and those who practise it, the *Satyagrahis*, have universal acceptance and application of the same. The rules prescribed for a *Satyagrahi*, in fact, applies to all those who seek to follow truth and achieve their objectives. Gandhi's insistence on a truthful, non-violent, and peaceful end is an important contribution to mankind. Galtung's (1996) seminal work on 'Peace by Peaceful Means' highlights the philosophical depth of Gandhi's ideas. Accordingly, this book positions Gandhi as a philosopher politician and as a surplus philosopher.

Continuing the discussion, it is also safe to position Gandhi as one of the greatest anti-imperialist thinkers. It is important to broaden the scope of his ideas to understand his struggle against the imperialism. A popular conception limits Gandhi's non-violent struggle for independence against the colonial British until the latter's withdrawal from India's territory. Beyond the territorial aspects of anti-colonial struggles, Gandhi's ideas also offer liberation to humanity from the imperialist conditioning. Gandhi's struggle against imperialism is a result of his anxiety regarding the threats of the modern western civilisation, an offshoot of colonialism. Although much of his anti-imperial struggle was directed against the British rule and was operated in India, the essence of his ideas had significant implications on many colonised countries across the globe. Gandhi's strong criticism on the Western modern civilisation, which continues to have hegemonic influence in most parts of the world, portends the fact that the colonised countries like India, as Bilgrami (2012) argues, will decline in terms of politics and political economy that has characterised a transition in Europe from early to late phase of modernity. Whilst Gandhi was sceptical and highly critical of the western modern civilisation, he also offered an alternate to it. Whilst it is a cliché that Gandhi rejected the Western modernity and its imperial motives, it is unfair to allege Gandhi being against modernity. Gandhi's rejection of Western modern sciences and its values is founded on the premise that the latter flourishes under the aegis of power and unnecessary wealth, which necessarily generates a culture of control and subjugation of others. The effectiveness of anti-imperialist ideas of Gandhi had significant influence on many third world countries, and they continue to be relevant in the present scenario.

As discussed previously, Gandhi's precepts, as a philosopher and social thinker, reflect on his activities in bringing substantial changes in social policy in India. It is safe to root him as one of the most influential social reformers in India. His initiatives for the abolition of apartheid, untouchability, caste discrimination, and women empowerment are some of the most important contributions in reforming social interactions. His fight against untouchability and initiatives for the women empowerment are widely recognized in India; whilst non-violent struggle against racial discrimination, offering a sense of empowerment to the downtrodden, has worldwide acceptance. This is clear from the fact that following Gandhi's assassination, an American Black Women leader expressed: 'A great warm light has been extinguished…his spirit, reached to the stars and sought to win a world without gun or bayonet or blood…As we, mothers of the earth, stand in awesome fear of the roar of the jet planes, the crash of atom bombs, and the unknown horrors of germ warfare, we must turn our eyes in hope to the East, where the sun of the Mahatma blazes' (As cited in Pyarelal, 1958). An important aspect of Gandhi as a social reformer is that he strongly criticized and denied the bad practices in social interactions and did not follow a militant approach to do so. He managed to bring social changes very much within the societal system. Accordingly, he once said, 'it is good to swim in the waters of the tradition, but to sink in them is suicide' (Gandhi, 1925). This position of Gandhi in terms of empowering the women also merits further investigation.

His efforts for women empowerment functioned at three different levels: social, political, and personal. At the personal level, Gandhi, unlike many others, positioned women on an independent platform. In the process, Gandhi envisioned an independent role of women in the society. For Gandhi, women could play paramount roles in the society both as moral guardians and social workers, without competing with men in the sphere of power and politics. He opined that any attempt by women to compete with men in the sphere of power and politics would be 'reversion to barbarity' (Gandhi, 1940). Further, Gandhi also believed in the ability of women to carry out the non-violent struggle against the social evils and the British colonialism simultaneously. Arguably, he is one of the first social thinkers and reformers who identified the unique potential of women to sacrifice and take lead in peacebuilding. What Gandhi prophesized as women's role in peacebuilding has become a truth in the present scenario. In many Indian states, affected by violent conflicts, we have been witnessing the active roles of women in the respective societies in containing violence and bringing peace. Gandhi's position on women's leadership in peacebuilding was founded on the logic that the world had been too long dominated by 'masculine' aggressive qualities, and it was time that 'feminine' qualities came to the fore (Kishwar, 1985). He played a crucial role in mobilising the women in participating in the independence movement. The large-scale participation of women in India's freedom movement had crucial social implications in challenging and breaking down the oppressive practices that had put women in secondary position. As Kishwar (1985) rightly asseverated, 'it is only with Gandhi's emergence as a political leader when he confronted the problem of mass mobilisation, that became aware of women not only in terms of their problems but also as a powerful potential force in society, hitherto overlooked and suppressed'. Moreover, it was Gandhi who realised that the national movement against the British could not succeed without the women's participation in the struggle (Patel, 1988). His contributions, apart from empowering women, in fighting untouchability and caste discrimination establish him as one of the greatest social reformers.

Gandhi completely rejected the social practices of caste based discrimination and untouchability. For him untouchability is a sin. To quote him, 'My fight against untouchability is a fight against impure humanity' (Gandhi as cited in Kumar, 2007). In September 1930, whilst he was imprisoned in Yeravda jail, Gandhi protested the untouchable practices. The impact of this protest led to opening of temples and wells for the *Harijans* (a term used by Gandhi for low caste people). The foundation of Harijan Sevak Sangh to combat untouchability and the magazine titled *Harijan*, started by Gandhi, were some of the important developments that played vital roles in the struggle against caste discrimination in India. Gandhi adopted a pragmatic intervention in changing the caste interactions in Indian society. He was aware of the subordinate position that forever tied the *Harijans* to superordinate position of the upper caste Hindus (Kumar, 2007). It was this realisation of Gandhi that propelled him to distinguish between what he called as *Varnashrama Dharma* (a prescriptive value necessarily based on hierarchical rigidity) and caste as an existential reality (an arrangement of division of labour without any hierarchy in the society). Accordingly, he found out an indirect rather than a direct attack on the evil practices of caste discrimination. He appealed,

> Fight, by all means, the monster that passes for varnashrama today, and you will find me working side by side with you. My varnashrama accommodates many Panchama families with whom I dine with the greatest pleasure to dine with whom is a privilege. My varnashrama refuses to bow the head before the greatest potentate on earth, but my varnashrama compels me to bow down my head in all humility before knowledge, before purity, before every person, where I see God face to face. (Gandhi, 1927).

An important aspect of Gandhi's fight against the vile practices of untouchability is to integrate it with the national movement. Such ideas on social reformation demonstrate his stature as a politician and political activist. His politics is based on his own philosophical grounds. Gandhi's stance on larger welfarism of people, his ideas of *Swaraj*, democracy, and the role of political leaders in a democracy are some of his notable contributions to politics. We will now discuss Gandhi's political views on *Swaraj* and democracy. The main objective of delving into these aspects is to contextualize Gandhi as a politician and political thinker.

Gandhi's views on *Swaraj*, arguably, portrays his political ideas the most. Affirming the aspects of larger good of people Gandhi says: 'By Swaraj, I mean the welfare of the whole people and if I could secure it at the hands of English, I should bow down my head to them' (Tendulkar, 1951). This position of Gandhi might create some misunderstanding: if greater welfare of people is guaranteed, the agency who governs the people matter very little. Here the confusion is regarding the primacy of good governance, for welfarism without ensuring that a legitimate agency governs the people, could potentially dilute the very essence of *Swaraj*. To address this confusion, putting Gandhi's perspective on *Swaraj* in a larger context is necessary. In a broader context beyond welfarism, Gandhi's *Swaraj* is equivalent to his idea of *Ramraj*.[1] In Gandhi's *Ramraj*, the moral authority and the political power are the basic foundations of the sovereignty of the people (Gandhi, 1931). The idea of a *Swaraj* can be put into various integrated perspectives. The social factor in *Swaraj* talks of an experience where the individual and the collective of

---

[1] Gandhi defined his understanding of *Ramraj* during Indian National Congress (INC) session in Faizpore, 1936. He mentioned that: 'By this I do not mean a mere imitation of the British House of Commons or the Soviet rule of Russia or the Fascist rule of Italy or the Nazi rule of Germany. They have systems suited to their genius. We must have systems suited to our genius. What that can be is more than I can tell. I have described it as *Ramraj*, that is sovereignty of the people based on moral authority' (cited in Pandey, 1988).

the people learn to rule themselves. One of the features of *Swaraj* is the combination of the individual and the collective of the people where the *Swaraj* of one individual does not conflict with the *Swaraj* of the other. To put it differently, they complement each other. In this regard, Gandhi emphasizes: 'it is *Swaraj*, where we learn to rule ourselves…the *Swaraj* that I wish to picture is such that, after once we realized it, we shall endeavour to the end of our lifetime to persuade others to do likewise. But such *Swaraj* should be experienced by each one for himself' (Gandhi, 1969). *Swaraj*, for Gandhi, is an ideal society, a state of 'enlightened anarchy' where social life becomes perfect as to be self-regulated (Pandey, 1988). Accordingly, for Gandhi, a perfect social life can be achieved through enabling the social communities in terms of making them self-sufficient in governance and economy. Gandhi would prescribe such interactions towards perfect social life at the village levels. The smaller units of societies, self-reliant villages, should possess economic independence to achieve *Swaraj*. According to Gandhi, an economically self-sufficient society is necessarily a culture in which every individual knows what they want and knows that no one should desire anything that others cannot have without equal labour (Khosal & Khosal, 1973). Gandhi's Hind Swaraj (1909) detailed his ideas of *Swaraj*. Gandhi, in general, was highly critical, if not rejective, of the parliamentary form of democracy as advocated by the modern Western civilisation. In one of his most scathing attacks, he declared the parliament as a 'prostitute and sterile woman' (Gandhi, 1969). His alternative views on a meaningful democracy very much integrated it with total freedom of people. According to him, democracy is 'freeing man from political and social enslavement and economic exploitation' (Gandhi, 1969) and is not merely confined to governance mechanism. Rather, it is a system that ensures abolition of all forms of exploitations. A critical investigation of Gandhi's position reveals that his insistence on the non-violent nature of the state and its legitimacy, opposition to the ethos of capitalism and principles of utilitarianism steered his ideas on democracy (Pantham, 1983). The role of democracy, as desired by Gandhi, is to devise a government that secures freedom of individuals without any scope for subjugation, promotes individual integrity, and non-violence (Terchek, 1986). Moreover, the legitimacy of that democratic system is decided by the extent to which a governance mechanism effectively endorses the 'greatest good for all.' As Pantham (1986) rightly expressed, 'Gandhi believed that capitalist ethos and utilitarian principles militate against participatory and substantive democracy. He realized that 'this age of awakening of the poorest of the poor' is 'the age of democracy' and that 'the states that are today nominally democratic have either to become frankly totalitarian or, if they are to become truly democratic, they must become courageously non-violent' (Ibid).

Gandhi's concern for the poorest of the poor in a non-violent democracy is mirrored in his views on economic issues. The foundation of Gandhi's desire for economic welfare of people centres on satisfying basic needs. In his words, 'a certain degree of physical harmony and comfort is necessary, but above that level, it becomes a hindrance instead of help. Therefore, the idea of creating an unlimited number of wants and satisfying them seems to be a delusion and a snare. The satisfaction of one's narrow self, must meet at a certain point, a dead stop, before it degenerates into physical and intellectual voluptuousness' (Gandhi, 1936). From this assertion of Gandhi, it can be interpreted that the pursuit of abundant wealth would lead to unhealthy competition in the society, and it has an impact on disturbing the social harmony. The role of a self-sufficient village as an economic hub is very crucial for Gandhi to ensure the basic needs of people. The concept of *Swadeshi* and interdependence between the neighbourhoods to exchange goods, Gandhi proposed, could be a sustainable model for economic security in India. Such views of Gandhi seem to be in a contrary position against the model that favoured establishment of large-scale industries which post-independent India eventually followed for economic development. Gandhi never supported the establishment of large-scale industries, but he did not protest the initiatives either. As a matter of fact, Gandhi certainly remonstrated the social disruption that the large-scale industrialisation might cause (Rivett, 1959). From this position one can derive that his views on economic welfare of the people are greatly integrated with social harmony. In his opposition against industrialisation, he emphasized on finding jobs for humans first than for the machines. He regarded development from a people's point of view. Gandhi knew that any economic initiative leading to profit-making leads to accumulation of wealth in few hands and that would eventually result in social disharmony. To minimise the risk of accumulation of wealth and economic inequality, Gandhi's ideas of trusteeship limit the rich holding the property as trustees. Gandhi's ideas on trusteeship and its relevance in the contemporary societies are discussed in chapter of this book. Further, to reduce the risk of profit-making and economic inequality, Gandhi objected to the idea of allocation of all productive resources based on capital values.

Apart from the economic issues, the relevance of Gandhian thoughts on the question of relationship of the rural people to their land in India is important. As Narayan (1969) once highlighted, *Gramdan* (change from private ownership to community ownership) and *Bhoodan* (voluntary donation of land rights to the landless by the private landowner) can be considered as some of the most radical reformations India witnessed as a part of peaceful exchange of land rights in India. Contestably, in post-independent India, more land has been distributed to the landless through the acts of voluntary donations (Bhoodan) than through any land related legislations. Similarly, no political party in India has such radical, yet peaceful, land legislation plans as compared to the Gandhian ideas discussed here. Gandhi contributed in two pivotal ways by favouring economic development through a self-sufficient village as the hub of economic activities: first, it offered a common villager several economic activities to be engaged with; second, it entitled the villagers with the responsibilities along with series of disciplines (Rivett, 1959) that guided them on the path of spiritual purity.

It is important to analyse the relevance of Gandhian ideas in the twenty-first century in relation to the multiple aspects discussed earlier. It may well be argued that the twenty-first century offers more challenges than solutions. As we witness more economic progress based on higher rates of Gross Domestic Production (GDP) and proliferation of industrialisation and urbanisation, there is also a social disharmony as an outcome of factors like growing economic inequality, land alienation and dispossession, large-scale displacements, poverty, internal conflicts induced by assertion of identities and, perennial migration from rural to urban centres in search of livelihood. Though the respective state machineries take concrete steps to minimise the risks involved with the challenges mentioned above and many others, it will be an exaggeration to conclude that they have been successful in their endeavours. With this background, the book attempts to bring in Gandhi and his ideas to examine their relevance in encountering these challenges in the twenty-first century. This book adopts a multidisciplinary approach to understand Gandhi in addressing specific contemporary societal issues. The concerns highlighted in the book through fifteen distinct, interrelated chapters offer solutions to some of the societal challenges through the prism of Gandhian thought process. The next section introduces the major themes of Gandhian ideas and beliefs pertaining to the contemporary challenges as discussed in the book.

Themes of the Book

With an aim to revisit Gandhi's ideas and its relevance in the twenty-first century, the essays collected in this volume are placed under four major themes. The subsequent section following the introduction chapter is on making sense with Gandhi's ideas and thoughts on 'democracy, development and governance'. Considering the critical developments that we witness on the functioning of democracies in terms of rising inter-group conflicts and shrinking authorities of the state as the corporate bodies are increasingly influencing the decision making, and, moreover, the desire for sustainable development, as outlined by the United Nations (UN), interrogating the issues related to democracy, development, and governance through the prism of Gandhian thoughts offers interesting and alternative perspectives.

The first essay in this section titled 'Gandhi, Oceanic Circle and Participatory Democracy' takes the stand that Gandhi's thoughts on democracy are not merely relevant in a post-colonial nation. This essay highlights Gandhi's criticism of the Western civilisation for reproducing alienating self and its subjugated nature. Criticising its relevance for the West and the craze for Western technologies in ex-colonies, Gandhi would argue for self-rule or Swaraj for both East and West. He pleads for reconstruction of democracy from within the self and its relations with community. He adopts a concept of oceanic circle which presupposes flow of democratic power from within and from below in 'ever widening circles'. It begins with numerous primary (village) communities. Oceanic circle also assumes multiple Sangam communities existing with *Bhaichara* (brotherhood) tradition horizontally. The concept refers to communities existing in widening and horizontal relations. His idea of Swaraj is realizable through several paths: *Antyodaya*, Sarvodaya, Satyagraha, and so on. His idea of village communities is reformative idea, not an empirical concept. It is to be reconstituted via social reformation of existing village communities to ensure development of all. Gandhi's Satyagraha critically hinges on the method of dialogue. Without dialogue and without respect for *Anekantavad*, a true Satyagraha cannot be ensured. All these are different aspects of Gandhi's participatory democracy.

The next essay is on the theme of 'Sustainable Development Goals in Gandhi's Thought Perspective. The idea of sustainable development, as desired in contemporary times, whilst matches with the Gandhian vision of development, it also departs from each other on many counts. For Gandhi, development aimed at finding peace and harmony with self, with others and with nature. There could be a possibility that the rational and material world of the day would dub the Gandhian concept as bordering over spirituality and hence of restricted relevance to humanity at large. By doing so would reflect failure to see practical wisdom in it for sustainable human development that has become humanity's most recent concern. The importance of localized nature of economy and social development, as prescribed by Gandhi could be critical guiding force towards sustainable developments. Accordingly, the essay gets into the seventeen specific goals of the UN document and juxtaposes them with Gandhi's ideas to identify the convergences and divergences.

The 'Ethics of Gandhi's politics' is the central theme of the next essay. This essay argues that a concern for justice constituted the ethics of Gandhi's politics. Differing the Liberal accounts of justice (whether they emphasized utility or rights) has rested upon the idea that justice is primarily a function of a consent-based state authority. Such liberal accounts accept the rule of law through third party justice and an abstract equality before the law. On the contrary, Gandhi argues that justice as a virtue of social institutions rested upon an *ahimsanat* individual sense of deference to the *other*—whether major- or minor-oppressed or colonizing oppressor. In this context this essay refers to the concepts—*swabhava ramrajya* swaraj and *tapasya*—that Gandhi employed to resolve conflicts with hostile others. On a historical side it is interesting to recall that it was Rabindranath Tagore who had first recognized the significance of *tapasya* or self-imposed pain/austerity in Gandhian ethics when he described Gandhi as '*the great tapasvi*'.

Recalling Gandhi and his thoughts in the contemporary context is important to examine the need for inclusive and holistic governance and public policy. The market-led governance and public policy paradigm have limited the scope for autonomy and universalism, for instance, '*Swaraj*' and '*Sarvodaya*'—in governance and public policy. The Gandhian paradigm of development provides an appropriate context to examine the ills of the dominant paradigm of neo-liberal inspired market-led rational choice approach on governance and public policy. On the issues of public policy and governance, the next essay discusses the context, meaning, and issues associated with 'good governance' emerging out of the Washington Consensus for the developing societies as the dominant paradigm of governance and development. Contrary to this backdrop, this essay argues that the Gandhian paradigm of governance provides an appropriate alternative to the dominant paradigm of governance and public policy for inclusive and sustainable development.

Talking about democracy and development of individuals the issues of values (read ethics and morality) and play a vital role. On the theme of Gandhi's philosophy on values and education, the next section of the book has three essays. The first essay in this section is on 'Making of a Man: A Reading of Gandhi's Philosophy in twenty-first century'. Humanity in twenty-first century is faced with several challenges which are, arguably, deeply rooted in human attitude and aspirations grounded on a materialistic view of life. A thoughtful reading of Gandhi's philosophical thoughts offers some help in overcoming this challenge. This essay discusses the flaw in materialistic conceptualization and celebration of man as a super functional entity. On the contrary, Gandhi conceptualizes the notion of human not merely a combination of mind and body, but rather having a spiritual element as an integrating metaphysical principle that cannot be reduced to the materiality of life. To comprehend this integral existence of human life, we need to reflect deeply into Gandhi's experiments and engagements that unfold truth following the path of non-violence. Gandhi's commitment to truth and non-violence, the essay argues, has epistemic power to awaken the humanity to a realm of self-knowledge leading towards in making a man that a flourishing civilization need.

The next essay under this theme is titled 'Between Fact and Value: Locating Gandhian Science'. From the writings of Gandhi, this essay investigates the nature and representation of science in modern India. The problem posed by Gandhian Science (GS)—the quandary between not an 'unmixed' admirer of science and not a 'sentimental' proponent of tradition—lies at the heart of current debates about what science means for the non-West. Outlining a concept of GS, the paper explores its potential role in advancing the ideas of postcolonial science more generally. There are four broad strands to this argument. First, Gandhian science is not only a philosophical and literary vocation but also everyone's practice without the dichotomy of expert and the layperson. Second, Gandhian science emphasizes upon data collection to understand reality without being content with impressionistic contents/management. Third, GS sought to contest Western presumptions of a monopoly over science and to ground the anti-vivisectionist approach through the indigenous systems of medicine in India's cultural traditions. Fourth, GS presented social responsibility of science which was not just concerned with fact alone, but in the creation of meanings (value) in all activities in terms of reconciling science and ethics.

The last essay of this section reflects upon the Gandhian principles of 'Education for an un-alienated life'. As overarching social transformations are underway, one can find an increasingly palpable sense of the extent and intensity of 'alienation' as a psychological and social phenomenon involving the perceived loss or the 'problematic separation' of 'self' from 'itself' or 'other'. The essay contends that Gandhi's ideas on education are worth revisiting at this juncture to find out if we live any answer to this crisis. Whilst the current policy impetus is focused on equitable, inclusive, affordable, flexible, and quality education, it is reckoned that the Gandhi's ideas of basic education and '*nai talim*' can be revived to influence the spontaneous concern for education in its varied forms in such a way that we 'learn to know', 'learn to do', 'learn to live together', and 'learn to be' for realizing the ideal of un-alienated life, without getting into the trap of the never-ending inherent contradictions between the central ideals of the western political enlightenment such as liberty, equality, and rights.

Considering the urgency involved, the next section of the book is on the theme of 'environment and public health'. Of the three essays in this section, 'Resolving Environmental Crises: A Gandhian Approach' reasons with Gandhian ideas to offer possible resolutions for the environmental crises. The essay argues that, for Gandhi, the steppingstone of the process of self-realization is self-restraint that involves certain virtues like *ahimsā, aparigraha* (non-possession), *asteya* (non-stealing), *brahmacharya* (celibacy), braid labour, etc. The very process of self-realization does not confine merely to the inner perfection of humans, yet it encompasses the safety and security of every living creature and the environment as a collective. This paper highlights that though Gandhi's ideas for the protection of the environment is premodern it is not impossible provided someone peruses her desire. In this process, the virtues like *ahimsā, aparigraha*, etc. which makes a philosophical foundation to the protection of the environment and to demonstrate how Gandhi's different moral principles can be harmlessly employed in resolving environmental crises are discussed.

The following essay in this section is on 'Mahatma Gandhi's insights on Air Pollution'. The issue of air pollution and its adverse effect on public health cannot be more direly felt and understood than during a period when the humanity is passing through an unprecedented pandemic of COVID-19. Whilst the urgency of access to clean air and concerns against air pollution are a common challenge to the entire humanity, Gandhi recognized these issues in early twentieth century. The issues related to air pollution and access to clean air that Gandhi identified continue to have relevance in the twenty-first century. This essay revisits Gandhi's insights on air pollution and reasons with their relevance in present day context. Echoing prophetic ideas of Gandhi that in modern civilisation clean air would not be available free of cost, the essay engages with Gandhi's ideas under four major themes. It begins engaging Gandhi's ideas on air pollution and clean air from spiritual perspectives. Subsequently, it highlights Gandhi's concerns over air pollution as a public health issue. The essay also engages with Gandhi's ideas linking air pollution with Swaraj, governance, and educational perspectives.

The next essay, titled 'Gandhi and Public health in India', provides detailed accounts of Gandhi's experience and ideas on the health-related issues. The essay reflects on Gandhi's realization on the importance of health and its association with poverty, socio-economic conditions, poor living conditions, and food habits of common Indians. For Gandhi, a simple but very effective solution to deal with the health issues was focused on cleanliness as this was directly related to cause many problems. Providing a brief description on Gandhi's major health conditions that he had experienced in different stages of his life, the essay highlights on two important aspects for healthy lifestyle, as articulated by Gandhi: vegetarianism and physical fitness. This essay also discusses medical legacies of Mahatma Gandhi in terms of his role in nursing patients, treating specific medical conditions like dog and scorpion bite, leprosy is discussed in detail.

The last major section of the book is on understanding the issues of conflict and peace building through Gandhian perspectives. This section begins with an essay titled 'Peaceful Resolution of Violent Conflicts in India: The Gandhian Way'. Offering a brief note on the existing violent conflicts in India: the Maoist conflict, ethnic conflicts in Northeast, separatism in Kashmir, and religious tensions, this essay engages with the critical aspects of Gandhian ideas for peaceful conflict resolution. Gandhi's ideas like engaging with the conflict parties, early solution of hostilities, and positive social construction in the post conflict societies are discussed in detail. The essay argues that the Indian State, following Gandhi, should start engaging with the violent groups operating in different parts of India. Moreover, there should be the political will to resolve these conflicts at the earliest. The issues of violent conflicts should not be pushed under the carpet. Efforts like initiating negotiation with multiple violent groups holds the key for successful and peaceful resolution of these conflicts.

The importance of *Satya*, truth, in ensuring peace is the next essay in this section. The experiential truth of Gandhi does not exclude epistemological, metaphysical, or moral facets of truth, but is an unequivocal acknowledgement of the subjective basis of the pursuit of objectivity. In admitting my truth, your truth, our truth, their truth, etc., Gandhi brought into clear focus the reality of I and we—the subjects (or viewpoints) of subjective experiences (views). The totality of these subjective viewpoints, along with their mutual relationships, constitutes an objective frame of reference for reconciling or putting together seemingly irreconcilable perceptions into a unitary whole of mutual understanding and an ever more refined comprehension of reality, thereby engendering peace. Considering the generality of the basic tenet—viewpoint dependence of views—of Gandhi's *satyagraha* and in view of the kinship between positive conception of peace and unity, this essay puts forwards '*satyagraha* for science' as a method to address numerous foundational problems in various branches of science centred on unity such as the binding problem in neuroscience.

Contrary to the desirability of peace, we witness the proliferation of protest movements in various forms and shades across the globe. The acts of violence that result during these protest movements dilutes the desire for peace. The essay on revisiting Gandhi's ideas of peaceful protest tries to make sense of Gandhian notion of dissent and protest in the twenty-first century. In this process, the paper investigates the contemporary protest movements to identify how and where they depart from Gandhi on carrying out the activities peacefully.

The last essay of this section is on 'Mahatma Gandhi: Architect of Non-violent Conflict Resolution'. Whilst Gandhi's ideas of *Ahmisa* (Non-violence) and *Satyagraha* found to be discussed in popular discourses, the use of Gandhian ideas to resolve internal conflicts in many countries outside India merits greater attention. This essay begins with reflecting on the concepts of Soul force and truth force and their influence in peaceful resolution of conflicts globally. Highlighting the philosophy behind Gandhi's strong belief in *Satyagraha* in resolving violent conflicts, the paper offers an account of the influence and effectiveness of Gandhi's own experience with non-violent conflict resolution and role of Gandhian principles globally.

References

Appadurai, A. (2011). Our Gandhi, our times. *Public Culture, 23*(2), 263–264.
Bilgrami, A. (2002). Gandhi's integrity: The philosophy behind the politics. *Postcolonial Studies, 5*(1), 79–93.
Bilgrami, A. (2012). Gandhi and marx. *Social Scientist, 40*(9/10), 3–25.

Bilgrami, A. (2003). Gandhi, the philosopher. *Economic and Political Weekly, 38*(39), 4159–4165.
Galtung, J. (1996). *Peace by peaceful means: Peace and conflict*. Sage Publications.
Gandhi, M.K. (1927). *Young India*.
Gandhi, M. (1936). *Harijan*.
Gandhi, M. (1931). *Young India*.
Gandhi, M. (1940). *Harijan. Collected works* (vol. LXXI, pp. 207–08).
Gandhi, M. (1909). *Hind Swaraj or the Indian home-rule*. Madras. G A Natesan & Co.
Gandhi, M. (1925). *Collected works* (vol. XXVIII, p.308).
Gandhi, M. (1969). *Hind Swaraj* (p. 65). Ahmedabad, Navajivan.
Galtung, J. (2011). Arne naess, peace and Gandhi. *Inquiry, 54*(1), 31–41.
Khosal, R. K., & Khosal, M. (1973). Gandhian economic philosophy. *The American Journal of Economics and Sociology, 32*(2), 191–209.
Kishwar, M. (1985). Gandhi on women. *Economic and Political Weekly, 20*(40), 1691–1702.
Kumar, R. (2007). Gandhi, Ambedkar and the poona pact, 1932. *South Asia: Journal of South Asian Studies, 8*(1–2), 87–101.
Narayan, J. (1969). *The relevance of Gandhi. A speech delivered at Indian Committee for Cultural Freedom*. New Delhi.
Pandey, J. (1988). Democratic ideal state and the hind Swaraj. *The Indian Journal of Political Science, 49*(1), 40–46.
Pani, N., & Behera, A. (2018). *Reasoning Indian politics: Philosopher politicians to politicians seeking philosophy*. Routledge.
Pantham, T. (1986). Beyond liberal democracy: Thinking with Mahatma Gandhi. In T. Pantham & K. L. Deutsch (Eds.), *Political thought in modern India* (p. 319). Sage Publications.
Pantham, T. (1983). Thinking with Mahatma Gandhi: Beyond liberal democracy. *Political Theory, 11*(2), 165–188.
Patel, S. (1988). Construction and reconstruction of woman in Gandhi. *Economic and Political Weekly, 23*(8), 377–387.
Pyarelal, (1958). *Mahatma Gandhi-the last phase* (vol. 2). Navajivan Publishing House.
Rivett, K. (1959). The economic thought of Mahatma Gandhi. *The British Journal of Sociology, 10*(1), 1–15.
Srivastava, K. L. (1968). The relevance of Gandhian political thought in the contemporary world. *Indian Journal of Political Science, 29*(3), 212–217.
Tendulkar, D. G. (1951). *Mahatma: life of M K Gandhi* (p. 106). New Delhi. Ministry of Information. Government of India.
Terchek, R. J. (1986). Gandhi and democratic theory. In T. Pantham & K. L. Deutsch (Eds.), *Political thought in modern India* (pp. 299–316). Sage Publications India Ltd.

Dr. Anshuman Behera is Associate Professor at the National Institute of Advanced Studies (NIAS), Bengaluru. Dr. Behera writes on internal conflicts in India, Bangladesh, and Nepal and on political processes in South Asia.

Dr. Shailesh Nayak is the Director, National Institute of Advanced Studies, Bengaluru and the Chancellor, TERI Institute of Advanced Studies, New Delhi. He obtained his Ph.D. degree in Geology from the M.S University of Baroda in 1980. He was the Secretary, Ministry of Earth Sciences, and Chair, Earth System Science Organisation (ESSO) during 2008–2015.

Part II
Democracy, Development and Swaraj

Chapter 2
Gandhi, Oceanic Circle, and Participatory Democracy

Arun Kumar Patnaik

Abstract Gandhi's thoughts on democracy are not merely relevant in a postcolonial nation. His criticism of Western civilisation for reproducing alienating self and subjugated nature is very suitable for the West. Gandhi argues for self-rule or Swaraj for East and West. He pleads for the reconstruction of democracy from within the self. He adopts a concept of the oceanic circle, which presupposes the flow of democratic power from within and from below in 'ever-widening circles. It begins with numerous primary (village) communities. Oceanic circle also assumes multiple Sangam communities existing with *Bhaichara* (brotherhood) tradition horizontally. The concept refers to communities living in widening and horizontal relations. His idea of Swaraj is realizable through several paths: Antyodaya, Sarvodaya, Satyagraha, and so on. His idea of village communities is reformative, not an empirical concept. It is to be reconstituted via social reformation of existing village communities to ensure the development of all. Gandhi's Satyagraha critically hinges on the method of dialogue. Without dialogue and respect for Anekantavad, a true Satyagraha cannot be ensured. All these are different aspects of Gandhi's participatory democracy.

Keywords Swaraj · Antyodaya · Sarvodaya · Technology as Upas tree · Technology for Justice · Satyagraha · Anekantavad

Introduction

> A nation that runs its affairs smoothly and effectively without much state interference is truly democratic. Where such condition is absent, the form of government is democratic in name. (Gandhi as cited in Jahanbegloo, 2015)

> Western democracy is on its trial if it has not already proved its failure. May it not be reserved to India to evolve the true science of democracy by demonstrating this fitness? Corruption and hypocrisy ought not to be inevitable products of democracy as they are undoubtedly are today, nor bulk a true test of democracy. …… I hold that forcible methods cannot evolve

A. K. Patnaik (✉)
Department of Political Science, University of Hyderabad, Hyderabad, Telangana, India

© National Institute of Advanced Studies 2022
A. Behera and S. Nayak (eds.), *Gandhi in the Twenty First Century*,
https://doi.org/10.1007/978-981-16-8476-0_2

democracy. The spirit of democracy cannot be posed from without. It has to come from within. (Gandhi)[1]

Gandhi's thoughts on democracy are not just relevant in a postcolonial country. As the above passages indicate, Gandhi remains critical of Western democracy for failing to live up to the hopes of the ordinary people. The highly centralized western state with the monopoly uses of violence can never achieve popular participation in governance except during elections. It is not a democracy to "come from within". Large democracies in the West have failed to establish 'self-rule' or Swaraj. They have not able to integrate nature with democratic societies. In India also we witness similar things. With the sole exception of Jayaprakash Narayan's 1959 essay (Prasad, 1980: pp. 209–242), Gandhian scholars of India have not explored Gandhi's notion of democracy connected with his concept of India's oceanic circle. As Jayaprakash proposes, Gandhi's ideals, including his participatory democracy, are based on an Indian communitarian perspective quite different from Western communitarian perspectives.

Western theorists have ignored Gandhi's participatory model of democracy and his criticism of the Westminster model (Jahanbegloo, 2015). However, in recent times, a few Gandhi commentators (Mehta, 2010; Jahanbegloo, 2015; Singh, 1997) have paid attention to his reflection on democracy in connection with his thoughts on non-violence. But they are singularly focused on democracy's relationship with his concept of Swaraj. Yet, his notion of religious tolerance deeply connected with the idea of democracy in India's diverse religious setting is hardly explored. For example, democracy is not simply political but also a cultural ideal in India's religious diversities. The science of democracy in India ought to learn from his critique of inter-religious domination.

Similarly, Dallymayr (2013) explores Swaraj as political self-rule but does not say anything on Satyagraha as a method of reconciling different elements of truth. Democracy as a method of truth-telling and reconciliation of truth elements is inherent in Gandhi's dialogue. Dallymayr (2013) mentions 'dialogue' in his subtitle without exploring connections between democracy and dialogue inherent in Gandhi's concept of Satyagraha. Mehta and Mantena say that Gandhi's concept of the oceanic circle is a critical innovation but do not examine its relevance in individual-community relation (Mehta, 1996: p. 268) or its connection with his critique of the modern state. (Mantena, 2012) Similarly, Joseph's interesting essay (2018) on Gandhi's contributions to deliberative democracy is not explicitly connected with Gandhi's foundational concept of oceanic circle.

This paper is divided into four sections. First, it examines the potential in his concept of the oceanic circle for widening and convergent relations of communities. Second, it is proposed to discuss Gandhi's critique of Western civilization and its inherent tendencies to dominate others. It calls for the democratization of the West internally and externally. Third, it will focus on his critique of the Westminster model of representative democracy and his alternative model of democracy based on

---

[1] Collected Works of Mahatma Gandhi (CWMG), Gandhi Sevagram Ashram, Wardha, Vol. 65, p. 12. (e-books), brought to my attention by Satya Narayan Sahu, a well-known Gandhi scholar.

a social ontology of the oceanic circle in India. Fourth, his analysis of inter-religious domination will be examined. Finally, his concept of Satyagraha as a dialogic method of conflict resolution will be discussed.

The Concept of Oceanic Circle

Gandhi's conception of self is very different from Western conceptions of self, advocated by liberals and communitarian thinkers. Though Jayaprakash Narayan discusses Gandhi's innovative concept in some detail, he mistakenly locates it as part of Indian communitarian tradition different from the Western communitarian thinking. For Gandhi, the foundational unit of India's oceanic circle is individual rather than community. However, for him, Indian society's fulcrum is not about the individual alone. Gandhi does not see any contradiction between individual and community. In the West, the community is seen as a melting pot or its opposite as an independent circle. Many scholars have drawn our attention to his critical assessment of Western individualism. But nobody seems to have systematically examined Gandhi's alternative model of the oceanic circle concerning individual and community relations.

Gandhi (1997: p. 189), commenting on the oceanic circle, says, "In this structure composed of innumerable villages, there will be ever-widening, never-ascending circles. Life will not be a pyramid with the apex sustained by the bottom. But it will be an oceanic circle whose centre will be the individual always ready to perish for the village, the latter ready to perish for the circle of villages, till at last, the whole becomes one life composed of individuals, never aggressive in their arrogance but ever humble, sharing the majesty of the oceanic circle of which they are integral units."[2]

First, in the oceanic circle, the individual is a prime unit. The individual is an independent unit but not autonomous of others. She enjoys independence by depending on others and nature. She is thus locked with inter-dependent circles. Unlike in western liberalism, she is not an atomistic individual and is not independent of each other. If she has rights, she has duties too. As Gandhi famously says that all her rights point towards responsibilities towards others. Oceanic circle assumes the existence of independent and inter-dependent widening circles. The basic unit of the oceanic circle is an individual. Gandhi turns Manu's Mastya Naya upside down. According to Manusmriti, big fish devours small fish and recommends a strong King reign in big fish. Gandhi gives a positive spin via his concept of oceanic principle. Small fish also depends on giant mammals and vice versa for their survival. Gandhi draws a positive lesson from a stark negative experience noticed by many thinkers.

Second, just as in the ocean, currents flow from below. In the oceanic circles, movements take place from the bottom. Ocean metaphorically stands for a seamless

---

[2] The famous quote from Gandhi is from Parel (1997: p. 189), brought to my attention by Siby K. Joseph, Institute of Gandhian Studies, Wardha.

movement of its species. There is a bottom-up approach to life, and the top also moves below. There is a hierarchy—the top and the bottom—but the top and the bottom are without contradiction. There is a seamless flow of activities from one to another. Gandhi admits no hierarchy where the top units dominate the bottom units. The national community is higher than the village community and the world community higher than the national community. Though, unlike Jayaprakash, Gandhi does not say explicitly on this subject, his idea of cosmic community as a higher ideal assumes the possibility of such a description of the bottom and up relationship. In the bottom-up relations, all units are equal. He admits no ascending order as in a pyramid. He rejects a pyramidical view of power. His dual path is from Loksakti (people's power) to Cosmic Order and back.

Third, the principles of interdependence amongst units are a crucial feature of the oceanic circle. What is the nature of interdependence? Everyone is independent and is yet connected with family, village, or town. The village/town is a primary community in the custody of specific activities. Its surplus activities that the primary unit cannot do are left to the district community. The governance process moves in wider circles to reach out to the regional/national/world community. Only a few tasks are left to be done by the national community. What the bottom units cannot perform are left up to the top units to undertake. One unit's limitation is another's strength. An individual's limit is a family's strength, a family's limit is the strength of a village, and so on. That is how the units of the oceanic circle are inter-dependent.

Fourth, as units borrow from each other's strengths, they also operate as convergent circles horizontally. As they feed into each other, they assimilate from each other. A method of assimilation is a critical element in the formation of communities in the oceanic circle. The wider vertical communities feed into each other, horizontal communities assimilate from each other. Horizontally, communities form convergent circles. Each community is politically self-reliant but is dependent on others what cannot be done by it. It feeds into others. Its autonomy is recognized and respected by higher-up units that do not interfere in its activities except facilitating them. So, the handholding of a community's work whilst carrying out surplus activities are twin functions of Gandhi's pyramid. Horizontally, communities follow a method of assimilation from each other without doing violence to their autonomy. Whether caste or occupational communities or Hindu-non-Hindu relationships, communities are not afraid of losing their diversities due to the assimilation of others. Brahminism assimilated cultures of non-Brahmins, and non-Hindus assimilated cultures of Hindus, including the contentious caste system. The method of assimilation is based on recognition, respect, and dialogue with each other. This method minimizes the propensity to violence in society. Gandhi's greatness lies in recognizing positive normative principles in negative and vile experiences of caste and communal contexts. He discovers alternatives to caste and religion-based unsociability from within. Many commentators who prefer to take an outsider's view of caste or Hinduism mistakenly think that Gandhi's views are pro-caste and Hindu fanatic. That is far from true.

If we compare Gandhi's notion of self and community, one may notice an ever-expanding notion of self. As stated above, this expansion is both vertical and horizontal. The western idea of community is different from Gandhi's oceanic circle. In the Western tradition, the community is not merely independent but also autonomous of each other. Western communitarian tradition posits a conflict between primary community and national community and opposes the assimilative tendency of the nation-state or the majority community. Mahajan (2002:84), with empathy for western communitarianism, says "... preservation is predicated on the view that members of a particular culture wish to continue with a specific practice or tradition; and multiculturalists seek to create conditions in which communities can resist pressures to assimilate." Mahajan does not notice that there are crucial differences in India in the methods of assimilation. In the west, assimilation is resisted to maintain the community's autonomy, India's oceanic circle is based on a method of assimilation over time, as stated above. Western communitarian thinkers offer bridges of social capital to foster national and international bonding. Such bridges are necessary as communities are not seen as sharing each other's cultural or civilisation norms.

Whilst bridging social capital is built from the outside by reconstructing national community in the West, the story is not identical in India.[3] Here bridging social capital by the state may be partly necessary. But the other survives in the very existence of a self in India's community circles. In India, a community-level mediation pre-dates mediation of the national community. The lesson from Gandhi's approach is obvious. Take an extreme case. It will be easier to comprehend what he means by this. In the case of communal conflict or caste conflict, look for community mediation rather than state-mediation with which our secular intellectuals are obsessed. Gandhi departs from this state-centric approach trying to create bridges across divided communities. Maulana Azad's Sangam humanities across India have the strength to solve the polarization of communities, indicating such a possibility to overcome the statolatry mindsets of most secular intellectuals and politicians. Gandhi's oceanic circle leaves behind a set of ideas that depart from the notion of expanded self in Western communitarian thinking.

Gandhi's oceanic circle posits a development story from below. A primary community must seek to initiate development in the primary sector and leave the rest to higher bodies to plan and carry out their respective duties. Growth and social reform are combined in the primary sector. Social reform ensures better participation of ordinary people so that growth-oriented projects benefit all.

---

[3] Putnam's account of bridging social capital by communities and the state. He assumes bridges are absent in social capital formation. So, they need to be built separately from outside by a political community. This is old social contract idea which argues that the state is necessary to build bridges across individuals lacking in trust. Putnam extends this idea of building trust networks to autonomy seeking communities in civil society. It is like a bridge built on two separate riverbanks. In the West, there is nothing in the Self that connects with the Other. It needs to be built from outside. In India, the Self remains incomplete without the Other. The Self manifests by sharing elements from the Other by a method of assimilation. For a Western view, Putnam, (2000), *Bowling alone: The collapse and revival of American community.* New York, NY: Simon and Schuster.

Critique of Western Civilisation

True, he is very critical of Western civilization promoting individualism. Its model of democracy is based on the atomistic view of the individual. He argues that western culture (modernity) is based on a self-centered individual seeking freedom from social/political control. Whilst it may emphasize the least governance or reduced government, it is founded on the individuals seeking contract providing benefits to each other. It has diminished society as a means for individual self-aggrandizement. Western societies are built on an extractive contractual principle. It has a duality: it extracts everything from community and nature. So, western modernity is like the Upas tree under whose shadow no society or nature can ever grow (Parel, 1997: p. lvii). It sucks their essence and empties both. He supports Western communitarianism based on dichotomous views of affectual/rational, individual/community, and community/nation pairs.

Unjust Technology: Alienating Self

Gandhi's critique of western civilization is not necessarily a criticism of Western Christianity. Gandhi associates his criticism with Western modernity rather than Christianity. Western modernity has produced a craze for its technology. It has made a driftnet in non-western societies like India. Western technology is like a 'Upas tree' destroying the growth of every other form of science and knowledge under its shadow. It affects villages and subjugates them by the power of technology. It disempowers the masses and does injustice to them. It violates the Dharma of people. It has produced a vast chasm between town dying with a craze of modernity and countryside denuded by its craze. A craze is a blind imitation.

By blindly imitating western technology, masses are made to suffer. They are made to sacrifice their habitus and paddy fields instead of cash. Rural labour does not get anything as they do not own assets or own marginally only. Modern technology has done Adharma (injustice) to non-modern masses. Take a post-Independence history of imitation of western technology in Rourkela, Durgapur, Bhilai, Bokaro, and so on. We may likely find that modern steel technologies have absorbed 50,000 people, whereas it has uprooted nearly three times in their surroundings. It may have benefitted roughly the population at the rate of 1:3 ratio. Technology meant to alleviate poverty has expanded due to blind imitation of technology and cheap profits. Nehru government did not alter the British policy during the 'growth poles' of development. This Western craze is challenged by displaced populations everywhere as the technological craze cannot address their existence. It is important to note that Gandhi's critique of the craze for western technology is developed in the pre-independent period. Yet, his thinking is more applicable in India's post-independence history of industrialization and urbanization, which has not prevented a turn towards the Western craze, despite India gaining Independence. Gandhi anticipates this problem sharply and argues that it is not enough to transfer power from British Government to Indians. It is more important for Indians to comprehend the nature of Western civilization, its obsessive concern for significant technologies, and its adverse impact on the masses in the colonies.

It may be pointed out that Gandhi is for appropriate technology so that masses could control masses. He is not opposed to modern innovative technologies. He did not oppose telephone or locomotives, or electricity which could not have produced without large scale industrialization. But he wants masses to control such processes. He wants 'technology with justice'. He advocates a critical adoption of new technology which delivers Dharma to groups. It must wipe out the tears of ordinary people. Thus, what is needed is to overcome the craze for technology in India and do justice to the masses whilst going for technological innovation under Independent India. In his plea for technology for justice, Gandhi recognizes the role of groups with the capacity to control and run it. Thus, Gandhi lays down a new principle for delineating technology in an alternative civilization which is not just part of postcolonial thinking but also reordering Western societies. This is indeed the universality of Gandhi's advocacy for new technology for the East and the West.

Unjust Technology: Alienating Nature

There is still one more side in his thought on technology with justice: the role of nature. As stated above, the problem of alienated self is a significant fall out of the predatory technology as it uproots masses from their habitus, agriculture, and urban job. It makes them passive users of it if it touches their life. It creates a dichotomy between rural and urban societies in colonies as it spreads urban centres more and more at the cost of rural masses. As stated before, its capacity to displace or overthrow is more than its capacity to absorb or assimilate rural people. But it produces alienating nature. Nature is increasingly marginalized and alienated from the human self. It induces passivity in nature. It treats nature as a thing of resources to be mobilized, mobilized, and conquered. It valorizes human power. Western modernity has interfered in nature beyond recognition. As a result, human civilization in the pandemic times today is gasping for oxygen!

Rousseau, long before Gandhi and Tolstoy, drew our attention to the limits of human intervention and warned us not to think of violation of nature as a persona. Rousseau argues western civil society is responsible for the privatization of nature and its social contract is thus evil. Nature is a public persona. Gandhi extends his line of thinking and blames the civilization mission of the West to dominate nature. Therefore, Gandhi argues forcefully that the technological gaze and control over nature based on human greed are rapacious. Gandhi famously said that nature has everything for human need, not for human greed. The pandemic today is nature's revenge against excessive human intrusion. Nature, too, must be respected. Gandhi's critique of western civilization is twofold: the loss of self and the alienation of nature. When human greed out manoeuvres human need over centuries, when the exploitation of nature has become truly global, the world is forced to witness a new phenomenon of climate change, the melting of glaciers, the depletion of the ozone layer, unpredictable acid rain, the rising of the seabed, and now the pandemic COVID-19, threatening the very survival of human species. I submit Gandhi's critique of Western civilization is no more a critical reflection of Western modernity in colonies. It is essentially a critique of the craze for modernity in the East as well as the West. Therefore, Gandhi's critique of Western civilization is genuinely universal and not simply valid for understanding a postcolonial context.

Critique of Liberal State

The modern liberal state, an extension of liberal philosophy in the British context, is politically based on an atomistic conception of an individual or what Macpherson calls possessive individualism. Possessive individualism has the following features in society and the state. First, society consists of autonomous individuals busy pursuing economic interests unhindered by societal norms or state power. Society is instead a vehicle for self-fulfillment. It remains a free association of individuals. Second, the market responsible for exchanging goods produced by private property owners is free from state control. The market is thus an institution for private bodies to trade what they have and own privately. No extra-economic coercion by a religion or a political force like the state is tolerable for expanding the free market. Third, if I may add, nature is like a resource for private agents in the modern economy to exploit private profits. Nature must be controlled and manipulated for market development. Fourth, market development takes place through competition over consumers. Competition leads to innovation. Innovation leads to the production of technology which in turn increases economic productivity and private profits. Fifth, private property owners cannot compete over consumer support unless they control and mobilize the labour force by a cooperative principle in marketplaces. Sixth, the free market produces risks. There is a fear of theft of private property. There is a threat of an 'invisible hand'. There is no universal player in the market. There is a threat to competition from market players themselves and so on. There is a threat to monopolize labour as well and force unfreedom on labour for higher profits. The need for a universal player is felt in the nook and corner of the market. Seventh, the universal political society is borne on the foundations of fear of disintegrating market or private property. Eighth, the universal state must be present everywhere. The liberal thinkers argue that it must be led by an elected body representing all. The entire violent apparatus is invested in the state. The modern state is a Leviathan of coercive powers. It is a centralized organ. It has a monopoly right to violence. It protects private property and confines the labouring majority from challenging private property. That is how the liberal democratic state is founded.

As Parekh (1997: p. 99) says, "Gandhi was deeply uneasy with the modern state. It was abstracted from society, centralized, bureaucratic, obsessed with homogeneity, and suffused with the spirit of violence." The liberal democratic state, one of the better versions of the modern state, cannot establish integration of the state with society and nature. It has failed to involve citizens in the decision-making process except voting. It has been unable to ensure participatory governance. It has failed to reduce the depth of violence inherent in its monopoly powers. It is thus founded on the principles of possessive individualism, atomist individuals, free market seeking private profits, competitive ethos, and an ever-expanding technology ruining the future of labour and nature. Therefore, Gandhi remains critical of the modern liberal state. Its democracy is constitutive of representation of voters through the political parties. As in the market, private property owners compete for profits on the shoulder of consumers. In the state, political parties compete for power and control based on the consent of ordinary voters. Neither voters nor consumers have any say in the governance processes of the state or market.

Parekh (ibid.) argues that Swaraj or true democracy is the only ethical alternative to the modern state for Gandhi. In Hind Swaraj, Gandhi subtly distinguishes Swaraj as self-government and Swaraj as self-rule. Those forces like the Congress who believe in Swaraj as self-government want a transfer of power from the British Tigers to the Indian Tigers. Gandhi says that such a process would entrap India in "English rule without the Englishman" (ibid.). Indians would be trapped within the tiger's nature, even though the tiger is gone. Gandhi is of the firm opinion that if this is what Swaraj means to Congress and others, "This is not the Swaraj that I want." India must liberate itself from slavish mindsets, not simply become masters of its destiny. As Parel (1997, p. iv) argues so cogently, "The tiger is Gandhi's metaphor for the modern state: all tigers seek their prey, but it makes no difference whether the tiger is British or Indian." The tiger's nature would remain the same. Therefore, look inwards and transform mindsets.

Gandhi challenges the orthodox idea of Swaraj as self-government. For Swaraj is about self-rule or the rule of Self by Self. For Congress, Swaraj is about removing external barriers or hindrances. For Gandhi, Swaraj means self-transformation, an inner spiritual transformation of self, and gradual expansion through oceanic circles.

Individual remains at the heart of Gandhi's Swaraj. But she is in a flux of movement towards larger units of society. She has rights and duties. For Gandhi, rights are at once tasks. As the individual has autonomy, she is aware of being part of a series of collective units. She has duties towards others but is aware of her rights. She retains rational application of her mind to the higher units to which she owes obligations or responsibilities. A typical example of Gandhi's concept of self can be explained in his duties to Hindu scriptures which occupy a higher ideal. Gandhi says, "I do not believe in the exclusive divinity of the Vedas. I believe the Bible, the Quran, and the Zend-Avesta to be divinity inspired as the Vedas. My belief in the Hindu scriptures does not require me to accept every word and every verse as divinely inspired. Nor do I claim to have any first-hand knowledge of these wonderful books. But I do claim to know and feel the truths of the essential teaching of the scriptures. I decline to be bound by any interpretation, however, learned it might be if it is repugnant to reason or moral sense" (Gandhi quoted in Kapur, 2002, p. 126).

The passage indicates how Gandhi takes the question of individual autonomy seriously. Gandhi tries to argue that a person has the freedom to accept a religious doctrine provided such wise views are consistent with our time's rational or moral order. A person may thus distinguish between essential truths and non-essential truths of scripture according to their application in our time. A person's empathetic understanding of scripture shall have to rhyme well in our time. Gandhi shows that as a Hindu, one may be a devotee of the Vedas. However, it may not be appropriate to claim exclusive divinity of the Vedas in modern India, which is essentially a multi-religious society. Unlike Vedic and post-Vedic times, India is no more a Hindu nation in a religious sense. There are many forms of divinity or religious texts, including the Bible or the Quran.

Moreover, all their statements cannot be accepted literally. One must apply one's creative imagination to understand sacred texts with empathy. Gandhi's position on individual autonomy is like the Western liberal views. But there is a crucial difference. He is not defending a liberal atomistic person exclusively interested in self-promotion. He demands empathy of self with a religious community and its forms of divinity instead of expressing a religion's dismissal. Unlike Western liberals who insist on a person's obligations to faith in private life, Gandhi sees no theocratic problem if persons express their religious duties in public life. He disapproves of religious dogmas in public life. A person's empathy for a larger ideal—religious or otherwise—may be guided by reason or the moral order of the time. A person may be part of a larger whole or circle of circles, but her moral or rational judgement of everything is crucial for her individuality. Gandhi rejects the idea of the surrender of self to divinity or collective bodies. Self retains reason and moral concerns to assess all the higher ideals to which it is duty-bound. Gandhi draws inspiration from Bhakti/Sufi saints who believe in the creative application of the mind in love for God, which may involve a critical reflection of human faculty to many religious injunctions or God's muted response to these injunctions issued by the clergy.

Gandhi imagines, the "Swaraj-polity" (Parekh, 1997: p. 99) is based on the oceanic circle. It moves from each person to the primary village community and the district, regional, national, and world communities. Ultimately, the world community is integrated with the cosmic order of nature and paradise. Unlike under modern liberal state, both self and nature are in sync with the Swaraj-polity. The modern liberal state is highly centralized with heartless bureaucracy. Its decentralised processes, if any, flow from above. Gandhi argues for decentralized Swaraj-polity based on a flow of activities from below to higher units above the primary units. Gandhi has not established a scheme of activities for each unit. However, Jayaprakash greatly narrates an outline of what Gandhi calls Loksakti (people's power). Jayaprakash's concept of Lokniti is based on Gandhi's political ideals. Loksakti or Lokniti may be discussed below. A story from the primary community may be narrated.

Gandhi rejects the state-centred model of development, which alienates the public from the decision-making process. It may be helpful to recall Gandhi at length here. He says, "I hold that self-government is not an end, but only a means to good government. And true democracy is that promotes the welfare of the people. The test of a good government lies in the largest good of people with minimum control. The test of autocracy, socialism, capitalism, etc. is also people's welfare or good government. In themselves, they are of no value. Any system of government can fail if people do not have honesty and a feeling of brotherhood. There may be work, there may be men to do the work and tools with which to do it, yet in my view, a system that admits of poverty and unemployment is not fit to survive even for a day" (Gandhi, 98: pp. 139–140).[4] The measure of a good government is how it wipes out tears of the poor and the unemployed. In his famous concept of Antyodaya—reaching out to the last mile person—Gandhi outlines a democratic path for a government. A primary community may marginalize the poor, the unemployed, and the untouchables. It is crucial to initiate social reforms to involve them in the path of Antyodaya.

It may be helpful to take a development story to understand difficulties with the statist development approach followed in India and the modern West. The Hindi film Swadesh by Ashutosh Gowariker, made in 2004, reflects Gandhi's development alternative below. The story is based on a real-life experiment carried out by the villagers of Sangli district, Maharashtra. The villagers put in 2000 person-days of Shramdaan to make their village energy sufficient. The story is reported to be inspired by the Kannada movie Chigurida Kanasu (Sprouting Dream) made by the film maker K Shivaram Karanth in 2003. The story revolves around the need for an independent micro-hydro power project due to the frequent failure of electricity supply from the state-controlled department, affecting studies of children and the increase in the struggle of women and men in several aspects. A centralized power system fails to live up to its promise to supply electricity amongst the rural masses. It affects the future of studies in the village. It involves people's daily management of life. Finally, people gather steam around an engineer who returned from NASA to initiate social reform and build a micro power project by harnessing the rainwater gushing down the nearby hills. They decide to use its flow and tap its energy by constructing a check dam and placing a generator to produce electricity in the village.

Whilst mobilizing villagers to create the micro hydel power project, the villagers resisted the idea mooted by a teacher and the engineer to let untouchables participate in the development process and benefit from it. The upper castes fought the egalitarian view and ridiculed it. Finally, they realized the value of the labour contribution of the lower castes and conceded their participation in development. With the sacrifice of untouchability by the upper castes and the Shramdan (sharing/sacrifice of labour) of the lower castes, a primary community is formed. A mutual give and take are very crucial for an immediate community to emerge. The project takes off brilliantly, and the story of growth from below starts experiencing new positive results in the social and economic spheres. The NASA returnee does not get back to the USA. The spirit of Swadesh gains a new height in the village, which overcomes the dependence on the centralized state supply of electricity. A new Swaraj (freedom) is founded in the village. The story indicates the successful formation of a primary community through the path of Antyodaya. Social reforms are necessary to incorporate the "last mile persons" everywhere in any growth story.

Without social reforms, the story of Antyodaya cannot be carried out. Without Antyodaya, a primary community can never be formed. Gandhi's ideal of self-rule or Swaraj is deeply connected with his concept of Antyodaya. Deendayal translates

---

[4] This is brought to my attention by Satya Narayan Sahu.

this very correctly and calls it "the rise of last-mile persons". Notice the word: 'rise' pointing towards participation. Without participation in a development project, their rise is not possible. Antyodaya means that the last mile persons cannot be simply seen as receivers. They need to be viewed as givers or donors in the development process. By merely covering them as targets of development as in a contemporary policy process, their rise or participation cannot be ensured. Deendayal's interpretation of the Gandhian doctrine is a very poignant reminder for policymakers today. The film truly captures micro details of Antyodaya by depicting "the rise of last-mile persons" in a village excluded from electricity and education and tells us a brilliant story of the formation of the primary community.

When Gandhi talks about village communities, it is essential to note that such communities do not exist empirically. However, their potential exists. But their potential needs to be harnessed through social reform. A primary community thus needs to be formed by an extraordinary effort of social reformation. With its formation, the development of all (or Sarvodaya) happens. Gandhi's concept of Sarvodaya (development of all) is linked with Antyodaya (the rise of the last mile persons). The film depicts a successful struggle of villagers to form a primary community and ensure the development of all by following the path of Antyodaya. Whilst celebrating 12 years of the film, the actor Shah Rukh Khan who acted as Mohan, the NASA engineer, said recently that the film shooting produced a patriotic fervour in the film unit. The film was his all-time favourite.

Critique of Religious Supremacy

Gandhi's ideal of Swaraj needs to relate to democracy as an inter-religious act. Unlike the West, India has remained a multi-religious society for centuries. It has both the tendencies of inter-religious domination and its antidote in inter-religious harmony operating in India since long, traditionally absent in the West. Gandhi's critique of religious supremacy is very challenging for a secular democracy. The Constitution of India has not spelt out this domain to expand secularism in India. Even though it safeguards minority rights to religious freedom, its reform narrative is weakened by not absorbing Gandhi's multisided critique of conversion/Suddhi/Tabligh. Everybody needs religious liberty protected by the Constitution.

Gandhi argues that religious communities exist side by side in India. They are each other's neighbours (Bose, 1996: p. 234). Their co-existence is horizontal. They are inter-linked and convergent communities. Many forms of syncretic practices operate amongst them. They absorb different forms of worship or rituals from each other. Religious communities co-exist in convergent horizontal circles in India. In the west, multicultural thinkers resist assimilation of a community to retain its autonomy. In India, religious communities follow assimilation methods from each other without any threat to their religious traditions. Thus, Indian history is replete with evidence of solutions to isolation problems faced by a religious community.

The problems of alienation from other religious traditions arise only when each religion carries out an aggressive campaign at Suddhi/Conversion/Tabligh. The alienating experience happens when each religion takes up a 'civilizing mission' in public life.

First, echoing Tolstoy's critique of conversion by organized Christianity, Gandhi shares his sentiment that any attempt to convert any non-Christian domination is a form of corruption of its religion. It looks down upon a neighbouring religion as inferior status and tries to impose itself on others. It is a form of bribery because Jesus says, "Love thy neighbours". In an attempt to convert neighbours via a public or community campaign, Christianity looks down on them. By carrying out a public campaign, Christians not merely distort the moral import of Jesus's saying but also knock on their neighbours' doors to come out and follow Jesus. In his book Experiments with Truth, Gandhi expressed frustration at the attempts made by pastors in his village community centres in denouncing idol-worshipping of the Hindu religion. He expresses his anguish in adult life long after such conversion attempts were made in public during his school days. Gandhi resents similar attempts of Hindus or Muslims in denouncing other religions in public life. In the public campaign for Suddhi or Tabligh, he sees identical forms of corruption of Hinduism or Islam. In his Treaty of Medina, the Prophet asks Islam to protect non-Islamic communities. Hinduism advocates many pathways to reach God. So, extending Tolstoy's formulation, Gandhi argues that all religious communities need to learn from their scriptures and classical *Paramparas* (traditions) that any attempt to look down upon a neighbouring religion is a form of corruption of preaching Upanishad or Jesus or the Prophet or Nanak. Guru Nanak says, "God is one known in diverse names". As the Jain doctrine of Anekantavada profoundly influenced him, he accepted many religious paths and practised their prayers in his Ashram. I have argued elsewhere, "Arguably the public campaigns for Suddhi (purification) by Hindus, conversion by Christians and Tabligh (spreading faith) by Muslims cannot be claimed as part of the intrinsic faith of these religious communities and are incompatible with a secular order" (Patnaik & Mudiam, 2014: p. 10).

Second, such a public campaign is also hurtful to other religions. It smacks of a form of domination over the neighbours. It produces a backlash from neighbours who are increasingly frustrated with the public condemnation of their rituals, symbols, God, or forms of worship, their religious sites and so on. This sort of supremacist perspective is a source of conflict between religious communities. Following Bhargava, this may be called a form of inter-religious domination.

Third, Gandhi rejects the idea of a theocratic state. He believes that the state shall not identify with the civilizing mission of religion. Commenting on the new national government in October 1947, Gandhi said that the new state should follow secular policy and remain vigilant of any religion's missionary activity. In contrast with the British state, which did not prevent the missionary activity of Christians, the new state should not patronize such religious supremacist ideology of any religious community. Gandhi does not offer any anti-secular manifesto. He is for a secular democracy. The state must restrain a religious community from exhibiting a supremacist mindset. He says, 'The State should undoubtedly be secular …. There should be no interference with missionary effort, but no mission could enjoy the State's patronage as it did during the foreign regime' (Gandhi, 1999).

Fourth, Gandhi is not opposed to the idea of Suddhi or conversion or Tabligh. He stands for Sarva Dharma Samabhava: equal respect for all religions. Following moral or rational thinking, Gandhi believes in all religions carrying out Suddhikaran (purification) of its goals. All religions must keep their doors open to new devotees in public life. For him, religion is a personal rather than private matter. His position in the scriptures is examined before. But religious activity may be a public activity rather than a household or private activity. When it is a public activity, all religions may keep doors open for conversion or Suddhi or Tabligh. He believes in the religious freedom of a person to profess and practise any religion. For him, religious conversion must be an internal spiritual transformation. It is like a change of heart.

Moreover, every religion will have to educate its public with its moral and intellectual lessons to better one's life. A belief in Suddhi is a must for all faiths. What is believed internally and cultivated through one's heart need not be exhibited against others in public? Gandhi remains firmly opposed to supremacist tendencies in religion as it is a corrupted religion. Gandhi wants a Hindu or Christian or a Muslim proud of their faith. He declared so many times that he was a proud Hindu and respected all other religions and their own 'essential' doctrines.

A democratic path cannot be unitary. Gandhi offers many forms of self-realization through plural paths to paradise laid down in all religions. His critique of religious supremacy in a multi-religious context like India is highly stimulating. If only the Constitution of India had incorporated all moral lessons from Gandhi's critique in its legal provision, the crisis of secularism arising today due to supremacist tendencies could have been addressed better. It may be helpful to return to this issue once more in the next section through a case study of Kandhamal, Odisha.

Satyagraha as a Model of Conflict Resolution

Finally, it must be stressed that Gandhi's approach to Swaraj or genuine democracy is laid down in his method of Satyagraha (holding on to truth).

First, interest in speaking and practising truth has many sides. In the Jain philosophy of Anekantavad, truth has many aspects or forms. Each person may hold on to some elements of truth. Jains construct a positive story of the fable of seven blind men and the elephant. As this fable is well known, it may be stated here that for Jains, each person knows some aspects of truth at a time. It is incorrect to claim that some people may know a whole story. Absolute negation of any story or complete adherence to reality is not tenable at any time. If the truth is the entire picture, then Jains argue that persons describe only partial truth or truths, not the whole picture, just as each blind man in the fable can get only a partial view.

Second, Gandhi makes another fascinating argument. He detests avoiding truth due to political correctness. That will paralyse truth-telling. In the case of conflict over truth, it will complicate solutions. The courage to speak the truth is a very decisive way out of a conflict situation where truth is fragmented or polarized between conflicting parties or social groups. Satyagraha is about the courage to stand up to truth no matter what views fragment it. Satyagraha is about submission to the truth no matter how inconvenient it may pose to a person.

Third, since nobody has a monopoly right to truth, resist falsifying or mystifying truth passively or non-violently. His non-violent method is primarily linked with the Jain rejection of absolute negation. No absolute negation is by and large possible. It is permitted under three exceptional situations only. Violence is valid in a minority of cases. It is legitimate under three conditions: 1. There is a condition of involuntary violence. Out of the fear of religion, the 'meat eating' Hindus may stop eating non-vegetarian food. Religion may sanction freedom from moral culpability. 2. Violence may be adopted to do good to others. For example, the war against Hitler's fascism is meant to restore peace and democracy. 3. Violence may be adopted in self-defence as well. Indian law courts permit it. But non-violence must be followed in most cases dealing with human conflict.

Non-violence is a force or vital energy. It is not a passive or timid observer's path. It is indeed a path of an energetic activist. One needs to have soul-force or Atmabal. Swaraj or self-rule is not possible without many forms of Atambal: love-force (Prembal), compassion-force (Dayabal), suffering (Tapbal), justice (Nitibal), and truth-force (Satyabal). These forces represent different pathways of the Satyagraha method (Parel, 1997: p. lvi).

Fourth, Satyagraha (Juergensmeyer, 2005: p. 21) has five steps in a conflict resolution process.

1. First, recognize the truthful or untruthful elements in each side.
2. Second, put the truth elements from each side together.
3. Third, form a narrow side and adopt it whilst struggling with your opponent.
4. Fourth, revise the new position even as the fight continues.
5. Fifth, end the struggle only when both sides agree to occupy the same side.

Thus, Satyagraha attempts to find a new position by affirming aspects of truth present in all sides in conflict situations. It adopts a more inclusive position than the pre-existing old positions responsible for a sharp conflict.[5] In contrast, arbitration neglects one side of truth in the loser's position, which may be relevant in a minority of cases. Satyagraha seems to offer the best possible solutions to peace and development in mob violence or community conflicts.

A story from Kandhamal will validate Gandhi's Satyagraha method. Before the story is discussed, it may be helpful to remember what Gandhi calls Satyagraha, which may be called dialogue. Satyagraha involves dialogue or discussion and then a back and forth movement in unlocking the nitty–gritty of conflicting positions. Dialogue requires respect for each conflict position and may include isolating essential from non-essential elements in collating truth elements together from opposite sides. Without dialogue, it is not possible to seek solutions to many intractable

---

[5] Mark Juergensmeyer, *Gandhi's Way: A Handbook of Conflict Resolution*. Berkeley: University of California Press, 2005, pp. 18–26.

conflicts. Recent studies by Ranabir Samaddar claim that democratic dialogue means "allowing the dialogic situation to inhere and absorb the conflict and conflictive positions" (Samaddar, 2013, p. 13). Democratic dialogue admits no fear of being politically correct.

Most secular intellectuals are afraid of speaking inconvenient truths. The first point of Satyagraha is lost sight of. Speak inconvenient truth or adopt a politically incorrect position. For example, in the case of Kandhamal violence 2007–2008, it may be found that most of them are silent on conversion drives made by Pentecostal churches during the 1990s. A few Catholic priests admit in private meetings. But that is not the official line of the All India Christian Council. It blames the Sangh Parivar for the destruction of life and property of Christians. The emphasis is one-sided. Those who talk about the religious supremacist tendency of new Churches are shouted down by pointing out that the attackers did not even spare other Christian denominations. But what is missed out by this argument is the logic of silence by all other denominations since 1990 and the collaboration of the AICC and its fallout. For the ordinary tribes, there is hardly any difference between old and new Church, especially when the old Church cries over the aggressive missionary activity of the new Church in the wilderness only.

Similarly, missionary activity of the new Church since 1990 has led to a backlash by animistic Kandhas during 2007–2008. The Peace Tribunals and National Minority Commission panels formed to enquire into the nature of violence are also silent on supremacist tendencies shown by the new Church. Thus, the private confession of Catholic priests or public narratives of animistic Kandhas (ST) is heavily censored out of the fear of legitimizing the Hindutva narratives. The first principle of Satyagraha is heavily compromised in most of the secular narratives on the Kandhamal riots.

However, that is not the story of the ordinary masses of Kandhamal who suffered the most of these riots. They are not trained in ideological correctness. In several villages, they have gone by their experiences to resort to violence, legal retribution, and finally Satyagraha. The ordinary masses from amongst the Kandha (Scheduled Tribe-ST), Paik (Other Backward Caste-OBC), and Pana Christians (Dalit) are true Gandhians without knowing his method of Satyagraha. They have gone by what Gramsci would call their 'good sense', forced by polarization and costly legal path, which made them suffer immensely even after violent events are long over. They revived dialogue with each other to follow up with 'ice breaking' measures. In Brahmanigaon circle and Katiangia villages, despite the destruction of life, property and Church, dialogue based on Satyagraha steps of conflict resolution as stated above has ushered a new beginning that respects religious differences different food habits and forms of religious freedom. Communities discovered their egos or cultural supremacy were responsible for conflicts. These community centred narratives are entirely missing in official secular discussions.

Tribes confessed to killing Dalit Christians and Pastors. Yet, both the groups regretted their cultural domination. The Church was rebuilt by Hindus, Tribes, and Christians in Brahaminigaon, followed by a massive communal feast to celebrate the occasion. Christians confessed their ego that led to conflict, showing off cultural arrogance, cutting dead cows in open space or so on. The Paikas or Kandhas confessed that they over-reacted to humiliating experiences. Through a mutual process of truth-telling and sacrifices, communities came together in solidarity. They recalled *Bhaichara* traditions built over the years preceding the 1990s. Memories of the 'good sense' of each religious community finally produced a true Satyagraha. Whilst Gandhian scholars run away from a true Satyagraha, the ordinary masses of Kandhas, Paikas, and Dalit Christians forced by circumstances of suffering discover dialogue resulting in a true Satyagraha ultimately usher in peace and 'normal' development (Patnaik & Bag, 2016).[6]

In the above story, Gandhi's oceanic circle is revealed. Communities share each other's cultural resources. Communities may sacrifice communal ego in favour of collective solidarity. They realise that they exist in horizontal circles and mature through dialogue and Satyagraha. Through the path of Satyagraha, they recall solidarity from Parampara (tradition) and rebuild their lives. A primary community is reborn. That is why it is significant to recognise how Gandhi's oceanic circle can develop his ideas of Swaraj, Antyodaya, Sarvodaya, and Satyagraha (SASS). The concept of oceanic circles thus provides many forms of participatory democracy as each of his above idea (SASS) relates to participation in peace or development. His concept of the oceanic circle propels a new way of looking at communities and their convergent circles. India's Sagam humanities represent another convergent circle in a horizontal relationship. However, a detailed theoretical exploration of the oceanic circle in its vertical and horizontal relations and its application in India's present history are beyond the scope of the present paper. There may be critical limitations of his conception of democracy from a Dalit and a socialist perspective. These competing perspectives are not examined here. However, it is important to recognize his strength before his limitations are discussed.

References

Bose, N. (1996). *Selections from Gandhi's writings*. Navajivan Press, Ahmedabad.
Dallymayr, F. (2013). *Being in the world: dialogue and cosmopolis* (pp. 151–161). University Press of Kentucky, Lexington.
Gandhi, M. K. (1999). Collected Works of Mahatma Gandhi (CWMG). *Gandhi sevagram ashram, Wardha* (vol. 65) (e-books).
Jahanbegloo, R. (2015). The Gandhian vision of democracy. In *Democratic theory* (vol. 2, no 2, pp. 59–70). Winter.
Joseph, S. (2018). Deliberative democracy, public sphere and the search for alternative politics in India: Gandhian contributions. In T. Joseph & S. K. Joseph (Eds.), *Deliberative democracy* (pp. 59–74). Routledge, London.
Juergensmeyer, M. (2005). *Gandhi's way: A handbook on conflict resolution*. University of California Press, Berkeley.
Kapur, S. (2002). Gandhi and hindutva: Two conflicting visions of Swaraj. In A. J. Parel (Ed.), *Gandhi, freedom, and self-rule*. Vistaar Publications, New Delhi.
Mahajan, G. (2002). *The multicultural path: Issues of diversity and discrimination in democracy*. Sage, New Delhi.

---

[6] https://ncds.nic.in/sites/default/files/WorkingandOccasionalPapers/WP64NCDS.pdf, 2016.

Mantena, K. (2012). On Gandhi's critique of the state: Sources, contexts, and conjunctures. In *Modern intellectual history* (vol. 9, no 3, pp. 535–563).

Mehta, U. S. (2010). 'Gandhi on democracy, politics and the ethics of everyday life. *Modern Intellectual History,* 7(2), 355–371.

Mehta, V. R. (1996). *Indian political thought.* Manohar, Delhi.

Parekh, B. (1997). *Gandhi: A very short introduction.* Oxford, New Delhi.

Parel, A. J. (1997). Editor's introduction. In Gandhi (Ed.), *Hindu Swaraj and other writings author* (pp. xiii-lxii). CUP, Delhi.

Patnaik, A. K., & Bag, R. (2016). *Dialogue, sacrifice and reconciliation: A study of Kandhamal violence, Odisha.* https://ncds.nic.in/sites/default/files/WorkingandOccasionalPapers/WP64NCDS.pdf

Patnaik, A. K., & Mudiam, P. R. (2014). Indian secularism, dialogue and the Ayodhya dispute. In *Religion, state and society* (vol. 42, no 4, pp. 1–15).

Prasad, B. (Ed.) (1980). *A revolutionary's quest: Selected writings of Jayaprakash Narayan.* OUP, Delhi

Putnam, R. D. (2000). *Bowling alone: The collapse and revival of American community.* Simon and Schuster, New York.

Samaddar, R. (2011). *The dialogic subject.* Paper presented for the Calcutta research group, Kolkata, at the centre for the study of social exclusion and inclusive policy. School of Social Sciences, University of Hyderabad, India. (February 7).

Singh, R. (1997). Gandhi's conception of democracy. In R. Bontekoe, & M. Stepaniants (Eds.), *Justice and democracy: Cross-cultural perspectives* (pp. 231–240). University of Hawai Press, Honolulu.

Dr. Arun Kumar Patnaik is a Professor in Political Science at University of Hyderabad, Telengana. A leading scholar on Political theory and India's political thinking Prof. Patnaik has contributed extensively to the field.

Chapter 3
Sustainable Development Goals in Gandhi's Thought Perspective

Sudarshan Iyengar

Abstract This chapter is on the theme of 'Sustainable Development Goals in Gandhi's Thought Perspective'. The Sustainable Development Goals (SDG), the Global Goals, otherwise known, is a universal call by the United Nations (UN) to work towards ending poverty, protecting the planet, and ensuring peace and prosperity for all the individuals by 2030. The idea of sustainable development, as desired in contemporary times, whilst matches with the Gandhian vision of development, it also departs from each other on many counts. The paper argues that, for Gandhi, development was for aiming at peace and harmony with self, with others, and with nature. There could be a possibility that the rational and material world of the day would dub the Gandhian concept as bordering over spirituality and hence of restricted relevance to humanity at large. The author argues that by doing so would reflect failure to see practical wisdom in it for sustainable human development that has become humanity's most recent concern. This paper highlights ideas of development as explained in Gandhi's Hind Swaraj. The importance of localized nature of economy and social development, as prescribed by Gandhi could be critical guiding force towards sustainable developments. This paper gets into the seventeen specific goals of the UN documents and juxtaposes them with Gandhi's ideas to identify the convergences and divergences.

Keywords Gandhi · Sustainable Development Goals · Hind Swaraj · Global Goals · UN document

---

[1] *Hind Swaraj* is a kind of treatise that Gandhi wrote in November 1909. It is necessary reading for all those who wish to understand Gandhi's criticism of modernity, industrialization, and his vision of a non-violent society where human dignity and bread labour were celebrated as key ethical values. He argued that modern industrial civilization was based on brute force or violence and non-violent society could be reconstructed with love force, truth force, and soul force. Those who wish to read *Hind Swaraj* with elaborate commentary may refer to Parel (Editor). 1997. *Gandhi—Hind Swaraj and other writing*. Cambridge University Press. First South Asian Edition. Reprinted 2005.

S. Iyengar (✉)
Action Research in Community Health and Development (ARCH), Valsad, Gujarat, India

Introduction

Gandhi's idea of human society around the principle of Love Force or Soul Force as evident in his work *Hind Swaraj*[1] has not been duly acknowledged by the forces promoting material development driven by the rapidly expanding scope of science and technology in economic and social affairs. The leaders of post-independence India also did not engage with Gandhi's ideas of the development of human society, let alone implementing them. For Gandhi development meant an overall development of the human persona that would be self-regulating and that it pursued limited economic prosperity. To rebuild such a society, Gandhi envisaged a simple economy that was based mainly on agriculture by a large section of the population living in villages. This world vision was hardly shared and in the years that followed the second the beginning of the twentieth century development and especially economic development meant an industrial society with most population living and working in cities known as urban areas. Twenty-first century has ushered in a post-industrial knowledge economy where technology determines development. This is believed to be consistent with the evolution of humanity. But the humanity continues to face serious problems such as hunger, extreme poverty, social and economic inequity, exploitation, and unbridled use of limited natural resources resulting in serious environmental and ecological damages. Despite such a situation modern development thinkers, technologists and historians hardly see any potential in alternatives offered by people like Gandhi. For instance, in recent times a popular historian Yuval Noah Harari has mentioned Mahatma Gandhi in discussing the potential in religions to solve the problems of humanity in the present in the following manner.

> Not that there aren't any economic ideas in the Bible, the Quran, or the Vedas—it is just that these ideas are not up to date. Mahatma Gandhi's reading of the Vedas caused him to envision independent India as a collection of self-sufficient agrarian communities, each spinning its own Khadi cloths, exporting little, and importing even less. The most famous photograph of him shows him spinning cotton with his own hands, and he made the humble spinning wheel the symbol of the Indian nationalist movement. Yet this Arcadian vision was simply incompatible with the realities of modern economics, and hence not much has remained of it save for Gandhi's radiant image on billions of rupee notes. (Harari, 2018)

Harari has perhaps not understood Gandhi in depth. For Gandhi, development implied peace and harmony with self, with others, and with nature. There is a possibility that the Gandhian concept was bordering over spirituality and hence of restricted relevance to the humanity at large that stops at rationality and does not want to venture into the areas where rationality has no answer, and a person has to go beyond in search of self. However, there is a clear recognition in most quarters that the present status of humanity as it lives and develops has serious problems some of which do not yield to the current state of knowledge, technology, and economics.

In the first decade of twenty-first century, there has been an agreement that environmental and ecological problems that are likely to threaten human existence are real. Hence there is a felt need that humanity should try to work in the direction of sustainable development. The concern was first reflected in UN World Commission on Environment and Development: *Our Common Future* in 1987. Many international conclaves were held and eventually the Millennium Developments Goals were framed by the UN. It was implemented by all the member countries between 2000 and 2015. This was followed by framing Sustainable Development Goals (SDGs) which are under implementation (2015–30). The Sustainable Development Goals address the issue of development with the ultimate objective of peace amongst nations and harmony with nature. Humanity has set SDGs and is making an honest attempt to move towards them. However, Techno deterministic solutions do not have the potential to lead to such desired peace and harmony. In this chapter, an attempt is made to understand SDGs from a Gandhian thought perspective since the latter transcends the material existence and brings the individual self to the centre. It is argued that viewed in Gandhi's thought perspective there are better chances to achieve the SDGs. This chapter consists of two sections. The first section discusses Gandhi's concept of sustainable human development. The second section discusses the convergence and the divergence between the two sets of concepts. The section is concluded by recommending that whilst the SDGs have a better case to address the concern for people, prosperity, and the planet if they are viewed in the Gandhian Thought perspective.

Gandhi's Idea of Human Beings' Sustainable Development

Gandhi lived, thought, and wrote about human civilisation based on truth and non-violence. His first organised thoughts on what he considered true human civilisation are found in his book *Hind Swaraj* written in November 1909 when he was 40. It must be understood at the outset that he wrote in the Gujarati language that was his mother tongue. Hence, it can be safely inferred that his thinking process, whilst he was writing, was in Gujarati. The context and reference for Gandhi then were not environment and ecology as the concepts were decades away. Therefore, he was not writing any prescription for sustainable development. His concern was that the industrialised societies that he had witnessed in England and South Africa promoted violence and did not have the potential for peaceful and harmonious human survival. The process of development also did not allow individual peace. The industrial civilisation was called the modern civilisation. Gandhi visualised both strengths and weaknesses in modernity, and he concluded that the weaknesses far outweighed the strengths. He, therefore, criticised the modern civilisation in *Hind Swaraj* and tried to present an alternative vision of human society that was constructed on non-violence or what he called love force or soul force. Parel (1997) has listed six reasons why Gandhi wrote *Hind Swaraj*. First, Gandhi felt illuminated with some deep understanding of where humanity was going and where it should be going and that he wanted to communicate urgently. Second, he wanted to explain the meaning of swaraj by making a clear distinction between Home Rule (freedom from British) and training oneself for own swaraj or self-regulation. Thirdly, he wanted to convey to the young patriots that violence and political terrorism was not the way to gain Home Rule and political freedom. Fourthly, he wanted to show that colonialism and modern civilisation were not the same. Modern civilisation led to colonialism and hence efforts should be to resist modern civilisation the way it was unfolding. Fifthly, he sought reconciliation of British and Indian as people both grounded in religious soil. British were also the victim of modern civilisation as they had given up the *dharma*. The last and most important reason for writing *Hind Swaraj*, according to Parel (1997) was Gandhi though the *Hind Swaraj* wanted to guide Indians to the formation of a new society based on 'updated conception of Dharama'. Parel writes,

> Finally, Gandhi believed that through *Hind Swaraj* he would be able to give Indians a practical philosophy, an updated conception of dharma, that would fit them for life in the modern world. In the past dharma was tied to a hierarchical system of duties and obligations and to the preservation of status. It gave little or no attention to the idea of democratic citizenship. Gandhi felt that time had come to redefine the scope of dharma to include notions of citizenship, equality, liberty, fraternity, and mutual assistance. And in *Hind Swaraj*, he presents in simple language his notion of such a redefined dharma, the vision of a new Indian or Gandhian civic humanism, one that the *Gita* and the *Ramayana* had always contained in *potential*, but something which Indian civilisation had not actualised fully in practice.

Gandhiji's concern was that the patriots who were fighting for India's independence believed in armed revolution using violence. Secondly, most of them appreciated the modern industrial civilisation as the only path of desirable development of human society. Gandhi disagreed with both. For the political activists fighting with the British for *Swaraj* the Indian term for Independence was for Home Rule. For Gandhi political *swaraj* was not only not enough but it was also secondary. His philosophy of *Swaraj* was self-regulation in leading one's life. The seeds for sustainable development of humanity in Gandhi's vision are contained in *Hind Swaraj*. This is his vision document. We must reinterpret it as times change. However, there are certain non-negotiable values specified in *Hind Swaraj*. Let us briefly look at Gandhiji's criticism of modern civilisation first.

Chapter 6 in the *Hind Swaraj* is titled *Sudharanu Darshan*. It should be noted that this is the only work of his that he translated from Gujarati into English. He did this for his close friend Hermann Kallenbach. Gandhi translated *Sudharanu Darshan* as 'Civilisation'. In Gujarati one of the meanings of *Sudhaaro* is civilisation. In translation, he avoided *darshan* which means philosophy. He did not title it as 'Philosophy of Civilisation.' The discussion in the text begins with the 'Reader' asking a question to the 'Editor' that the latter should now explain what he means by civilisation because in the opinion of the Editor it is *kudharo*. Now the word *kudharo* in Gujarati is not an antonym of civilisation, i.e. it does not mean barbarianism. It means harmful sociocultural reforms. Gandhi the Editor in response himself switches over to this meaning and begins by saying that even some Englishmen call the *sudharo as kudhaaro*. The English translation that he has rendered reads: *It is not a question of what I mean. Several English writers refuse to call that civilisation which passes under the name.* It appears that to both the English and the native audiences Gandhi wanted to convey that he is offering not the philosophy of civilisation, but a criticism which has also been made by some thinking English people.

Let us see his main criticism.

Let us first consider what state of things is described by the word "civilization". Its true test lies in the fact that people living in it make bodily welfare the object of life… The people of Europe today live in better-built houses than they did a hundred years ago. This is considered an emblem of civilization, and this is also a matter to promote bodily happiness. Formerly, they wore skins and used spears as their weapons. Now, they wear long trousers, and, for embellishing their bodies, they wear a variety of clothing and, instead of spears, they carry with them revolvers containing five or more chambers. If people of a certain country, who have hitherto not been in the habit of wearing much clothing, boots, etc. adopt European clothing, they are supposed to have become civilized out of savagery. (CWMG, vol. 10, 1963)

Gandhi was also prophetic about the future. He wrote,

Formerly, men travelled in wagons. Now, they fly through the air in trains at the rate of four hundred and more miles per day. This is considered the height of civilization. It has been stated that, as men progress, they shall be able to travel in airships and reach any part of the world in a few hours. Men will not need the use of their hands and feet. They will press a button, and they will have their clothing by their side. They will press another button, and they will have their newspaper. A third and a motor-car will be in waiting for them. They will have a variety of delicately dished up food. Everything will be done by machinery. Formerly, when people wanted to fight with one another, they measured between them their bodily strength; now it is possible to take away thousands of lives by one man working behind a gun from a hill. This is civilization. (ibid, p. 20)

In 1909, India was still mostly rural. Agriculture and animal husbandry were the mainstay. People lived simply and dressed in their traditional clothes. But today one can see how true Gandhi then was. We have mostly copied the West in almost every walk of life. Our lifestyle also is almost similar. One may argue that what is so wrong with it? It is indeed more comfortable now compared to the hardships in life in the past. Whilst it is true to an extent, Gandhiji's main criticism about body focus sticks. Today's civilization world over is characterized by fancy food, fancy clothes, and accessories, motorized vehicles, luxurious houses, machines for all types of work including those that can be easily done using hands and legs and nuclear armaments for war. There is a constant threat to the very existence of human beings on earth. It has taken about six to seven decades before realising a new threat because of over emphasis on the material development for pampering the body. The material resources that humanity uses today at an increasing rate from nature have created two adverse impacts. One, it is being realised that material resources in nature are ultimately limited, innovation or invention of substitutes and economic pricing notwithstanding. Secondly, a serious unintended consequence has shown up in terms of a rise in pollution levels that threatens human health and the health of nature. So, the spaceship earth is facing a reduction in resources for survival due to overuse and depletion due to pollution. Until recent times this issue was debated, but it appears that it is settled and there is a widespread agreement that the spaceship earth's environment and ecology are under threat.

In Gandhi's definition of civilisation seeds of sustainability are inherent. The vision of civilisation and its perspective are significantly different. Let us try to understand it. Gandhi defined civilisation in *Hind Swaraj* in Chap. 13 titled 'What is True Civilisation?'

> Civilization is that mode of conduct that points out to man the path of duty. Performance of duty and observance of morality are convertible terms. To observe morality is to attain mastery over our minds and our passions. So doing, we know ourselves. The Gujarati equivalent for civilisation is good Conduct. (ibid, p. 30)

The Gujarati text is important because in it Gandhi communicates to the native audience. In Volume 10 of Collected Works of Mahatma Gandhi, the editor has introduced a footnote on this part of the English text. It reads: Literally, "This is the meaning of *su,* that is, good, *dharo* [way of life]." The original adds: "The opposite is *Kudharo* [bad way of life]" (Ibid, p. 37). Thus, for Gandhi, a true civilization is one where every citizen is performing his/her duty with utmost sincerity. Ajit Dasgupta using Dworkin's classification of political theories states that Gandhi's political theory falls under duty-based theories. In Dasgupta's words,

> For duty-based theories, it is the performance of a duty or duties that is the fundamental concern. Other goals, rights, and duties could also be valued by an exponent of the theory in question but they would have to be treated as either subordinates or derivative…Gandhi's approach to political theory could be interpreted either as goal-based or as duty-based, for both elements can found in his thought, but it is certainly not right-based. (Dasgupta, 1996)

Dasgupta explains well that Gandhi's discussion on rights contains two main ideas. One is that rights and duties are correlated, and second, it is duties that have priority. In the current debate on sustainable development, Gandhi's this discourse about citizen's duty is missing. It must be considered. If we let it go as has been done in the past, irrespective of the serious efforts by the intergovernmental panels on climate change and studies and recommendations of the scientists and technologists, the solution of might continue to elude us. It should be remembered that Gandhi did not stop at this point after he penned *Hind Swaraj*. He continued to reflect and comment on it. Most importantly, his response to Julian Huxley in October 1947, then Director-General of the United Nations Educational, Scientific and Cultural Organization (UNESCO) about UN's proposal of declaration of Human Rights was the following.

> The very right to live accrues to us only when we do the duty of the citizenship of the world. From this one fundamental statement perhaps it is easy enough to define the duties of man and woman and correlate every right to some corresponding duty to be first performed. Every other right can be shown to be usurpation hardly worth fighting for. (CWMG, vol. 89, 1983:347)

The practice of swaraj by every individual was a basic duty of every citizen of the society. This feature was there in Indian society for thousands of years. Hence, Indian civilisation survived long. Gandhi reminds us of this aspect in *Hind Swaraj*. Mashruwala (1951), a profound thinker and a Gandhian scholar, suggests that civilisation is recognised by its socio-economic systems and individual behavioural ethics that establish a culture. According to him, western society's culture is elitist. He calls it *bhadra sanskriti*. Ramesh Shah, an economist and Gandhian scholar, has described it as follows. The elitist civilisation (culture) is characterised by the development of the reasoning and power of imagination. Scholars, experts, religious scholars, poets, and fine arts people represent the cultural arena. Lawyers, doctors, teachers, masters, and clerks represent the arena of worldly affairs. The British have developed some white-collar professions that require both labour and brain. Elitist civilisation is not founded on the principles of equality. Philosophically, it would show equality not only amongst human beings but also with evil, but in the practical world, it says that not only there is disparity amongst individuals but also differences should obtain. Hence, for managing, such society violence and animal force were unavoidable and state that the society should continuously wield the state power to keep individuals within limits. In practice, the elitist civilisation includes within it only those individuals who are in elitist professions and work. Rest is outside it (Shah, 1998).

Mashruwala (1951) has termed Gandhi's vision of culture and civilisation as *sant sanskriti*—saint culture. The goal of a human being is to live with values where material prosperity is not the aim. The aim is to live according to the indication given in Ishawasya Upanishad's first verse that reads *Ishavasyam idam sarvam Yatkinchit Jagatyam Jagat; Ten tyaktena bhunjitha maa grudha kasyaswid dhanam*—Whatever there is changeful in this ephemeral world, all that must be enveloped by the Lord. By this renunciation (of the World), support yourself. Do not covet the wealth of anyone.

This is a moral value. Thus, to consider one's duty to self, others, and nature is inherent in Gandhi's vision of true civilisation. A possible confusion may occur here. *Sant Sanskrit* appears to have a strong element of spirituality in it. It may have been for Gandhi a personal agenda but for all, he advocated the practice of *dharma* which is the duty-centred behaviour of an individual. In Gandhi's model of sustainability, an individual is at the centre and responsible. The state and technology are auxiliary forces to conduct human affairs in the material world. The point being belaboured here is that modern economics is not as objective as it is made out to be. The civilization and culture arising out of a set of value systems influence economic analysis and behaviour. The tastes and preferences are not given, they are created. The demand is not there always, supply is planned by the entrepreneur, and then the good or service is marketed. Marketing means creating demand. The Gandhian thought helps us in understanding the source from which unsustainability arises. It also enables us to understand that why the solution does not lie where it is being looked for. He suggested duty-based behaviour which leads an individual to live with less material wealth. It helps in reducing and regulating the use of limited natural resources and adverse consequences such as pollution.

Gandhi visualized a rural society where people led simple lives, and no one would be extraordinarily rich, and no one will die of hunger. Aspiring and making supreme efforts to attain material prosperity promote violence and the use of brute force. By using brute force and violence one cannot arrive at a peaceful and harmonious society. Means—end continuum is an important formulation and theme in *Hind Swaraj*. In arguing about the means Gandhi believed that the English gained power and prosperity using brute force, but what they had got was not desirable. He wrote,

> Your belief that there is no connection between the means and the end is a great mistake. Through that mistake, even men who have been considered religious have committed grievous crimes. Your reasoning is the same as saying that we can get a rose through planting a noxious weed. If I want to cross the ocean, I can do so only by means of a vessel; if I were

to use a cart for that purpose, both the cart and I would soon find the bottom. "As is the God, so is the votary", is a maxim worth considering. I am not likely to obtain the result flowing from the worship of God by laying myself prostrate before Satan. If, therefore, anyone was to say: "I want to worship God; it does not matter that I do so by means of Satan," it would be set down as ignorant folly. We reap exactly as we sow (CWMG, vol. 10 p. 43)

Between 1909 and 1945 the world of science and technology had rapidly progressed. The power of destruction in wars had increased many folds. Material prosperity and variety had increased substantially. Hundreds of inventions and scores of innovations were happening every day. Most of it was for material betterment and bodily survival. Gandhi was witness to all of it. He used motor cars for travel, he travelled in trains, and he also had a telephone connection. He used modern amenities. Did he yet hold the view that he held in *Hind Swaraj*? Answer to this is available in his correspondence with Nehru in October 1945. Gandhi wanted to be clear about the vision around which free India was to be reconstructed. He clarified his position in the following way.

> I have said that I fully stand by the kind of governance which I have described in *Hind Swaraj*. It is not just a way of speaking. My experience has confirmed the truth of what I wrote in 1909…I believe that if India, and through India the world, is to achieve real freedom, then sooner or later we shall have to go and live in the villages-in huts, not in palaces. Millions of people can never live-in cities and palaces in comfort and peace. Nor can they do so by killing one another, that is, by resorting to violence and untruth…. It does not frighten me at all that the world seems to be going in the opposite direction. For the matter of that, when the moth approaches its doom it whirls around faster and faster till it is burnt up. It is possible that India will not be able to escape this moth-like circling. It is my duty to try, till my last breath, to save India and through it the world from such a fate (CWMG, vol. 81, 1976. P. 319).

He had mentioned in the *Hind Swaraj* that Indian villages were not free of issues, vices, and problems. But his village existed in his imagination. It is the form of settlement and society that he was talking about. He was also not against modernity. He had learned so much from it. He also knew about the status of villages in India. Yet he had strong reason to hold his belief that a village society had more likeliness to be nearer to society based on non-violence. He wrote to Nehru in the same letter the following.

> While I appreciate modern thought, I find that an ancient thing, considered in the light of this thought looks so sweet. You will not be able to understand me if you think that I am talking about the villages of today. My ideal village still exists only in my imagination. After all, every human being lives in the world of his own imagination. In this village of my dreams, the villager will not be dull—he will be all awareness. He will not live like an animal in filth and darkness. Men and women will live in freedom, prepared to face the whole world. There will be no plague, no cholera and no smallpox. Nobody will be allowed to be idle or to wallow in luxury. Everyone will have to do body labour. Granting all this, I can still envisage a number of things that will have to be organized on a large scale. Perhaps there will even be railways and also post and telegraph offices. I do not know what things there will be or will not be. Nor am I bothered about it. If I can make sure of the essential thing, other things will follow in due course. But if I give up the essential thing, I give up everything (Ibid, p. 320)

A sustainable world came to Gandhi from a non-violent economy. He argued that modernity despite aiming at a civilised society with virtues promoted stealing and possession (acquisitiveness). In the early 1920s, he had suggested to Sabarmati Ashram dwellers eleven vows that each inmate should follow to be able to perform *Dharma*—duty to self and others and nature. Two of the eleven vows are *Asteya* and *Aparigraha*—Non-stealing and being non-possessive. He later evolved the idea and advocated trusteeship. Being a trustee served two purposes; one, indulgence in the material world by the creator of the wealth would be avoided, and two, a trustee would utilize such wealth for the material and social welfare of the deprived. Revisiting his writings in today's context where sustainability is a critical issue in human survival, one can find that he laid down principles and values for the SDGs he had set for India. In a statement in Aden made to a Reuter correspondent en route England for the Second Round Table Conference, Gandhiji's said,

> I shall strive for a constitution which will release India from all thraldom and patronage, and give her if need be, the right to sin. I shall work for an India in which the poorest shall feel that it is their country in whose making they have an effective voice; an India in which there shall be no high class and low class of people; an India in which all communities shall live in perfect harmony.
>
> There can be no room in such an India for the curse of untouchability or the curse of intoxicating drinks and drugs. Women will enjoy the same rights as men. Since we shall be at peace with all the rest of the world, neither exploiting nor being exploited, we should have the smallest army imaginable.
>
> All interests not in conflict with the interests of the dumb millions will be scrupulously respected, whether foreign or indigenous. Personally, I hate distinction between foreign and indigenous.
>
> This is the India of my dreams for which I shall struggle at the next Round Table Conference. I may fail, but if I am to deserve the confidence of the Congress, I shall be satisfied with nothing less. (CWMG, vol. 47, 1959, p. 388–9)

Eradicating poverty, ending hunger, constructing an equitable society, gender empowerment, non-exploitative mode of production, and limiting consumption by regulating one's behaviour including limiting one's material wants forms the crux of a sustainable society for Gandhiji.

SDGs and Gandhi: Commonalities and Differences of Ideas

The United Nations General Assembly has committed and dedicated itself in favour of People, Planet, Prosperity, Peace, and Partnership in that order. The outcome document says that the goals and targets will stimulate action over the next fifteen years in areas of critical importance for humanity and the planet.[2] Five components are described as important for humanity and the planet. Let us revisit each of the components and compare what modern humanity's wisdom has to say and how

---
[2] Those interested in referring to the SDGs and the targets may access a pdf copy published by UNDP at https://sustainabledevelopment.un.org/content/documents/21252030%20Agenda%20for%20Sustainable%20Development%20web.pdf.

Gandhi reflected it in his thought framework. The first eight SDGs are directly devoted to people. The goals relate to poverty, hunger, health, education, gender, water and sanitation, clean energy, and work. Each of them has been dealt with in detail, and each one is linked to specific targets. As mentioned, detailed analytical work has been done on each of these targets, improvements are suggested by experts, and there are some additions as well.

People are indeed at the centre in Gandhi's thought framework too. He would have been in complete agreement with the statement made by the UN about people. However, the difference between the UN approach and Gandhi's approach is significant.

No Poverty and Zero Hunger

The SDG's targets are specific, quantitative, and measurable. The experts have modified the approach for the first goal of eradicating poverty. The UN assumes the responsibility of eradicating poverty in less developed countries (LDCs) by significant global resource mobilization and distribution from rich to poor countries. It also recommends appropriate policies at the local, regional, national, and global levels for social protection and solidarity (UNDP, 2015). This modified approach is top-down. Developed or rich countries are expected to support LDCs, and each country must make appropriate policy at multiple levels.

Consistent with his philosophy and vision Gandhi recommends poverty removal efforts from below. The village has primary responsibility in this process. Basic needs, food, clothing and shelter, and other basic amenities are to be met at the village level in a self-reliant manner. His vision for removing poverty and hunger forever was working through *Gram Swaraj*—Village Swaraj. Answering a question on village Swaraj Gandhi viewed that:

> My idea of village swaraj is that it is a complete republic, independent of its neighbours for its own vital wants, and yet interdependent for many others in which dependence is a necessity. Thus, every village's first concern will be to grow its own food crops and cotton for its cloth. It should have a reserve for its cattle, recreation, and playground for adults and children. Then if there is more land available, it will grow *useful* money crops……..The government of the village will be conducted by a Panchayat of five persons annually elected by the adult villagers, male and female, possessing minimum prescribed qualifications. These will have all the authority and jurisdiction required. Since there will be no system of punishments in the accepted sense, this Panchayat will be the legislature, judiciary and executive combined to operate for its year of office (CWMG, vol. 76, 1979, pp. 308–9)

Gandhi had evolved the concept of *Swadeshi* from his approach to development. Village Swaraj cannot be achieved if *Swadeshi* is not followed. This concept stands in stark contrast to the way the world lives now under globalization. If we examine SDG-Two of ending hunger, achieving food security, improving nutritional status, and promotion of sustainable agriculture, the suggested approach to achieve targets is once again top-down. Increased investment by the suffering country, international cooperation in agriculture research and extension, increase agriculture productivity, correcting trade restrictions and distortions by negotiations at the World Trade Organisation, removing of all export subsidies on agricultural products, proper functioning of community markets, and providing access to information to correct market failures, etc. How did Gandhi solve it using *the Swadeshi* concept is equally interesting?

> Swadeshi is the spirit in us that restricts us to the use and service of our immediate surroundings to the exclusion of more remote… Much of the deep poverty of the masses is due to the ruinous departure from the Swadeshi in economic and industrial life… If we follow the Swadeshi doctrine, it would be your duty and mine to find out neighbours who can supply your wants and reach them to supply them where they do not know how to proceed, assuming that there are neighbours who are in want of healthy occupation. Then every village of India will almost be a self-supporting and self-contained unit, exchanging only such necessary commodities with other villages as are not locally producible (Gandhi, 1947).

Gandhi believed that India should not rely on other countries for food items. Thus, his suggestion to the Less Developed Countries (LDCs) to come out of hunger and poverty would not be only through international cooperation, and free trade, but primarily by being self-sufficient at local levels. Gandhi was not against trade amongst regions and countries, but he advocated self-sufficiency in basic needs. For achieving SDG one and two, he would strongly recommend Swadeshi and self-reliance as the key. Gandhi did not neglect agriculture. If a village has to be self-reliant in food and clothing, agricultural productivity is to be at the centre. According to him, every village's first concern was to grow its own food crops and cotton for cloth. Land use plan must provide for recreation, playground, cremation, etc. For improving productivity in agriculture, he was a practitioner and votary of using local nature-based inputs that could be produced by simple skills using hands. In a compilation of his writings on Gram Swaraj Gandhi has written methods of preparing farm year manure and cattle feed at great length (Gandhi, 1962)[3]. After decades of modern agriculture in the whole world, low input organic agriculture with local seeds, and farmyard manure is on the return and perhaps this holds the key to sustainable agriculture which would help to eradicate hunger and poverty. SDGs' strategy has practically ignored this aspect.

Good Health and Well-Being

The third SDG aims at ensuring healthy lives and promoting well-being for all ages. Gandhi would not disagree on this broad goal. But when one gets to specific targets that are laid down, most of them deal with intervention through curative services in and for disadvantaged areas and people. There are 9 specific targets and 4 supportive targets to be achieved. One of the targets is to 'strengthen the prevention and treatment

---

[3] Hariprasad Vyas compiled Gandhiji's writings on various issues related to Gram Swaraj. In English, it was titled Village Swaraj. Chapters 14–18 are on Agriculture and Animal Husbandry. Chapter 17 in the series is on Manure. See M.K. Gandhi. 1962. *Village Swaraj*. Compiled by Hariprasad Vyas. Navajivan Publishing House, Ahmedabad.

of substance abuse, including narcotic drug abuse and harmful use of alcohol.' Gandhi was one step ahead, and he would not allow growing tobacco as a crop. The world order of humanity is hesitant to categorically suggest that alcohol and substance use should be gradually discontinued in society. If there is an admission that there is a freedom to intoxicate oneself with life-threatening material, it will promote illicit trade and affect the poor most. SDG 3 has nine targets that deal with controlling morbidity and mortality through programmes, campaigns, infrastructure, finance, and of course research for a cure. Modernity has developed public health very well, but the major emphasis is on curative medicine. For Gandhiji, health is the responsibility of the individual first. In gaining one's *Swaraj*[4] (self-regulation) one has to regulate one's behaviour for keeping the body and mind healthy. One may argue that it is abstract and in a forum such as the UN the global goals must be concrete. But the WHO defines health as wellness of body, mind, and spirit. So, the SDG should have incorporated Gandhi's concept of health. For sustainable health and well-being of human beings, Gandhi's approach was the following.

> In a well-ordered society, the citizens know and observe the laws of health and hygiene. It is established beyond doubt that ignorance and neglect of the law of health and hygiene are responsible for most of the diseases to which mankind is heir...*Mens sana in copore sano* is perhaps the first law for humanity. 'A healthy mind in a healthy body' is a self-evident truth...The fundamental laws of health and hygiene are simple and easily learned. The difficulty is their observance (Gandhi, 2000).

Gandhi would not have disagreed with any of the targets spelled out for SDG-three, but the approach would have been focusing in a major way on educating the population about health and hygiene. Bringing a healthy body and mind on the agenda would shift the paradigm from cure to prevention and maintenance.

Quality Education

The targets laid down for SDG Four are about ensuring inclusive and equitable quality education and promoting lifelong learning opportunities for all. This fits well in Gandhi's experiments and thoughts on education. However, there is a fundamental difference. Education in the SDG framework is for an evolving society which is taken as given. In the Gandhian framework education is de novo, designed to reconstruct a new world.

Inclusive and equitable quality education is in the design of Gandhi's basic education. No boy or girl in a village or city can be left out if Gandhiji's basic education is followed. Gandhiji's basic education is a philosophy where heart, hand, and head are to be educated with values, skill, and knowledge with an objective of reconstruction of

---

[4] The word Swaraj is a word in Hindi originating in Sanskrit. It means political freedom. However, Gandhi used the word to mean self-regulation as well. *Swa- Rajya* meaning rule of self. He held individuals responsible for regulating behaviour. He has explained in detail in his book *Hind Swaraj*. Refer, CMMG Volume 10, p. 39.

non-violence society where a village is a basic unit and Swaraj is attained at that level. Education is imparted through work and learning by doing is the method. The community is made responsible for educating its children. Access must be to all without any discrimination on grounds of social and economic and gender factors. Both primary and secondary education is compulsory and free in the Gandhian education framework as the community bears the cost. Human values and values for sustainable survival are the core of Gandhi's basic education. For humanity's world order individual persona should be as important as the systems and technology. Individuals with a character alone will form a sustainable world.

Gender Equality

On gender equality and empowerment of women, there is almost full convergence between SDG's basic thrust and that of the Gandhian framework. Gandhi discussed women and girls in the Indian context. For him:

> A woman is the companion of a man, gifted with equal mental capacities. She has the right to participate in every minute detail in the activities of man she has an equal right of freedom and liberty with him. She is entitled to a supreme place in her own sphere of activity as man in his… By sheer force of vicious custom, even the most ignorant and worthless men have been enjoying a superiority over women which they do not deserve and not ought to have (Gandhi, 1947).

The Gender issue is addressed by changing values, attitudes, and behaviour by men towards women and girl children, but it is also very important to think and act in the Gandhian thought framework of promoting an economy that runs with non-violent forces and not by brute force. If the basic approach is not altered significantly that is if the driving force of the society is brute force (structural violence) then gender equality and dignity will also be as difficult as the economic inequality.

Clean Water and Sanitation

Availability and sustainable management of water and sanitation (WATSAN) is a goal that Gandhi also cherished. Gandhi was opposed to open defecation. In case of contingent situations, he was a strong practitioner and votary of *Tatti pe Mitti*, covering the night soil under the earth. He considered human excreta to be highly valuable and developed techniques to convert it into manure. In the Ashrams of Gandhi, sanitation and hygiene was a high priority. He wanted every person to be a scavenger. He encouraged innovations in collecting and treating faecal materials. Today, good technologies are available to build toilets in the villages and convert the faecal material into good manure. Modern WATSAN science, technology, and practices promote clean and potable water sources for drinking and adequate supply for domestic use, and drainage with sewage treatment at a very high capital cost. Also, with WATSAN-related SDGs most targets are set against the present urban-industrial society where water will have to be sourced brought from distant locations. The sustainability of supplies from such sources has remained always doubtful. Hardly any LDC will be able to achieve the targets in the stipulated period and hence the goal is likely to remain severely underachieved.

Gandhi had placed his priority on local sources and community management. Once again there is a basic contradiction between Gandhiji's vision and that of the SDGs. SDGs visualise an urban industrial society by 2030 (which may be a reality if the paradigm of development does not shift decisively soon). Gandhi had visualized a rural society. Gandhiji's recommendation is in concurrence with target 6.6 of the SDG Six which calls for protection and restoration of water-related ecosystems, and the strategy spelled out in SDG 6b which says that supporting and strengthening local communities in improving water and sanitation management. In the Gandhian framework target 6.6 and approach, 6b would top the list. It would become clear from the following quotes from Gandhiji's writings:

> Village sanitation is, perhaps, the most difficult task… No Government can change the habits of a people without their hearty co-operation. And if the latter is forthcoming, a Government will have little to do in the matter. The intelligentsia—medical men and students—can deal with the problem successfully if they would conscientiously, intelligently, jealously, and regularly *do the work* in the villages. Attention to personal and corporate hygiene is the beginning of all education…The things to attend to in the villages are cleaning tanks and wells and keeping them clean, getting rid of dung heaps (CWMG, vol. 60, 1974, p. 190).

He also had very clear ideas for solid waste management. He wrote,

> Lanes and streets have to be cleansed of all the rubbish, which should be classified. There are portions which can be turned into manure, portions which have simply to be buried, and portions which can be directly turned into wealth. Every bone picked up is valuable raw material from which useful articles can be made or which can be crushed into rich manure. Rags and waste paper can be turned into paper, and excreta picked up are golden manure for the village fields (Ibid, p. 191).

Gandhi learned a great deal from how municipalities worked in England. He, therefore, commented on the municipality's function and citizen's responsibilities during series of articles he wrote in 1924–25. He wrote,

> The one thing which we can and must learn from the West is the science of municipal sanitation…We must modify western methods of sanitation to suit our requirements…No municipality can cope with insanitation and congestion by the simple process of taxation and paid services. This vital reform is possible only by wholesale and voluntary co-operation of the people both rich and poor (Gandhi, 1947).

Affordable and Clean Energy

SDG 7 is about ensuring access to affordable, reliable, and modern energy for all. The targets set for achieving the goal do emphasise renewable energy and clean technologies using fossil fuels. However, Gandhiji prioritised human and animal energy as far as it was feasible and free of drudgery. From his main criticism of industrial society, one can infer that he was a votary of input production and consumption systems. This would drastically reduce the energy demand. Adding his preference for human and animal energy, the economies would be by design using low energy. He had opposed railways and motorised vehicles for the speed. However, he was not averse to such development. Importantly, he was not against science and technology per se. Use of hand for spinning cloth was not to be done like a zombie. Kulkarni examining the question 'was Gandhi opposed to Science and Technology quotes Gandhi and notes,

> The spinning wheel, he repeatedly said, will not become a power for the liberation of India in our hands unless we have made a deep study of the various sciences related to it. 'The science of Khadi,' he wrote, 'requires technical and mechanical skill of a high order and demands as much concentration as is given by Sir J.C. Bose to the tiny leaves of plants in his laboratory before he wrests from them the secrets of nature.' On another occasion, he wrote that 'the rediscovery of the "cunning of the hands", which had earlier brought fame to Indian textiles but had been lost later, would require the same kind of scientific attention that Bose and (C.V.) Raman gave to their work (Kulkarni, 2012).

Kulkarni further notes that Gandhi was a strong votary of the electrification of every village in India. But it is important to note that he preferred community owned electricity generation and distribution. About the source, he was not clear then, but about scale he was. In a conversation of Gandhi's position on machines, a socialist asked that what did Gandhi think of great inventions, and would he not have electricity? Gandhi responded,

> Who said so? If we could have electricity in every village home, I should not mind villagers plying their implements and tools with the help of electricity. But then the village communities or the State would own power-houses, just as they have their grazing pastures. But where there is no electricity and no machinery, what are idle hands to do? Will you give them work, or would you have their owners cut them down for want of work? (CWMG, vol, 61, 1975, p. 187).

He would have been in favour of clean energy as far as possible. But most important point is that he would have taken energy consumption per capita as an indicator of economic development with serious reservations. The targets set under the goal for energy do not contain any mention about reducing the energy consumption in the countries and population in the developed countries. There is a specific target to reduce energy inequality. For Gandhi reduction in economic inequality would have necessarily meant reducing excessive energy consumption by a section of the population.

Decent Work and Economic Growth

The focus is on inclusive economic growth and decent and full employment for all who seek work with special emphasis on youth. Economic growth, per se, does not appear in the Gandhian framework. One of the targets in SDG 8 is ensuring sustained economic growth of seven percent per annum until at least 2030 in the developing economies and LDCs. This is already proving difficult for a large country like India and is not going to be easy for the LDCs. The experts have also expressed reservations about achieving this target.

In the Gandhian framework, the rural economy offers scope for decent livelihood for all those who seek work. This target would go well with the Gandhian framework of sustainability in employment generation provided such a framework is accepted by the governments. Even if India accepts the Gandhian framework for employment, the sustainable employment target could be achieved gradually. The developed economies that are a guide to the developing countries have been constantly moving towards automation at an increasing pace. Youth unemployment is going to be perhaps the gravest problem in the coming decades. Normally, rapid advancements in science and technology are identified as the cause for the automated machine-based production. Techno-economic models determine and seal fate. But this is deliberate and not evolutionary. Gandhi would have approved what Kirkpatrick Sale has called human-scale technology. Sales argues,

> …it is perfectly possible for Western nations to go on with their present large-scale, centralised technology until they reach the point, in the name of efficiency and rational allocation of resources, that they absorb all enterprises under their control…. Any alternative technology would need to be designed for and controlled by the individual and of being harmonious with the individual's role in the ecosphere…a human-scale technology would need to be designed according to human needs, human capabilities, and human forms (Sale, 1980).

Responding to an anticipated argument that did science for doing so existed, Sale argues that virtually all the scientific understanding necessary is available. There is a general agreement amongst the scientific community that, for most part, all the ideas and theories that are needed to construct any kind of technology humanity wants are there. The question is do we want to apply them. Gandhi was making a similar argument. But from this perspective, SDG 8 and its targets will meet very limited success.

Industry, Reduced Inequalities, and Sustainable Cities

The divergence between the SDGs (Nine to Eleven) and the sustainability discourse in the Gandhian framework is very high. Gandhi was against uncontrolled mechanization and industrialisation. The Gandhian model of industrialisation is different. The industry was to be in rural areas, and they would be farm-based and non-farm based as well. The core of the Gandhian approach lies in decentralisation of all production. Gandhi recommended and promoted innovations that helped the development of decentralized production systems. Gandhi was pragmatic enough to realize that there would be some large-scale production of goods and services as well and hence wealth concentration may take place. Innovators do make abnormal profits and so also the monopolists. Income inequalities arise from there. SDGs aim to reduce income inequalities within a country and amongst countries. This is easier said than done. Seven percent consistent growth in GDP for decades is not possible without a lopsided development and unequal creation of wealth. Poverty may be reduced but the income inequalities would grow. In the Gandhian framework, there is a way out. Gandhi advised the principle of trusteeship. His said,

> Suppose I have come by a fair amount of wealth either by way of legacy or by means of trade and industry, I must know that all that wealth does not belong to me, what belongs to me is the right to an honorable livelihood, no better than that enjoyed by millions of others. The rest of my wealth belongs to the community and must be used for the welfare of the community (Gandhi, 1947).

According to Gandhi, trusteeship was not a legal fiction but if people meditate constantly and tried to act up it, then life on earth would be governed far more by love than it is at present. SDG promoters have conveniently glossed over this value premise. Consistently high growth in GDP alone will not help to achieve the SDGs in any significant way. Arguing for the trickledown theory is to throw crumbs at the poor.

Responsible Production and Consumption

It is about ensuring sustainable consumption and production patterns. Sustainable production is all about clean production and efficiency; it says nothing about scale and level. In the case of consumption, the only advice is about reducing wasteful consumption and recycling materials. The SDGs promoters have practically assumed that whatever technologies develop in the developed world they are necessarily good for humanity and therefore they should be transferred. This lacks scrutiny in the context of cultural differences in the societies.

In contrast, Gandhi suggests alternative methods of production. This alternative is decentralized production for local units of human settlements taking account of the surrounding ecosystem services. It does not completely forbid regional, national, and international trade and exchange of goods and services, but it insists on prioritizing the local level production and consumption of the goods and services. This production must consider the overall constraints that the local eco-systems impose on the survival of species in harmony with all other species that constitute the total ecosystem.

It is believed that consumption is end. It is not. Consumption depends upon ethics, culture, and philosophy that govern a society. Wants have to be limited and limiting wants and limiting the choices would solve a lot of problems that have arisen in the present-day functioning of the economies. It is the determination of wants and types of preference that will support the local economies that function in the overall constraints of the local ecosystem services. SDGs should thus put consumption on its agenda because Gandhian thought has something very original to offer to the world.

In the above context, *prosperity* needs to be discussed since the UN document on SDG highlights the same. The declaration document announces prosperous and fulfilling lives and adds a rider that economic, social, and technological progress should be in harmony with nature. Without any express goal and target about values that need to be followed strictly by the society prosperity and fulfilling lives remain undefined and unclear. Each country and each section of human society is free to interpret prosperity in its own way. In the Gandhian framework, prosperity is decent material survival with limited wants and fulfilling lives is for non-material quality of life.

Climate Action. Life on Land and Below Water

In the Gandhian framework, one does not have to confront climate change and ecological degradation. Humanity is at peace with nature by its own regulated behaviour. During Gandhiji's times, the global population and population of India was indeed far less than what is it today, but the approach that is suggested and the values that are promoted in the Gandhian framework support a simple lifestyle where production and consumption are restrained voluntarily.

It has been argued above that although the UN document appears sincere in its commitment to ask the countries to take urgent action for climate change, it is non-committal about impacting consumption patterns and drastic lifestyle changes. Gandhian approach recommends it ab initio.

Peace and Justice and Partnership for Goals

The UN Documents presume that global solidarity around supporting the poor and vulnerable people and countries there would be peace and prosperity. However, on peace itself, the understanding revealed via the targets does not generate hope for peace that leads to harmony amongst people and with nature. The UN peace discourse that unfolds through ten targets and two strategies has focused on two main aspects. One is non-discriminatory laws and universal access to justice, and the second is to strengthen national level institutions with an international network and support to establish rule of law around the globe to counterterrorism and crime. The strategy critically ignores the community and local level peace initiatives. Gandhi was fully aware of conflicts that arise at various levels. Building a non-violence society was also visualized as a process by Gandhiji. The economy and its structure are vital for peace and harmony but working at the community level is equally important. Gandhi suggested the formation of *shanti senas*—peace brigades—who would risk their lives during riots and other disturbances.

The approach is not restricted to communal riots situations only, but in any sociopolitical tension peace brigade has an important role. A member of a peace brigade was to have specific attributes. The first and foremost qualification is that the member must have a living faith in non-violence. Secondly, the member should have equal regard for all religions and faiths, and opinions. The peace work must be taken up at local levels. The brigade should evolve locally and should chalk out its functions and do's and don'ts. Gandhi is consistent in his approach. The peace should be built from below. Starting from a village and an urban neighbourhood people with soul force must work hard for peace. Gandhi also believed that peace and harmony were necessary for sound and sustainable socio-economic development.

Gandhi is also deeply concerned with people, planet, prosperity, peace, and partnership as the SDGs are. But SDGs have a total focus on governments, institutions, technologies, and systems to guide sustainable human development. The approach ignores the individual significantly with respect to the sense of duty and responsibility. Gandhiji's approach begins with an individual. In the Indian cultural nuance to which Gandhi referred, the actors are *vyakti, samashti, and srushti*—Individual, society, and nature. Self-regulated individuals would build sustainable practices and institutions which would help draw sustainably from nature. SDGs may have better prospects under the Gandhian frame.

References

Dasgupta, A. K. (1996). *Gandhi's economic thought*. Routledge.
Gandhi, M. K. (2000). *Gandhi's health guide*. Crossing Press.
Gandhi, M. K. (1958–1994). *Collected works of Mahatma Gandhi* (100 *volumes*). Publications Division, Government of India, New Delhi. (Volumes referred to in this chapters, 10, 47, 60, 61, 76, 81, and 89).
Gandhi, M. K. (1962). *Village Swaraj*. Compiled by Hariprasad Vyas, Navajivan Prakashan Mandir, Ahmedabad.
Gandhi, M. K. (1947). *India of my dreams*. Compiled by R. K. Prabhu. Navajivan Trust, Ahmedabad. (Sixteenth reprint 2012).
Harari, Y. N. (2018). *21 Lessons for the 21st century*. Random House, UK.
Kulkarni, S. (2012). *Music of the spinning wheel: Mahatma Gandhi's manifesto for the internet age*. Manjul Publishing House, New Delhi.
Mashruwala, K. G. (1951). *Gandhi and marx*. Navajivan Press.
Parel A. J. (Ed.), (1997). *Gandhi—hind Swaraj and other writing*. Cambridge University Press. First South Asian Edition. (Reprinted 2005).
Sale, K. (1980). *Human scale*. New Catalyst Books.
Shah R. B. (1998). *(Gujarati) Gandhian lifestyle and economic system*. Gujarat Vidyapith, Ahmedabad.
UNDP. (2015). *Sustainable development goals*. https://sustainabledevelopment.un.org/content/documents/21252030%20Agenda%20for%20Sustainable%20Development%20web.pdf. Last accessed 1 Apr 2021.

Prof. Sudarshan Iyengar is one of the foremost scholars of Gandhi in India. He is former Vice Chancellor of Gujarat Vidyapith, Ahmedabad which was founded by Mahatma Gandhi. He is currently working with Action Research in Community Health and Development (ARCH) at Dharampur Centre, Valsad, Gujarat.

Chapter 4
The Great *Tapasvi*: The Ethics of Gandhi's Politics *Swabhava, Ramrajya, Satyagraha, Tapasya*

Bindu Puri

Abstract This paper argues that a concern for justice formed the organizing insight of the ethics of Gandhi's politics. It seems apparent that whether they emphasized utility or rights, liberal conceptions of justice, rested upon the idea that justice was the concern of a consent-based state authority. Such liberal accounts (no matter the differences between them) accepted the rule of law administered by a third party and an abstract equality before such law. On a somewhat contrary note, Gandhi had argued that justice as a virtue of social institutions rested upon an *ahimsanat* individual sense of deference to the *other*—whether major- or minor-oppressed or colonizing oppressor. In this context this paper will refer to the concepts—*swabhava ramrajya swaraj* and *tapasya*—which Gandhi used (both conceptually and practically) to resolve conflicts with hostile others. Going back in history, it is perhaps significant that it was Rabindranath Tagore who had first recognized the significance of *tapasya* or self-imposed pain/austerity in Gandhian ethics when he described Gandhi as *'the great tapasvi'*.

Keywords Swabhava · Ramrajya · Swaraj · Satyagraha · Justice · Tapasvi · Ethics

Introduction

This paper will philosophically re-construct the ethics of Gandhi's politics. Any such reconstruction must begin by stating that the ethics of Gandhi's politics could be no different from the ethics of the *properly* human life. This appears apparent given that Gandhi unequivocally rejected the distinction between the private and the public-the sphere of the individual and the *socius/politicus*. Gandhi had thought about the state and the relationship between citizens using metaphors of *Ramrajya*/the kingdom of righteousness and of kinship. The ideas of *Ramrajya* as the ideal state and of citizens being bound together not by fraternity but by extended ties of the family certainly seemed to be powerfully alternative to contemporary, and predominantly liberal

B. Puri (✉)
Jawaharlal Nehru University, New Delhi, India

© National Institute of Advanced Studies 2022
A. Behera and S. Nayak (eds.), *Gandhi in the Twenty First Century*,
https://doi.org/10.1007/978-981-16-8476-0_4

conceptions, of the ethics of the political. One might note in this context for instance the difference between Gandhi's account and that of the utilitarians or that of Rawls'. It seems fair to say that though there are differences of detail between them most of the liberal conceptions of the right and justice appear to have emphasized the notions of consent-based state authority, centralized representative parliamentary democracy, third party justice, abstract equality before law, and general responsibility.

It might seem natural that Gandhi should have been concerned with justice. Given the colonial context of his movements Gandhi was obviously seeking political and economic justice for Indians. However, this paper argues that such a concern for justice governed both the means and ends of Gandhi's politics. Further the paper makes the point that on a Gandhian view, justice as a virtue of social institutions was dependent on the individual capacity for a sense of justice. In this context, upon an individual capacity of deferring to/having respect for the-often hostile- *other*. It seems important now to ask what Gandhi might have meant by 'justice'. Gandhi seemed to have understood the term primarily in the sense of 'giving all human and non-human others their due'. One may note that this association between justice and being given one's due seems close enough to the ordinary usage of the term. There is a sense in which justice demands that we/others get our/their due even when we/others may not like the result. Gandhi understood what was due to others primarily in terms of *ahimsa* love and deference to all others—friendly or hostile human or non-human.

To unpack that which is due to others purely in terms of *ahimsa* as deference might seem far afield from contemporary liberal accounts of justice. Liberty equality and the distribution of benefits and burdens in society are values which have been central to liberal theory and practice. This is well reflected in the opening words of *A Theory of Justice* where Rawls (1958) famously declared that justice is the first virtue of institutions (and by implication not of individuals). It is significant to note the differences in detail between the utilitarian principle of justice (as the design of socio-political organizations in accordance with the principle of the maximization of utility), Rawls' theory of justice as fairness, Nozick's Libertarianism, the capabilities approach and Ronald Dworkin's equality of resources doctrine. However, it is equally important to note that notwithstanding the differences between them, these theories, shared the insight that it was justice that regulated the basic structure of society and guided the organization of the distribution of goods and burdens. Though the dominant liberal accounts might have differed from each other in emphasizing utility or rights, as the case may be, they seemed to have agreed in re-iterating that justice itself was primarily a function of the consent-based state, the rule of law through the third party and an abstract equality before the law. Rawls had argued that "the sense of justice as applied to practices" was primary or "basic" (Rawls, 1958). It followed that "Justice as a virtue of particular actions or of person's" would go "quite easily "once that basic sense of justice as applied to institutions had been understood (Rawls, 1958). Whilst it is indisputable that justice provides a framework to regulate the play of competing values and ends in society and in that sense, it is a virtue of social institutions it is also true that justice must have a sanction independent of the ends and values that men actually seek. Whilst Rawls located that sanction in the principles chosen by persons in a hypothetical original position Utilitarians located it in the principle of utility. Gandhi located such a sanction firmly in *individual swaraj/*self-rule and the human capacity to defer equally to all 'others'. It may be noted that when Gandhi was recommending deference/respect in the context of religious *others,* he was clear that deference/respect was a far more exacting term than tolerance:

> Sahishnuta' is a translation of the English word 'Tolerance'. I did not like that word... Kakasaheb, too, did not like that word. ...Tolerance may imply a gratuitous assumption of the inferiority of other faiths to one's own.... (Gandhi, CWMG, Vol. 50: 78).

Gandhi's primary insight about the nature of justice as a virtue of persons or practices seemed to have been that it was because human beings had the special virtue/*khaas lakshana* of recognizing what they owed to one another that there could be a just regulation of the basic structure of society and its patterns of distribution. Gandhi had often emphasized that a properly human life was a life that was lived in accordance with the human being's innermost/true nature/*swabhava.* Such a life would entail that individuals responded to *others* with equal deference no matter if such *others* were friendly or hostile to their own interest. This is borne out by examining some of the arguments that Gandhi had made in connection with conceptions that seemed central to his political thought and practice. Accordingly, this paper will refer to *swabhava Ramrajya swaraj and tapasya* which were important to Gandhi's ethical politics.

Though Gandhi emphasized justice as a virtue of persons it would be fair to say that he shared the liberal concern with liberty and equality. Mainstream liberalism had conceptualized the simultaneous freedom of differing individuals as equality. Paradoxically enough however Liberal equality was an equality between those who could be very unequal in their private spaces. This was because liberal equality was primarily conceived as an abstract equality before the law. However, Gandhi's emphasis on justice seemed to have led him to think about the simultaneous equality of differing others along more individual terms as an equality of deference to all *others.*[1]

Man's *Swabhava/*Nature

As evident from the preceding considerations Gandhi had argued that justice as a virtue of social institutions derived its sanction from the individual sense of deference to the 'other' whether major- or minor-oppressed or colonizing oppressor. The ethics of Gandhi's politics can be best unpacked in terms of such an unconditional individual commitment to giving all *others* their due. It was on account of such a commitment—one entailing an equality of respect—that Gandhi tried to organize the basic structure of the nation state in concentric circles around relationships between the people at a local level. On this understanding, it was only smaller and local organizations which would make it possible to keep in place the individual's responsibility to practice absolute equality of respect towards friendly or hostile *others.* It was this perhaps that led Gandhi to emphasize the oceanic circle model as a way of organizing the state (Prabhu & Rao, 2007: 374). It also led to the primacy he accorded to autonomy at the local level in the form of the *panchayat* (an elected council of five village elders serving to govern a village unit in the simultaneous form of the legislative executive and judiciary) *raj*. An examination of the alternative Gandhian approach could reveal that there are crucial inadequacies in any approach to justice that concentrates overwhelmingly (and one may add *exclusively*) on institutions and the basic structure of the state rather than on the relationships between people that make up those institutions.[2]

It is significant to bring out Gandhi's related emphasis on the fact that justice should be essentially contextual. Gandhi rejected a liberal conception of justice administered through the law courts with the judge as the measure. Gandhi thought of justice differently, without a measure, as emerging from the irreducibly particular experience of giving the different (even oppressing) 'other' his/her due as one might to one's kin in the family.

Gandhi's alternative conception of justice rested upon his argument that having a sense of justice (giving the other his/her due), constituted the 'special virtue' of the *properly* human life. In order to substantiate this last point, one may recall that Gandhi often invoked two ideas, that of man's *swabhava*/own most orientation/nature, and that of *farj*/duty/*kartavya*. In the *Hind Swaraj* Gandhi had argued that *satyagraha*/passive resistance was natural/*swabhavika* to man. In 1926 in two interesting essays on the *swabhava*/nature/own most orientation of man he had gone on to develop his argument about what came naturally to man and constituted the innermost orientation of the human person. In this context one might recall Gandhi's essay *'what is natural'* in *Young India* written in June 1926.

> No word seems more abused today than the word 'natural'… not everything that is natural to the brute is natural to man.… it must therefore be, and is, man's nature to know and find God. (Gandhi, CWMG, Vol. 35: 357–58).

In this essay Gandhi had clearly explained what it might mean to describe the human being's *swabhava* in terms of the search for God. He made it clear that by relating human nature to the quest for God he did not mean to relate it exclusively to a conventional religious system or quest;

> And if it is man's nature to know and find God.… his duty is to develop all his Godward faculties to perfection…Man's nature then is not himsa but ahimsa…And from that experience he evolves the ethics of subduing desire, anger, ignorance malice and other passions.… (Ibid: 358).

As Gandhi explained it God was the way to think about the human being because a human being was an image or a reflection of God. It followed that Gandhi should have argued that it was human nature to know and indeed to find God. In this context it is significant to recall that Gandhi had famously equated God with Truth:

> If it is possible for the human tongue to give the fullest description of God, I have come to the conclusion that for myself God is Truth. But two years ago, I went a step further and said that Truth is God. You will see the fine distinction between the two statements. (Gandhi in Murti (ed), 1970: 73)

This emphasis on the idea that the quest for God/truth was constitutive of the human *swabhava*/innermost nature and that the human being was essentially non-violent suggests a commitment to a complete transparency as a search for truth in the human being's moral life. A doctor had commented upon Gandhi's essay '*what is natural*' arguing that:

> ...to prevent violence is ...positively against man's nature. Man is animal first human afterwards...Ahimsa is the creed of civilization but not man's nature. (Gandhi, eCWMG, Vol. 36: 3).

This response occasioned further reflection and Gandhi laid forth his understanding of the human being's innermost nature;

> Hitherto one has been taught to believe that a species is recognized and differentiated from the rest by its special characteristics (khaas lakshana). Therefore, it would be wrong, I presume, that a horse is animal first and horse afterwards... (Gandhi, eCWMG, Vol. 36: 3).

In responding to the criticism Gandhi re-iterated that the special virtue of the human being was indeed "that ahimsa (love) not himsa (hate) rules man..." (Gandhi, *eCWMG*, Vol. 36: 3). He explained that this entailed that human beings had the special virtue/*khaas lakshana* as a species to own:

> ...Kinship with not merely the ape but the horse and the sheep, the lion and the leopard, the snake and the scorpion...the difficult dharma which rule my life, and I hold ought to rule that of every man and woman, impose this unilateral obligation (ekpakshi farj) on us. And it is so imposed because only the human is the image of God. (Gandhi, eCWMG, Vol. 36: 3).

Quite clearly a reference to the unilateral obligation of the human person to own kinship with non-human others—whether these be snakes, scorpions, or horses—was meant to be metaphorical. Gandhi invoked this metaphor perhaps because it was the most natural way of bringing up the idea of a unilateral obligation/*farj* towards the 'otherness' of the different (sometimes hostile) other. Witness that it is relationships in the family that invoke the sense of unconditional and unilateral duties owed to *other* family members. It was just such an association between kinship and unilateral obligation that lead Gandhi to bring up the idea of kinship in the context of the special virtue of humanity as lying in a unilateral obligation towards human and non-human others.

It may be noted that Gandhi used the idea of obligation duty/*farj* in connection with various aspects of justice frequently enough to make it significant. For instance, in his response to the framers of the universal declaration of human rights in 1948 he had said that it made no sense to speak of the rights of man without duties (Puri, 2015a). On such a view an individual could earn rights only by performing his/her duties to 'others'. In this context Gandhi also sometimes used the word *paropkar* in Gujarati. The word *par* means *paraya* or the other and *upkar* means to do good. For Gandhi the special virtue/*khaas lakshana* of man was to be just to human and non-human others and as the law of love *qua* deference such a sense of justice came naturally to human beings.

This special virtue of humanity was unpacked by Gandhi in terms of *ahimsa*. In a Gandhian understanding of the term, *ahimsa*, was much more than non-violence.

It was a form of personhood that gave the contentious 'other' his/her due. Gandhi explained;

> In its positive form, Ahimsa means the largest love, the greatest charity. If I am a follower of Ahimsa, I must love my enemy. I must apply the same rules to the wrong-doer, who is my enemy or a stranger to me, as I would to my wrongdoing father or son. (Gandhi in Narayan, 1968, Vol 6: 15).

It is significant that Gandhi used examples of kinship in connection with the ideas of *swabhava Satyagraha*, rights and duties. He often invoked relations in the family as examples of *earning* individual rights by giving intimate others what one owed to them-spouse parent or child. He spoke of passive resistance/*satyagraha* by a son to his unjust father through non-violent non-cooperation with him. In *Hind Swaraj* Gandhi gave the example of the armed man who came in to steal or thieve and recommended that the thief ought to be treated as a blood brother by the victim. In describing *ahimsa* and *satyagraha* in terms of the voluntary choice made by the *satyagrahi* not to retaliate but to defer (in the context of the argument in the *Hind Swaraj*) to the thief Gandhi patterned 'otherness' on the metaphor of kinship in order to bring out the idea that the ethics of a properly human life consisted in deferring equally to hostile 'others'. However, this last point should not be taken to suggest that Gandhi recommended that one ought to accept the other's injustice passively thereby surrendering one's sovereignty to hostile powerful or intimate, others. However, it did imply that even when resisting others in extreme cases of perceived injustice one should at the minimal defer to the 'other'-defer to his/her basic needs, physical and emotional integrity, and the truth that he/she believed in. This insight led Gandhi to *Satyagraha* or a non-violent insistence on truth as the only just (and in terms of this argument) *swabhavika*/natural means to redress injustice and end conflicts. Speaking about the basic assumptions of *Satyagraha* in 1938 Gandhi said;

> I have argued from the analogy of what we do in families or even clans. The humankind is one big family. And if the love expressed is intense enough, it must apply to all mankind. (Gandhi in Murti, 1970: 42).

It seems to follow that (in a Gandhian framework) *Satyagraha* was indeed the only *swabhavika*/natural means available to man to secure freedom/*swaraj* through what Gandhi termed *tapasya:*

> Passive resistance is a method of securing rights by personal suffering: it is the reverse of resistance by arms. (Parel, 1997: 88).

Tapasya was another category that Gandhi resurrected from tradition. In this context mention may be made of other terms that Gandhi used such as *yama niyama* and *yajna* (see Puri, 2015b). It performed two related functions in a Gandhian conception of justice. For one, it transformed abstract general responsibility into individual responsibility. For another, it was a resource to effect transformation in the 'otherness' of the 'other' by intensifying the passive resistance of the *satyagrahi*. This made it possible for the subject to *secure* justice from that other without doing injustice to him/her.

Thinking Ramrajya–Gandhi's Insights About Justice

Significantly both the 'end' envisaged by Gandhian politics and the means proper to that 'end' were thought of as primarily governed by a sense of justice *swabhavik* to man. Gandhi's ideal state *Ramrajya* the reign of the just king Ram was not a metaphor for Hindu majoritarian rule but for the state, which would ensure perfect justice to the minor/subaltern. Gandhi declared often enough;

> Hind Swaraj is the rule of all people, is the rule of justice (Gandhi, 1947: 9).
>
> Poorna swaraj…. 'Poorna' complete because it is as much for the prince as for the peasent, as much for the rich landowner as for the landless tiller of the soil, as much for the Hindu as for the Mussalmans, as much for the Parsis and Christians as for the Jains, Jews and Sikhs irrespective of caste or creed or status in life (Gandhi, 1947: 9).

Gandhi emphasized that the ideal state would be one where perfect justice could be easily secured to the minor;

> By Ramrajya I do not mean Hindu Raj…Whether Rama of my imagination ever lived or not on this earth, the ancient ideal of Ramrajya is undoubtedly one of true democracy in which the meanest citizen could be sure of swift justice without an elaborate and costly procedure. Even the dog is described by the poet to have received justice under Ramrajya. (Gandhi, 1947: 326).

However, Gandhi was clear that though the aim of the National movement for India's freedom was to establish an ideal state as a state of perfect justice such an end, in itself, could not justify the use of unjust means to attain it. On this view no matter if the goal sought was political self-government, social equality, or economic redistribution of resources an assertion of individual or group rights in the quest for justice could only proceed by deferring to the hostile other.

Justice: An Alternative Gandhian Understanding

It may seem appropriate at this point to bring out some alternative Gandhian insights about justice that have emerged from the preceding considerations:

1. Gandhi's explanation of the special weight of considerations of justice in terms of the *swabhavik* /natural human sense of a "unilateral obligation" of kinship to 'otherness' went against a familiar way of thinking about justice. Going back to the Greek sophists this approach to justice rested upon the fundamental insight that the acceptance of principles of justice was always a compromise between parties who had equal power. On this account such parties/individuals would each seek to unilaterally pursue their own interest if only they had the power to do so. On all such accounts the only reason that a compromise between competing interests is sustained (albeit in the form of a precarious truce) and that force is not employed by competing parties, is that prudence compels them, to respect the equal force of one another. It may be recalled that Rawls' account, whilst

it differs in significant respects, from such a way of thinking about justice, still locates the concept of justice in "the conditions of reciprocity" (Rawls, 1958: 183–84) between "rational and mutually self-interested parties" (Rawls, 1958: 183). Gandhi's idea of unilateral obligation/*farj* is a complete rejection of the idea that justice is grounded in an acceptance of conditions of reciprocity.

2. Quite clearly (as already noted) Gandhi rejected the adequacy of liberal institutions, which secured justice for the basic structure of society. He argued in *Hind Swaraj* that the idea of third-party justice with the judge as the measure was not able to secure justice to the minor. On his view Justice was an irreducibly particular and contextual experience of arriving at the truth in situations of conflict whilst all the time remaining civil/deferring to the conflicting other. Gandhi argued (in 1909):

> It is wrong to consider that courts are established for the benefit of the people.... Surely the decision of a third party is not, always right? The parties alone know who is right. We, in our simplicity and ignorance imagine that a stranger, by taking our money, gives us justice. (Parel, 1997: 59)

The only mediation (in a Gandhian point of view) which would perhaps not disrupt or do violence to the particularity of the individual experience of seeking justice could be the voluntary decision by the parties concerned to accept the intervention of the near—the next to kin-the village elders or the *panch*.

3. In such an alternative framework questions of justice were inextricably involved with questions of truth. The equality involved in the Gandhian deference to all others was, in an important part, an equality of deference to the possibility that the truth could also lie in the position and beliefs of the contending *other*. Since truth could only be arrived at (in cases of conflict) between the parties at the site of the *supposed* injustice Gandhi's treatment of justice was essentially contextual. Consequently, it would seem to follow that Gandhi rejected the idea that there could be universal and a priori rights of man (Puri, 2015a), which could be invoked to settle conflicts, without paying attention to the particularities of the conflict. It was this aspect of justice—as essentially connected with the search for truth—that Gandhi meant to bring out when he used the metaphor of man as the image of God. This will become clear if we recall that Gandhi had famously equated Truth with God saying that Truth is the best name of God. Since one could never arrive at justice without searching for the truth in situations of conflicts, it seemed natural enough, that Gandhi should have insisted that justice was necessarily contextual.

4. Mention must be made of Gandhi's emphasis on the inseparable relationship between means adopted and end sought. It was on account of this intimate relationship between means and end that Gandhian justice could never be secured-political, economic, social, or individual-without giving 'others' their due. Consequently, the only appropriate Gandhian method to secure justice in the public sphere was one that simply extended that which came naturally to man in his most intimate conflicts. This law of love *atmabal* or the force of truth was to be brought into the arena of the conflicting relationship between

citizens in the political sphere. Therefore, *Satyagraha* as a non-violent *agraha* or insistence on *satya* or truth became the only appropriate Gandhian means to redress injustice.
5. The Gandhian *satyagrahas* and Gandhi's conception of justice shared the liberal concern with the freedom of the individual and Nation. However, Gandhi thought of such freedom differently in terms of *swaraj*. Gandhian *swaraj* was conceptualized both as political self-governance and individual self-control. Gandhis' quest for freedom was philosophically alive to the liberal concern for the simultaneous freedom of all humans as equality. However, Gandhi transformed the liberal abstract equality before the law that relegated actual inequalities to the private realm into an absolute equality that could be *practised*-an equality of deference to all human and non-human others.

Concluding Remarks

The *swabhava* of man as a sense of deference to the *otherness* of the other called forth a voluntary acceptance of pain rather than infliction of pain on the hostile other to resolve conflicts. It was in such a context that Gandhi brought in the idea of *tapas* as a means to transform both oneself and the otherness of the 'other'. A sense of justice as a function of the relationship of an equality of deference between individuals was indeed the first virtue in Gandhi and it was the organizing insight of the ethics of a Gandhian politics.

Notes

1. I owe the insight into a Gandhian understanding of equality as an equality of deference to Ajay Skaria. (Skaria, 2011: 206).
2. A further discussion of this point can be found in my forthcoming book *The Ambedkar-Gandhi Debate: On Identity, Community and Justice* in press with Springer Nature, New Delhi.

References

Gandhi, M. K., *Collected Works of Mahatma Gandhi (eCWMG)*, Vol. 1–97 (soft copy) available at http://www.gandhiserve.org/e/cwmg/cwmg.htm.
Gandhi, M. K. (1947). *India of my dreams*. In R. K. Prabhu (ed.) Ahmedabad: Navajivan Publishing House.
Gandhi, M. K. (1955). *Collected Works of Mahatma Gandhi, Volume 36, electronic edition (eCWMG)*, Ministry of Information and Broadcasting, GoI, New Delhi. accessible online at http://gandhiserve.org/cwmg/cwmg.html.
Narayan, S. (ed). (1968). *The selected works of Mahatma Gandhi*, Vol. 6, Navajivan Publishing House Ahmedabad.

Prabhu, R. K., & Rao, U. R. (Eds.). (2007). *The Mind of Mahatma Gandhi*. Navajivan Publishing House.
Parel Anthony, J. (Ed.). (1997). *M K Gandhi Hind swaraj and other Writings* Cambridge: Cambridge University Press.
Puri and (2015). "The Rights of man; A Gandhian intervention" in Jay Drydyk and Ashwini Peetush, Ashwani and Drydyk. Jay, , 2015.Puri, B. (2015). The rights of man; A Gandhian intervention. In J. Drydyk, A. Peetush, Ashwani, & D. Jay (Eds.), *Human rights: India and the West*, Oxford University Press, New Delhi.
Puri, B. (2015). The Gandhi Tagore Debate: On matters of Truth and Untruth. *Sophia : Studies in Cross-cultural Philosophy of Traditions and Cultures*, Vol. 9, Springer.
Ramana, M. V. V. (Ed). (1970). *Gandhi: Essential writings*, Gandhi Peace Foundation, New Delhi.
Rawls, J. (1958). Justice as Fairness. *The Philosophical Review, 67*(2), 164–194.
Skaria, A. (2011). Relinquishing Republican Democracy: Gandhi's Ramarajya. *Postcolonial Studies, 14*(2), 203–229.

Dr. Bindu Puri is Professor of contemporary Indian Philosophy at the Centre for Philosophy, Jawaharlal Nehru University, New Delhi, India. She is a leading scholar on the thought and practice of Mahatma Gandhi.

Chapter 5
Governance and Public Policy in India: Gandhian Perspective

Chetan Singai

Abstract Recalling Gandhi and his thoughts in the contemporary context is important to examine the need for inclusive and holistic governance and public policy. The market-led governance and public policy paradigm have limited the scope for autonomy and universalism, for instance, *'Swaraj'* and *'Sarvodaya'*—in governance and public policy. The Gandhian paradigm of development provides an appropriate context to examine the ills of the dominant paradigm of neoliberal inspired market-led rational choice approach on governance and public policy. The Chapter highlights the context, meaning, and issues associated with 'good governance' emerging out of the Washington Consensus for the developing societies as the dominant paradigm of governance and development. Against this backdrop, the Chapter argues that the Gandhian paradigm of governance provides an appropriate alternative to the dominant rational-choice paradigm of governance and public policy for inclusive and sustainable development.

Keywords Gandhi · Rational-choice · Good governance · Swaraj · New Public Management · Development

Introduction

Revisiting Gandhi and his thoughts in the contemporary context are critical to enable inclusive and holistic governance and public policy. The market-led governance and public policy paradigm have limited the scope for autonomy and inclusiveness—*'Swaraj'* and *'Sarvodaya'*—in governance and public policy, especially in the post-colonial societies. With the fall of the Soviet Union, the significance of rational choice led approach of governance and public policy has grown over the years challenging the conventional pluralistic political processes (Neimun & Stambough, 1998).

The Gandhian paradigm of development provides an appropriate context to examine the ills of the dominant paradigm of the twenty-first century, i.e. the rational

---

C. Singai (✉)
School of Social Sciences, Ramaiah University of Applied Sciences, Bengaluru, India

© National Institute of Advanced Studies 2022
A. Behera and S. Nayak (eds.), *Gandhi in the Twenty First Century*,
https://doi.org/10.1007/978-981-16-8476-0_5

choice model of governance and policy. The World Bank, along with other institutions emerging out of the 'Washington Consensus', has, over the years, integrated the neoliberal approach (inspired by rational choice model) of governance in response to the crisis of governance in the developing societies. The dominant neoliberal good governance paradigm has altered the way policy preferences are listed, designed, and implemented in most developing societies (Bhattacharya, 1998). As a result of the socio-economic and political crisis, most of the developing societies were dependent on the developed world. The World Bank report on Africa identified poor governance as the main reason for the crisis in Africa (World Bank, 1989). It argued that underlying the "litany of Africa's development problem is a crisis of governance by which was meant the exercise of political power to manage a nation's affairs" (World Bank, 1989, Pg. 23). The report argues that better 'governance' is essential for the recovery from the crisis (Pg. 8). Governance has become a checklist of criteria for managing public affairs. The World Bank-led governance prescribed and mandated a series of reforms in the public sector aligned to the New Public Management (NPM) and marketization, which the Bank believed will augment efficiency in governance (Santiso, 2001).

In the post-1990s, in response to the crisis, India was 'forced' to liberalize and reform as a 'conditionality' to seek aid by substituting the indigenous and traditional approaches of governance. Such an approach was instrumental in the loss of conviction about the state and society towards development (Manning, 2001). At this juncture, it is critical to unpack the issues with the rational choice paradigm for an inclusive agenda of development, especially for developing societies. The Gandhian paradigm of *swaraj, self-rule, and village republics* could be an appropriate alternative to the dominant paradigm. To this end, the Chapter provides a context and meaning of good governance and its implications to the state in adopting a people-centred approach in public policy in line with the Gandhian paradigm juxtaposed with the rational choice paradigm.

De-Constructing the Concept and Approach of 'Good Governance'

Government and governance are often considered to be synonymous to denote the exercise of authority over territory or system or in an institution, a state, or an organization. In recent times, governance has acquired a meaning quite distant from the government. Governance means "to steer and to pilot or be at the helm of things" (Medury, 2010, Pg. 185). According to Cleveland, governance will evolve to constitute "the organizations that get things done will no longer be hierarchical pyramids with most of the real control at the top. They will be systems—interlaced webs of tensions in which control is loose, power diffused, and centers of decision plural…because organizations will be horizontal, the way they are governed is likely to be more collegial, consensual, and consultative" (Cleveland, 1972, Pg. 13).

According to Rosenau and Czempiel (1992), "governance is a more encompassing phenomenon than government, it embraces governmental institutions, but it also subsumes informal, non-governmental mechanisms whereby those persons and organizations within its purview move ahead, satisfy their needs and fulfil their wants" (Pg. 4). Further, according to Chhotray and Stoker (2009), "governance is about rules of the collective decision-making in settings where there is a plurality of actors or organizations and where no formal control systems can dictate the terms of relationships between these actors and organizations" (Pg. 3).

The World Bank Report (1989) was supported by a series of pronouncements on governance, often linked with ideological overtures of democracy and development. The World Bank's report on 'Governance and Development' (1992) defined governance "as the manner in which power is exercised in the management of a country's economic and social resources for development." In other words, the Bank projected the importance of good governance as a critical factor in promoting sustainable and equitable development complementing the national and global economic policies (World Bank, 1989).

In line with the core idea of the Bank's prescriptions, the United Nations Development Programme (UNDP) elaborated the concept by underlining that governance is "the essence of economic, political and administrative authority to manage a country's affairs at all levels. It articulated governance in terms of eight major characteristics, that is, it should be "participatory, consensus-oriented, accountable, transparent, responsive, effective, and efficient, be equitable and inclusive and follow the rule of law" (UNDP, 1997, Pg. 44). Such an agenda of good governance seems "naïve and simplistic" (Leftwich, 1994, Pg. 365); however, the Bank in the name of good governance has touted a set of technical and economistic solutions for economic development, especially for the developing world. Arguably, as result of such "technicist illusion" (Bhattacharya, 1998), the developing world witnessed the emergence of a neo-managerial approach based on the principles of rational-choice approach influencing governance and policymaking in managing the political and economic spheres 'development' in the developing societies. As a result of such shifts, governance is now being conceptualized as the point of separation between administration and politics (Das, 1998).

Such a conception of governance has challenged the conventional bureaucratic public administration. In the present times, governance is about rationalizing and revisiting the linkages between the state, market, and the civil society to ensure participatory and people-centric development agenda. Whilst the concept and approach of (good) governance are inclusive, the implications of the same for developing societies are noteworthy. Firstly, the surge of interest in governance is associated with Western and developed governments. It is more political and ideological vis-à-vis a mere package to support the economies of the countries in the global south. During the surge of interest, especially by the end of the Cold War (1985–1989), most of the countries in the global south, especially the post-colonial societies, adopted the socialist model of development. State played a pivotal role in all spheres of economic, political, and social life in the country. The World Bank-led governance paradigm has shattered and discredited the dominant post-war state-led development paradigm.

The World Bank-led governance paradigm promoted by the West towards open and free market economies with limited role for States in developing countries to overcome the development stagnation became the order of the day (Kiely, 1998). It also meant that the West could now attach explicit political and institutional conditions to its aid without fear of losing countries in the global south or developing economies to communism or socialism (Dorn & Ghodsee, 2012). As a result of these transitions, the World Bank mandated developing economies to adopt liberalization, privatization and globalization aligned to the Bank's conceptualization of good governance as a precondition for aid and development. For instance, India was exposed to such pressures in seeking development assistance by adapting to the 'new politics of good governance touted by the Bank' (Jayal, 1997).

The Emergence of New Public Management and Rational Choice Approach

Most scholars agree that the crisis of the developmental states in the developing world were manifested by issues related to limited compliance, inadequate financial resources, lack of administrative effectiveness leading to limited or no accountability and legitimacy (Krahmann, 2003; Dorn & Ghodsee, 2012; Kiely, 1998). Referring to the background conditions of the 'good governance and its implications to reforming the governance, Leftwich (1994, Pg. 369) points out that 'western aid and overseas development policy' are defined by promotion of market-friendly economy along with forced democratization linked to human rights and legitimacy as preconditions for structural adjustment lending.

The concept of governance promoted by the World Bank looks innocuous. As a matter of fact, in retrospect, such a concept was the major cause of promoting liberal democracy in India. Such intrusions into our local context have influenced the logic of market and individualism in organizing and identifying our governance and policy priorities.

As a result of this, there is a tendency in recent years to shift the balance between state and society towards the private sector, at the cost of ignoring the public sector. In other words, privatization and deregulation are fast emerging as the dominant approach in governance and public policy. Unfortunately, people-centric, collective problem-solving, and welfare society paradigms have been ignored or labelled as 'utopian,' 'idealistic,' or 'populistic' (Das, 1998). A state that was criticized as being unresponsive, invasive, overextended, and interventionist. The public image of the bureaucracy was one of inaccessibility, indifference, procedure-orientation, poor quality, sluggishness, corruption-prone, and non-accountability for results (Bhattacharya, 1998). At this juncture, the government of India had to assure its citizens of providing an open and accountable governance at all levels. Against this backdrop, the New Public Management (NPM) emerged as an alternate model to the market-centric model of governance. The NPM emerged as a market-based public administration model with three primary goals—economy, efficiency, and effectiveness (Gaebler & Osborne, 1995).

Such orientation and transition favoured the articulation of governance as a mode of public administration along with the rise of neoliberalism—an overarching philosophy behind the New Public Management (NPM). NPM is characterized by features such as downsizing, quasi-privatization, deregulation of labour markets, contracts, market mechanisms to foster competition, and stress on customers and quality (Hood, 1991; Pollitt, 1993). The neoliberal vision of governance demands a minimalist state as espoused under the NPM. The reinvented administration wanted the state to create an 'enabling environment' for the private sector through a series of administrative, legal, and economic reforms (Sandbrook, 1995).

However, the NPM model came under criticism for the corrosion of ethics and values of public service in administration. For instance, the basic norms of public service such as neutrality, accountability, responsiveness, representativeness, and rule-of-law being substituted by pro-market values such as competition, production, profit, and efficiency (Medury, 2010). Dissatisfaction with NPM also arose from an overemphasis on the economy and the limited role of citizens as consumers rather than as members of the communities which co-planned, designed, and managed services. With this view, especially from the later 1980s, good governance was extensively promoted and used by the developing world, including India.

Amidst such pressures and criticisms, India was exposed to the NPM approach along with the economic reforms in the 1990s (Minocha, 1998). There was a widespread agreement on achieving the aspirations of good governance—accountability, citizen-friendly government, right to information, transparency, and performance-driven administration at the Central and State levels. The Fifth Central Pay Commission Report (1995) provides a reference to rationalizing the cost and effectiveness of administration and its personnel (Sahni & Medury, 2002). The recommendation of the Commission suggests adopting methods used in countries like Britain, New Zealand, Malaysia, and Canada (Minocha, 1998). The Commission recommended sweeping changes to transform the government into efficient and effective administration. 'Doing more with less, based on the logic of the private sector, was the order of the day. Such an approach reflects the hidden agenda of capitalist neoliberalism embedded in the agenda of the World Bank's idea of good governance'.

Neoliberal policies emphasize innovation and competitiveness enabling an ecosystem for international competition and innovation. The emphasis is on economic policy rather than social policy. Such an emphasis will aid labour markets and the flow of capital to be more flexible as such the emphasis is on the cost of production rather than on means of redistribution and social cohesion. In sum, the neoliberal policies foster economic globalization supporting and sustaining the project of neoliberal democracy. The neoliberal agenda for good governance is ostensibly a search for solutions to the failure of the state through unrestricted freedom for the market. Against the backdrop of pressures of World Bank-led good governance and the dominance of NPM, the rational policymaking model has attained unprecedented attention by policymakers in India.

Rational Choice Model and Its Encounter in India

In the late 1980s, the rational choice model of policymaking replaced the bureaucratic and input–output model of public policy in India (Mishra, 1998). The bureaucratic model believes in top-down administration in fulfilling the needs of the citizens expressed as desires. A model which considers public policy as a limited task and as a continuous operation. A model of this kind benefits in attending to routine problems. During the initial years of independence, the Bureaucratic model became the preferred approach in addressing large-scale challenges and aspirations of the nation. Whilst such an approach enabled an ecosystem of governance, it was largely top-down than bottom-up. However, the Bureaucratic model, in the last few decades, has lost its strategic significance because the World Bank promoted good governance and the introduction of economic reforms in India.

The input–output model of public policy replaced the bureaucracy for pivotal policymaking decisions and crisis situations. In this model, the policymakers assess various environmental factors often raised by elected representatives as inputs leading to decisions of the government as policy outcomes. According to Mishra (1998), "the Indian public policy scenario points out that at the informal and unorganized level, the demand of public policy formulation and implementation is taken care of by this model" (Pg. 117).

The rational choice policymaking model emphasizes that policymaking is a choice amongst policy alternatives on rational grounds. Maximization of net value achievement is the central point of this model. To ensure maximum value with minimum resources, the rational choice model concerns itself with privatizing the allocation of societal resources for maximizing the social benefits during a given period. According to the rational choice model, rationality is considered the 'yardstick of wisdom' in policymaking. Rational policymaking is "to choose the best option" (Dye, 1972, Pg. 104). Thomas Dye argues, "a policy is rational when it is most efficient, that is if the ratio between the values it achieves and the values it sacrifices is positive and higher than any other policy alternative" (Dye, 1972, Pg. 106).

In such changing governance strategies due to the changing role of the state, market forces and individualism often trump social goals. The market based NPM model is driven by the profit and efficiency criterion; there is a need to revisit and examine the Gandhian paradigm of governance.

The Gandhian Paradigm of Governance

Gandhi believed in the concept and practice of the welfare state and encouraged people to work towards bettering the situation of the downtrodden in any ways in which a privileged man could. According to Gandhi, good governance is related to resolving problems of the poor and marginalized sections of the society. Gandhi's proposition of good governance is in terms of his concern, that is, "do the policies help the poorest and weakest man? If yes, that is good governance" (Amerjee, 2021, Pg. 768). This thought and perspective of Gandhi have been echoed by the World Bank and many renowned economists, who have emphasized the importance of working towards uplifting the lowest rung of the society. Former World Bank Chief Economist François Bourguignon said the welfare of a country could be assessed by measuring the living standards of the last decile of its population. As such, this is how our country's public policy and governance mechanism should be created. Such a thought of Gandhi was endorsed by Deen Dayal Upadhyay, who said that the real development of a country could only take place if the person who is at the lowest rung of the ladder is uplifted through his one of the most popular ideas of *Antyodaya*. In the present scenario of our nation, there exists an Economic and Social gap creating a divide amongst the urban elite and the rural masses. There exists a divide amongst the different sections of the society, like those who support the Western culture and those who do not.

This economic and cultural difference amongst the people goes against the very social fibre that Gandhi espoused (Nadkarni et al., 2017). This is an area where our policymakers and researchers in the field should create policies and governance structures that allow us to close these divides. Our established structures must strive to raise the living standard of those who are at the bottom of the ladder, in all aspects, be it education, health, social or economic benefit. To develop our country and uplift every person out of poverty, we as a nation should deep-dive into Gandhi's philosophy.

The panacea for issues and constraints in policymaking was sought to be discovered in the new system of 'good governance. There are the social contract theorists who propose that the government must resolve and safeguard the citizens from nasty social status to an orderly living condition. Further, the utilitarians prescribe the principle of 'the greatest good of the greatest number' as the mission of the government. According to J.S. Mill, "one criterion of the goodness of a government is the degree in which it tends to increase the sum of good quantities in the governed" (Bhattacharya, 1998, Pg. 290). In contrast to the utilitarians, the Gandhian paradigm prescribes a condition where everyone grows with special reference to the underprivileged sections being bailed out of the vicious cycle of poverty.

Modern society induced with a sense of materialism based on misleading ideas of wealth and merit have often led to unwarranted competition and violence. In contrast, Gandhi said, "real civilization would be found in enlightened villages unfettered by modernity" (Nadkarni et al., 2017: 26). To this end, Gandhi believed that satyagraha as a mode of social engagement would enable a social system driven by cooperation rather than competition resolving unwarranted tensions and violence in the society (Parel, 2010). In other words, Gandhi believed that it is only through morality and values, the nation can lead an independent and self-sufficient 'new' life.

The core principles of good governance rely on value and respect for human rights, rule-of-law, transparency, and accountability. An inclusive governance and policy-making approach is essential to address the needs and aspirations of the citizens (Rodrik, 2000). To this end, the local-self-government model proposed by Gandhi, the 'village republics' constitute as an effective mechanism in addressing the challenges of inclusive governance. Such an approach is not new to India. Since ancient times, villages have been one of the key units of administration and governance, embedded into the ideals of participatory democracy.

Similarly, Gandhi advocated the cause of *Vasudhaiva Kutumbakam*, i.e. 'the world is one family'. By saying so, he encouraged people to maintain an atmosphere of harmony and compassion not just amongst humans but also inclusive of the ecosystem. He emphasized eco-friendly growth and the idea of sustainable development. These ideas and thoughts carry not only value but gather extreme importance in today's times wherein any development program or policy scheme which India acquires requires to be focused on sustainable development, keeping in mind the wellbeing of our future generations.

Gandhi's idea of democratic decentralization bears testimony to his belief in the rule of law, strengthening of the democratic institutions starting from the grassroots level, promoting transparency and capacity in public administration. Gandhi favoured participatory democracy and advocated for 'a village-based political formation fostered by a stateless, classless society' for the creation of Gram Swaraj. Gram Swaraj is an ideal non-violent social order in which self-sufficient, self-reliant, self-governing village-states function independently in vital matters. It is a holistic concept of decentralized democracy (Nadkarni et al., 2017). It is a total revolution and a complete grassroots democracy in which people are awakened to their capabilities and are fully empowered. It is founded on spiritual values such as inner self-rule, love, compassion, service, and sacrifice and the reorientation of development, minimum government, universalism, individual, and the national. *Gram Swaraj*, as conceived by Gandhiji, is not the resurrection of the old village Panchayats but the formation of new independent village units of Swaraj in the context of the present-day world.

In a letter to Pandit Nehru dated 5–10-1945, Gandhiji wrote (Parel, 2010, Pg. 144),

> I am convinced that if India is to attain true freedom and through India the world also, then sooner or later the fact must be recognized that the people will have to live in villages, not in towns, in huts, not in palaces. Crores of people will never be able to live in peace with each other in towns and palaces. They will then have no recourse but to resort to both violence and untruth. I hold that without truth and non-violence, there can be nothing but destruction for humanity. We can realize truth and non-violence only in the simplicity of village life.

Gram Swaraj is the practical embodiment of truth and non-violence in the spheres of politics, economics, and sociology. He considered Gram Swaraj as an ideal society which is a stateless democracy with participatory governance where social life has become so perfect that it is self-regulated.

Gandhi elaborated on this village-centric theory in an article published in 1944 (in Friedman, 2008, Pg. 60), "Independence must begin at the bottom. Thus, every village will be a republic having full powers. It follows, therefore, that every village has to be self-sustained and capable of managing its affairs even to the extent of defending itself against the whole world. It will be trained and prepared to perish in the attempt to defend itself against any onslaught from without" (Pg. 60).

The Gandhian concept of Panchayat Raj was basically a state diminishing and society-enriching concept, reliance being placed on autonomous social groups. Gandhi's idea of self-sustained village republics was in response to the social and economic conditions around him. John Ruskin's 'Unto this last' (1907) and Henry Maine's 'Village Communities' (1871) in the East and West had a profound influence on Gandhi. Gandhi saw the great potential of local leadership in 'Gram Sevaks.' He opined that, to make the village folk self-sufficient, a skilled workforce that is ready to work in the rural areas is required. The selected Gram Sevaks would train the villagers in many fields like healthcare and medicine, education and agriculture, irrigation, and animal husbandry. However, before doing so, they would have to win the confidence of the villagers by developing a bond with them. The Gram Sevaks would have to teach the villagers how to help themselves and procure for them such help and materials which the villagers require. As a facilitator, the Gram Sevaks were intended to work hard to improve the capacity of village communities to take care of their own resources.

Gandhi's concern for modern civilization and *swaraj* expressed itself in his deep interest in the revitalization of India's villages. Not many thinkers in India had a better grasp of the truth that *swaraj* would mean little for India if the lives of the poor in the villages saw no significant improvement. The pragmatic side of Gandhi always believed that, in a country so overpopulated and heavily dependent on agriculture, the villages held the key to economic and political development (Chakrabarty, 2006, Pg. 103). Gandhi always believed that the unit of society would be the village where all the activities will be organized on a cooperative basis.

Gandhi advocated for a people-centred approach as the idea of good governance and development at the community level, which ensured that rural people had access to relevant information to make them informed citizens who can collaborate and participate in development (Nair & Sharma, 2016). The Gandhian idea of effective government and governance revolves around enhancing rural communication services at the grass-root level to empower local people to manage the rural development processes. Thus, Gandhi advocated for two main aspects of governance—'increased participation' and 'effective communication.'

Gandhian Paradigm for New and Emerging India

Gandhi's conceptualization of good governance juxtaposed the popular rational-choice model of governance, touted by the World Bank. "It is not the British who are responsible for the misfortunes of India," Gandhi writes in *Hind Swaraj*, "but we who have succumbed to modern civilization" (Parel, 2010, Pg. 126). Gandhi's approach propagates a moral framework of governance enabling a decentralized participatory model for inclusive and sustainable development. In other words, the attainment of Swaraj to pursue socio-economic and political stability, post-independence, was an appropriate and urgent task for India. In his book *Hind Swaraj*, Gandhi writes "that India will have nominal "self-rule" when the British disengages but will not have actual self-rule until India undergoes a spiritual regeneration" (Pg. 37). Gandhi believed in ensuring control over greed and violence as preconditions to ensure prosperity and well-being (Parel, 2010).

As a result of the neoliberal infused World Bank led good governance policies, the government as part of its reform agenda has favoured the market-led agenda of governance and development. The neoliberal paradigm of governance is a response to the economic crisis. The Gandhian paradigm of governance exposes the crisis in humanity to modern civilization, which has fostered materialism, indoctrinated false ideals of merit and wealth, and led to violence and competition as development. In *Hind Swaraj*, Gandhi emphasized that "the Western civilization which passes for civilization is disgusting to me" (Parel, 2010, Pg. 138).

Amidst such pressures, the government has espoused localized governance principles as envisaged by the Constitution of India. Aligned to the ethos of welfare state and the Gandhian principles, the Directive Principles of State Policy (DPSP), Part IV of the Constitution of India, envisioned an inclusive and participatory form of governance. These principles are positive instructions and do not refrain the state from enacting laws based on Directive Principles. Article 37 explicitly states that these principles are "fundamental in the governance of the country and that it is the duty of the state to apply these principles in making laws and policies". Article 39 urges the state to ensure that "the citizens, men, and women equally, have the right to adequate means to livelihood".

The Mahatma Gandhi Rural Employment Guarantee Act, 2005 (MNREGA) owes its existence to the Gandhian philosophy of village republics. The MNREGA addresses the needs of disadvantaged groups. The Gram Panchayat has been endowed with substantial responsibility for local governance. Similarly, embarking on the Gandhian thought juxtaposed to the rational choice model, followings are some of the programs as part of its governance and policy agenda inspired by the Gandhian paradigm—'*sab ka sath, sab ka Vikas, sabka vishwaas,*' '*swachh bharat; 'Atma Nirbhar'; 'Kaushal Vikas Yojana'; 'Swasth Bharat'; and 'Gram Swaraj,*' are a few initiatives reminding the significance of Gandhian paradigm for contemporary governance and public policies.

Conclusion

In the paradigm of good governance as espoused by the World Bank, the state has a new and important role to play in reconciling the interests of public and private institutions as well as in social action (Medury, 2010). The prospects of the rational choice dominant paradigm in developing countries like India are limited indeed, given the paucity of data and appropriate technology needed for policymaking. Also, such a paradigm has in the past evidenced serious exclusion of values such as equity and responsiveness. Policy and governance are central to Gandhian thought, especially in the Indian context.

Given the era of capitalist innovation, market laws have developed a tendency to exclude many people and even threaten to dominate holistic development. Market logic and influence have emerged as the dominant paradigm as contemporary discourse determines governance and public policy. Such a paradigm emerging in the developed world is fast influencing the developing world. India is no exception to this. Gandhi and his thoughts constitute an important part of the indigenous and alternative paradigm of governance.

References

Amerjee, A. (2012). Role of the CAG in meeting challenges of Good Governance. *Journal of Governance., 1*(6), 766–778.
Article 37. The Constitution of India, 1950.
Article 39. The Constitution of India, 1950.
Bhattacharya, M. (1998). Conceptualising good governance. *Indian Journal of Public Administration, 44*(3), 289–296.
Cleveland, H. (1972). *The future executive: A guide for tomorrow's managers.* Harper & Row.
Das, S. K. (1998). *Civil service reform and structural adjustment.* Oxford University Press.
Dorn, C., & Ghodsee, K. (2012). The Cold War politicization of literacy: Communism, UNESCO, and the World Bank. *Diplomatic History, 36*(2), 373–398.
Dye, T. R. (1972). Policy analysis and political science: Some problems at the interface. *Policy Studies Journal, 1*(2), 103–107.
Fifth Pay Commission. (1997). Report of the Fifth Pay Commission, Government of India, Ministry of Finance.
Frederickson, H. G. (2005). Whatever happened to public administration? Governance, governance everywhere. The Oxford handbook of public management, pp. 282–304.
Friedman, J. S. (2008). Mahatma Gandhi's vision for the future of India: The role of enlightened anarchy. *Penn History Review, 16*(1), 5.
Gandhi, M. (2019). Hind Swaraj (centenary edition). Rajpal & Sons: New Delhi.
Hood, C. (1991). A public management for all seasons? *Public Administration, 69*(1), 3–19.
Jayal, N. G. (1997). The governance agenda: Making democratic development dispensable. *Economic and Political Weekly,* 407–412.
Kiely, R. (1998). Neo liberalism revised? A critical account of World Bank concepts of good governance and market friendly intervention. *Capital & Class, 22*(1), 63–88.
Krahmann, E. (2003). National, regional, and global governance: One phenomenon or many. *Global Governance, 9,* 323.
Leftwich, A. (1994). Governance, the State, and the Politics of Development. *Development and Change, 25*(2), 363–386.
Maine, H. S. (1871). *Village communities in the east and west: Six lectures delivered at Oxford.* Spottiswoode and Co.
Manning, N. (2001). The legacy of the New Public Management in developing countries. *International Review of Administrative Sciences, 67*(2), 297–312.

Medury, U. (2010). *Public Administration in the Globalisation Era: The New Public Management Perspective*. Orient Blackswan.

Minocha, O. P. (1998). Good governance: New public management perspective. *Indian Journal of Public Administration, 44*(3), 271–280.

Mishra, R. K. (1998). Some Dimensions of Public Policy Management in India. *Indian Journal of Public Administration, 44*(2), 115–124.

Nadkarni, M. V., Sivanna, N., & Suresh, L. (2017). *Decentralised Democracy in India: Gandhi's Vision and Reality*. Routledge India.

Nair, P., & Sharma, S. (2016). Gandhi and Governance: Relooking Development at Grassroot Level. *Mainstream, 54*(41), 7–10.

Neimun, M., & Stambough, S. J. (1998). Rational choice theory and the evaluation of public policy. *Policy Studies Journal, 26*(3), 449–465.

Osborne, D., & Gaebler, T. (1995). Reinventing government. *Journal of Leisure Research, 27*(3), 302.

Parel, A. (2010). Gandhi and the Emergence of Indian Political Canon. *Comparative Political Theory: An Introduction*, New York, NY: Palgrave Macmillan.

Pollitt, C. (1993). *Managerialism and Public Services: Cuts or cultural change in the 1990s?* Blackwell Business.

Rodrik, D. (2000). Development strategies for the 21st century. In *Annual World Bank Conference on Development Economics*, pp. 85–108.

Rosenau, J. N., & Czempiel E. O. (1992). Governance without government: order and change in world politics. Cambridge: Cambridge University Press. http://doi.org/10.1017/CBO9780511521775

Ruskin, J. (1907). *Unto this last and other essays on art and political economy*. London: J. M. Dent & Sons. (Original work published 1860).

Sahni, P., & Medury, U. (2002). *Governance for development: Issues and strategies*. PHI Learning Private Ltd: New Delhi, India.

Sandbrook, R. (1995). Bringing politics back in? The World Bank and adjustment in Africa. *Canadian Journal of African Studies/la Revue Canadienne Des Études Africaines, 29*(2), 278–289.

Santiso, C. (2001). Good governance and aid effectiveness: The World Bank and conditionality. *The Georgetown Public Policy Review, 7*(1), 1–22.

Vasudha, C., & Stoker, G. (2009). Governance theory and practice: A cross-disciplinary approach. *Journal of Public Administration, 87*(4), 982–983.

World Bank. (1989). Sub-Saharan Africa: From Crisis to Sustainable Growth: a Long-term Perspective Study. Washington, D.C.: World Bank Group. Available at http://documents.worldbank.org/curated/en/498241468742846138/From-crisis-to-sustainable-growth-sub-Saharan-Africa-a-long-term-perspective-study, Retrieved on June 23, 2021.

Dr. Chetan Singai is an Associate Professor, School of Social Sciences, Ramaiah University of Applied Sciences Bengaluru.

Part III
Science, Values and Education

Chapter 6
Making of a Man: A Reading of Gandhi's Philosophy in 21st Century

Ranjan K. Panda

Abstract Humanity in the twenty-first century, despite its incredible progress, encounters several challenges which are, arguably, deeply rooted in human attitude and aspirations grounded on a materialistic view of life. A thoughtful reading of Gandhi's philosophical thoughts might help us overcome this crisis and rebuild society to celebrate humanity and its commitment to higher values of life. This paper discusses the flaw in materialistic conceptualization and celebration of man as a super functional entity. Such a conception is insufficient to transform society and save humanity from this current crisis. A human being is not a functional entity; instead, he/she has a substantive existence so far as the production of knowledge and values are concerned. Gandhi conceptualizes the notion of the human as not merely a combination of mind and body, but rather having a spiritual element as an integrating metaphysical principle that cannot be reduced to the materiality of life. To comprehend this integral existence of human life, we need to reflect deeply into his various experiments and engagements that unfold truth following the path of non-violence. Gandhi's commitment to truth and non-violence has tremendous epistemic power to awaken us to a realm of self-knowledge that would help humanity make a man that a flourishing civilization needs.

Keywords Gandhi · Making of a Man · Truth and Non-violence · Spirituality · Gandhi's Philosophy

Introduction

In the twenty-first century, though humanity has progressed tremendously in science, technology, information processing, and communication, it still encounters several challenging problems: social inequality, poverty, malnutrition, climate change, pollution, proxy wars and terrorism, and more recently, COVID-19 Pandemic. These encounters show that the crisis is deeply rooted in human attitude and aspirations

---

R. K. Panda (✉)
Department of Humanities and Social Sciences, Indian Institute of Technology Bombay, Mumbai, India
e-mail: ranjan.panda@iitb.ac.in

© National Institute of Advanced Studies 2022
A. Behera and S. Nayak (eds.), *Gandhi in the Twenty First Century*,
https://doi.org/10.1007/978-981-16-8476-0_6

grounded on a materialistic view of life that cultivates individualism, selfishness, brutishness, and a pleasure-centric lifestyle affected by anxiety, fear, and insecurity. A thoughtful reading of Gandhi's philosophical thoughts might help us overcome this crisis and rebuild society in a meaningful way to celebrate humanity and its commitment to higher life values. Thus, the paper discusses the flaw in materialistic conceptualization and celebrating man as a super functional entity. Such a conception is insufficient to transform society and save humanity from this current crisis. The materialistic attitude erodes the fundamental ethos of life, values, and existence. A human being is not a functional entity; instead, he/she has a substantive existence so far as the production of knowledge and values are concerned. Gandhi conceptualizes the notion of man not merely a combination of mind and body but instead having a spiritual element as an integrating metaphysical principle that cannot be reduced to the materiality of life. To comprehend this integral existence of human life, we need to reflect deeply into his various experiments and engagements that unfold truth following the path of non-violence. Gandhi's commitment to truth and non-violence has tremendous epistemic power to awaken us to a realm of self-knowledge that would help humanity make a man that a flourishing civilization needs.

Knowledge Age, Technological Convergence and Humanity in Troubled Times

Centuries have passed; humanity has encountered the emergence of many civilizations and seen the decline of a few. The fall of a civilization can be traced from the intent of violence, which is articulated in many languages. From globalization, high-tech-capitalism to the bureaucratization of politics, there is the complete absence of a bond that configures the entire community under the idea of humanity. The decline of present civilization–*decivilization* has put humanity in the crossroad. Like Plato's prisoners of the cave, we are trapped inside the world of meaninglessness and sources that fuel violence's re-emergence (Jahanbegloo, 2017). The multilingual form of violence terminates inter-cultural communication. Civilization represents the divergence of cultures, but if the expansion of one culture destroys the other cultures, it takes away the spiritual atmosphere of human civilization. The spirit of the civilization thrives on empathy, compassion, and mutual understanding. Unless these values are raised from individual self-consciousness to the collective societal consciousness and further cultivated for the larger goal of sustaining civilizations, humanity will keep bleeding.

Ramin Jahanbegloo's this observation concerning *decivilization* invites us to reflect upon the everyday life in which humanity encounters restlessness, anxiety, and fear. Judgements and values are digitized, quantified, and expressed in utilitarian terms as if everything is a business and measured by the scale of profit and loss. Life has no significance beyond its essential existence, whether about climate change, poverty, proxy wars, terrorism, abuses, rapes, or murders. The recent attack of the COVID-19 pandemic has aggravated this situation multiple times. Millions have succumbed to death, several have lost their livelihood, and many have become parentless (Jahanbegloo, 2020).

Consequently, all these have intensified the growth of poverty and inequality, and more importantly, pessimism about life has unpredictably increased the challenges of everyday life. Research in biotechnology and artificial intelligence has helped develop vaccines faster and quicker in processing information, advancing machine learning and e-commerce has increased to minimize the challenges. Human proximity and reliance on technology through augmented, the quality of life has not improved proportionately. Unfortunately, all these are happening when we are living in the 'age of knowledge century' (Devy, 2017).

Globally there has been a tremendous emphasis on education, knowledge production and dissemination. Researchers and academics have been persistent in widening the horizon of disciplinary knowledge and bringing cross-disciplinary studies to show the emergence of new fields of knowledge such as data science, nanotechnology, information technology, artificial intelligence, robotics, biotechnology, and bioinformatics, to name a few, (Devy, 2017) still in this century there is massive despair for everything. Human life is sinking rapidly in technology as it is flourishing inexhaustibly in every domain of human existence. "From artificial intelligence and "Big Data" to mapping the human genome and human cloning, recent research in computer science and the life sciences has posed profound questions about the meaning, limits and essence of the human" (Sitze, Sarat & Wolfson, 2015: 196). This century, technology has an overriding presence, from health appliances to a health diagnosis, space studies to measuring carbon footprints and weather prediction. The use of technology has defined human existence in all the spheres of life, such as economics, politics and religion. 'It is breeding its new wants. There is a need for a critical engagement to understand this enterprise that promotes mechanical means and new commodities influential in changing the habits of life and consciousness' (Jonas, 1979: 38–39).

So far as the technological transformation is concerned, it has succeeded in integrating private life with the social life that has redefined our identities. In multiple ways, technological knowledge production provides a solution to practical needs (Myllyntaus, 2010). This engagement with technology and technological knowledge production is deeply connected to capitalism and the market economy. Michael Peters, who reflects on technological convergence, writes that "we live in a global economy where nanotechnology, biotechnology, IT and Cognitive Sciences are converging into new capitalistic strategies or "advanced capitalism", which aims to accumulate profits by investing in the commodification of all that lives" (Peters, 2020: 244). He also calls this 'advanced capitalism' in the name of 'bio-informational capitalism' or 'algorithmic capitalism.' We must pay attention deeply to how this technoscience culture is motivated and nurtured. One example he cites is the use of 'fifth generation cybernetics capitalism, which benefited mostly from financialization and high-frequency trading.' It has some implications also in the domain of geopolitics. No doubt, the convergence of technology takes us to a new stage in advancing knowledge society. However, it has repercussions on health and security.

Peters reminds this referring to Boisvert, who claims that "intelligent technology is a slow form of violence rescripting the nervous system, which in turn affect physical wellbeing, inter-personal relationship, and by extension, the fabric of society" (Peters, 2020: 247). Thus, technological change underlines the greater risk for the future of humanity.

It is hard to give up technology because our horizon of thinking does not proceed beyond our materialistic needs. We are caught in the prison of desire and its immediate gratification, no matter at what cost it comes to us. Because essentially people believe that 'everything can be bought and sold. The market determines the value and plays a greater role in social life' (Sandel, 2012: 7–8). That very attitude covers everything. Hence the intent of globalization or industrialization is concealed, as if everything is well and fine, no matter what it brings to humanity in future. The convergence of technology is predicted to be highly disruptive as it has some consequences on the economy, norms, and governance as predicted by Brannen, Ahmed and Newton (2020), but we also need to look at its impact on climate change, as we will be competing with limited resources. Conflicts may arise concerning the shortage of food, water and health facilities. Seeing the fragile structures of our societal interests and climate change, Paola Spadaro writes, "The evolution of human civilization has come at the expense of the natural world. The unsustainable resources and modern human's creation of scarcity have unleashed unprecedented climate variability and ecosystem's collapse" (Spadaro, 2020: 58). The collapse of the ecosystem, in the reading of Spadaro, is not merely apprehensive about its impact on extinct species but also raising concern for eco-terrorism. Competition on local resources and livelihood always creates fear and anxiety, which engender violence. Thus, Devy is correct in stating that the 'scale in which violence occurs is unmatched with past years of human history' (2019: ix).

According to Devy, the root of violence has proliferated largely due to the mechanized form of wars that would involve the long strategic plan for developing sophisticated chemical and biological war weapons to spread fear and have premediated political-economic control and political hegemony over other nations. Globalization has favoured a majoritarian approach to development and annihilated the minorities (2019: x). The prosperity of a society is counted by its economic affluence and the ability to produce more and consume more; more importantly, "more than we need. This is the new ethic, the new *dharma*. The rhetoric of modernity and the ideology of progress boils down to what Gandhi called violence" (2019: 48). Gandhi's criticism of modernity has been resilient and spiritually active, providing an alternative ethical model against the culture of consumerism and materialism. Industrialization and globalization have spread the ethos of materialism and its values, putting civilization in crisis.

No civilization can sustain this crisis. Hence, both Jahangebloo and Devy recall Gandhi's moral and spiritual voice to counter the violence and rescue the civilization from decivilizing. However, before discussing Gandhi's philosophical ideas on saving civilization in troubling times, we need to reflect on the metaphysics of the notion of man that perpetuates materialistic consciousness in everyday life. Moreover, the possibility of transforming it.

Materialistic Life and Its Discontentment

The materialistic consciousness unfolds an attitude of possessing everything that an individual desires to achieve. It is a natural appetite that continuously drives for material possessions, in terms of money, wealth, houses, cars, luxurious accessories, etc. More importantly, the accumulation of properties and power for personal satisfaction and quality of life has been a determining criterion for living standards. In a materialistic society, human beings are consumers, and consumer satisfaction essentially plays a decisive role in the market economy. Consumptions are not about fulfilling the needs, but as observed, they get unconsciously into the realm of livelihood, where consumers proclaim self-esteem and self-actualization. In a particular income group, material aspirations are broadly comparable and that adds to their happiness (Easterlin, 2001). People are primarily concerned about living a quality life, and when their income increases, it will impact greater happiness (Sirgy et al., 2013). The increase in the income level accelerates the possibility of consumption on a large scale. However, it is not easy to assert that an increase in income level would increase happiness.

Happiness or consumer satisfaction largely depends on the expectations. Sometimes the expectancy level is so high that there is no coordination with the standard of living; as a result, they fail to accomplish their goal and bring dissatisfaction to their life. People get demotivated and frustrated unless they alter their negative self-evaluation. Hence, it is essential to look at how individuals relate to the material domains concerning income, wealth, health, family, leisure, etc. There are multiple ways of constructing this relation. Some would like to work less but have high expectations for income. Easy life and the tendency to spend more than income is a sign of a materialistic attitude (Sirgy, 1998). Hence, it is essential to take note of the motivational tendency on individual perception of self. Like the great Charvaka thinkers in one of the ancient schools of philosophy emphatically maintained that 'eat ghee, never mind even if you have to borrow', living happily or merrymaking cannot be compromised. People often quote this, but they do not consider the moral standard the Charvakas had towards borrowing conditions. It would be a prejudice to infer that Charvakas were irrational and unreasonable in their actions. Nevertheless, the crucial point is that the consumer must positively self-evaluate with worldly life to achieve satisfaction, but that consumer would rationally situate the end, which will match the basic living standard (Sirgy, 1998: 253).

In a socio-economic relationship, when we measure the quality of life of people concerning anxiety, stress, depression, drug abuse, child abuse, domestic violence, rapes, and murders happening around the globe, it would not be hard to relate them with them the consumeristic form of life. Such an inference seems reasonable because consumerism is not merely about accumulating wealth but also the tendency to possess and enjoy power towards the immediate gratification of desire. It represents a case of an expression of *natural appetite* in the language Thomas Hobbes that a consumer nurtures not only for the immediate gratification of desire, instead rears it for the future too, "as a result, but man also becomes the strongest, the most feared, the wisest and most dangerous animals"(Ratulea, 2015: 47). Strength, fear and knowledge are acquired to possess and rule; it is the power of the brutish force that one exercise over the other whilst controlling and exploiting for the sake of gaining pleasure, then that 'aspiration is measured as evil in man. This inclination of humanity consists of the perpetual and restless desire of power after which ceases only in death' (Ratulea, 2015: 47).

No doubt, in the Hobbesian framework, distrust and demotivation prevail in the absence of a robust central authority who can enforce laws. Without cooperation and convention, laws of the authority might fail to establish liberal social order. Distrust makes a case for an impossible market economy. In addition to that, greed for power and wealth causes inequality which is always a threat to security. Whilst reflecting on the economic dimension of the human condition, Peter Lawrence writes, "The increasing concentration of wealth and power in the hands of a small group of individuals corporate remains a global faultline that threatens democracy and human rights everywhere" (Lawrence, 2021: 31). Violation of human rights puts humanity in crisis. It raises grave concern for humanity as it destroys an ordinary world. Whilst reflecting on this question concerning humanity, Adam Sitze et al. remind us in the prophetic voice of Hanna Arendt: "Crisis ruins the common-sense that otherwise allows a coherent experience of the world" (2015: 193). It is indeed a challenge to develop a coherent view of the world within the framework of materialism. The underlying assumption of materialism thus illustrates that man is a material entity, and all the endeavours of man can be reduced to specific basic facts based on bodily needs and functions.

Materialists believe that 'matter is eternal and dialectical' (Fuchs, 2020: 31). Matter exists in a basic form of reality, and its nature is dynamic. The material existence and vitality disclose the existence of its being and possibilities of future existence. As Fuchs summarizes, "Materialism stresses that the whole world is a complex of production, in which matter produces and organizes itself and thereby develops. Materialism is opposed to idealism, dualism and religious worldviews" (2020: 39). The world includes the presence of man in it. Man is not a separate entity; instead, its existence can be defined concerning the material conditions of the world, that is, self-producing and self-reproducing.

Further, human beings can be better understood in a social and historical context. Everything about human life can be scientifically studied by looking at their historical and social conditions. The objectification of human behaviour was the larger project of human studies, which started in the eighteenth century and integrated human sciences with natural sciences (Teggert, 1919). This integration helps to predict or calculate human behaviour by treating humans as machines (Pradhan, 2020: 11). This outcome of materialism undermines the fact that 'life means much more than living', which cannot just be reduced to mechanical principles of matter and explain away all its civilizational meaningfulness.

There is a need to understand the intellectual and emotional nature of human life to transcend reductionism. Human life is much more than its corporeal existence and capabilities and must not be obsessed with measuring it within the theoretical framework of technoscience and using that knowledge to boost the realm of consumerism further. The culture of techno-science with its mutual alliance with consumerism engenders the pathos of alienation, which divides society and fractures the relationship between man and nature. The failure is not merely due to lack of trust but the experience of coercive forces in every sphere of life that breach the peaceful relationship in society. Furthermore, this added to the failure of imagination of new possibilities and its meaningfulness to see the value of humanity. Western civilisation's man-centric or anthropocentric philosophical outlook has affected the ecosystem in which human beings are figures at the centre of the universe. If men are the maker of their destiny, they cannot wake up with the normative attitude of commitment and responsibility towards the other beings and the universe.

Humanism has been proliferated in the name of essentialism, naturalism, existential humanism, etc. So far as *essentialism* is concerned human beings constitute a natural kind. The naturalists also maintain that 'humans are natural entities by their deeper features similar to other natural beings' (Cooper, 1999: 5). This kind of naturalism is also termed scientism, which provides a 'natural scientific account of the world which tries to explain human thoughts and culture' (Ibid). There have been many criticisms of Western philosophical traditions. More interestingly, he draws our attention to the philosophical significance of *second nature*. For Cooper, John McDowell (1994) following Cicero has recently critiqued philosophical naturalism and has highlighted the significance of the *second nature* of man. So far as this goes, for Cicero, 'culture, trade, and navigation are created by human beings themselves apart from other animals' (Cooper, 1999: 6).

Human life is culture-centric; whether materialistic or otherwise, culture defines the way of living. The entire classification of man's first and second nature has Aristotelian bearing and relevance in studying Hobbes' concept of man. Aristotle and Hobbes have theorized the *first nature* of man or the human beings, which is essentially described as the performer of actions exclusively desire centric—*akratic*, selfish, quarrelsome, and brutish. Human behaviours are guided by the attitude of seeking pleasure for the gratification of desire. To counter the akratic action, Aristotle articulates moral philosophy resorting to reason and virtue.

Similarly, for Hobbes, the function of *natural reason* provides a foundation for *natural law* for confirming the right to live for himself and others (Ratulea, 2015: 49). However, the reason alone will be sufficient to remove humanity's suffering caused by the culture of technoscience and consumerism, which is doubtful as we encounter *decivilization* in the *age of knowledge* (Jahanbegloo 2017; Devy, 2017). The contemporary knowledge society does not treat human beings and their meaningful existence beyond the theoretical framework of *reason* concerning materialism.

Gandhi Conceptualizing Humanity Beyond Materialism

The celebration of life in the knowledge age demands a holistic view of humanism that integrates life with values and defines man not merely on materialistic terms but also spirituality. In this connection, Mahatma Gandhi responds critically to the modern industrial civilization stating that man and his function in society cannot be just interpreted within the cognitive closure of materialism conceptualized by Hobbes, Marx, and Darwin. Rather man as a human is not a simple possessor of wealth, a greedy consumer who struggles to accumulate and flourish by defeating or controlling *the other*. Human success cannot be described in these terms of materialism that has characterized man as a selfish and power-hungry creature on this earth. Instead, there is a surplus to the life of man which needs to be grasped looking deeper into human consciousness and moral psychology that articulates a hermeneutic relation for sustainable and flourishing humanity (Gandhi, 2010). To elaborate on Gandhi Ji's vision for humanity, we need to reflect on the nature of man and translate its spiritual relationship, which has been part of his experiments with truth.

Gandhi has been an extraordinary freedom fighter, social worker, and saint in the modern era known for his striving for non-violence and tenacity to seek truth in everyday life. Gandhi's conceptualization of humanity is unique compared to the Hobbesian and the Marxian theorization of man that defines man looking at their first and second nature. 'Human beings are neither necessarily selfish and brutish as Hobbes defines nor the inequality between the classes will dissolve after transferring wealth to the labour class. In other words, human nature is not a social construct. The evil character cannot be abolished by imposing an external force or inducing greater fear through laws. Rather, the source of evil is the will to power—the ego—*ahamkara*; insatiable greed for more and more material possession' (Doctor, 1992: 152–153). The problem persists because of a faulty pedagogy concerning the nature of man by creating a categorical division between the body and the mind and consequently providing the reason for the non-existence of the mental. The modernist conceptualization of dualism and eliminating the mind from the deconstructive approach of post-modernism tries to locate the problem of humanity elsewhere, not within.

Gandhi, on the contrary, locates the issue by meditating on the moral psychology of humanity. According to him, moral progress is inevitable and evolutionary, where humanity is destined to lead a good life. Since human nature is infected by the preponderance of *rajasic* and *tamasic* attributes of life, we do not have the will to improve and grasp the innate goodness present in human life. The existing human conditions can be improved; the *sattvic* merits like non-attachment and sacrifice are given priority. *Sattva, rajas* and *tamas* are three fundamental attributes of *Prkrti* that constitute life and manifest in human beings' behavioural attitudes. When the *rajas* predominate, it exhibits possessing and conquering wealth and power, whereas the predominating character of tamas discloses greed, lust, jealousy, and lethargy. According to Gandhi, the source of evil is the *ahamkara* and *asakta*, that is, ego and attachment, which respectively manifest in producing the *rajasic* behaviour; unless the spirit of non-attachment and non-possession is thoughtfully cultivated in our psyche, the ego will not be contented, and one will not be awakened to understand the true spirit of consciousness—the *chetana*. The awakening consciousness unfolds the passage to inner goodness (Doctor, 1992: 157).

The inner goodness is realized by calling two important concepts that Gandhi emphasized: *agraha* and *tapasya*. By *agraha*, he refers to that which appeals to the heart, whereas *tapasya* signifies inculcation of self-effort. Gandhi referred to the natural *agraha* for truth. However, more importantly, how the effort was articulated is something philosophically interesting. *Tapasya*, the self-effort, generally means "concentration of consciousness and action to transcend the narrow limit given to oneself. It means living one's life for more enriching intimacy, a qualitatively different kind of togetherness in society. *Tapasya* means discovering the centre in oneself and the circle which can hold all of us together in our continued seeking and movement for transformation" (Giri, 2002: 90). Gandhi was a vigilant and thoughtful person, right from his childhood, as he watched his actions and put sincere effort into improving himself as a morally concerned person. Because he had "literally believed in the story of Harischandra and Sravana", and they were not mere plays for him (Gandhi, 1927: 6). The character Harishchandra represented the epitome of a *seeker of truth*, and Sravana was an astounding character of commitment and service to parents. Apart from his sincere adherence to truth, his commitment to nursing his father is noteworthy. In his later life in South Africa, he often resorted to nursing as his hobby and dedicated his life to serving humanity.

Tapasya was never an esoteric activity from him and never Gandhi decided to live the world to practice spirituality. Instead, his everyday activities were revered as 'spiritual whilst engaged in challenging social and political life content' (Nanda, 1997: 143). His spiritual thinking had a mystical presence and could be traced, as Nanda puts it, "When the inner voice spoke to Gandhi, it was only 'to tell him, what to do tomorrow—how to act more effectively to unite warring communities or how to hasten the end of untouchability'" (1997: 143–144). Gandhi was a man of *action*, and his saintly detachment—*anasakta bhava* is part of his everyday life. Whilst illustrating Chittaranjan Das' notion of *tapasya* and its connection with everyday life, Giri writes, "Everyday life of an individual is also the site of *tapashya*; our routine life is and can be *tapasya*. "If we agreed to be prepared for genuine streams of transcendence, then any instinct and occupation of our life can be a *tapashya*" (2002: 90–91). One may be curious to know: What kind of transcendence *tapasya* is? Whilst Gandhi was engaged in spinning, he could effortlessly do the spinning, not because it was his everyday routine work, but because he meditatively performed the act which facilitated him transcending the act itself. Thus, *tapasya* becomes meditatively experiential moments where the self is intimately absorbed in action without any rational division between agency, action, and consequences.

On a further note, on transcendence, Giri clarifies that "But this transcendence is possible only when we have the genuine reverence for transcendence, i.e. a genuine desire to transcend identities and loyalties and to be more and love more. Das also says that if we desire, then "our literature, culture, civilization, art, and our love for art can be *tapashya*" (2002: 91). Transcendence is not a mechanical shifting of consciousness—attention, rather a sincere effort in pursuing a meditative inquiry concerning reflection and imagination that sometimes transcends the space of reason that dwells in the realm of binaries of *this* and this *is not*. Rather, it unfolds a realm of reaching out and relating to the other with love. Gandhi's *ahimsa* or non-violence is an expression of love that transcends all other forms of language. As Akeel Bilgrami concisely puts it, 'violence has many languages, but non-violence has none' (Bilgrami, 2003). Thus,

Gandhi's acceptance of non-violence is the most effective means of understanding truth.

The transcending intentionality of *tapasya* is an expansion of self that substantiates the notion of self-awakening. In the Gandhian philosophical framework, this conceptualization of *tapasya* is accomplished by *sadhana* in everyday life. *Tapasya* and *sadhana* complement each other in the moral and spiritual endeavours of life. For Gandhi, spirituality is grounded on morality, and moral progress is measured by integrating thought and action. If *tapasya* is described as a contemplative mode of thinking, then *sadhana* pertains to the realm of both disciplined thinking and action. *Sadhana,* in its mode of active engagement, maintains transparency in action. Self-knowledge ought to be transparent (Bilgrami, 2006). The ashram is a locus of *sadhana* and transparent space for understanding Gandhi's experiment and commitment to humanity. As Tridip Suhrud writes, "An ashram or a community of co-religionists as Gandhi described it, is both an ancient and a modern institution. Gandhi's ashrams were one of India's greatest experiments with truth" (Suhrud, *Indian Express* 2010). As a collective institution for practising spirituality, politics, economics, and, more importantly, morality, the ashram offers scope for being transparently engaged with the other.

The long tenure of Gandhiji's life lived in various ashrams, which he established. Right from Phoenix Settlement to Tolstoy farm in South Africa, and Sabarmati and lastly at Sevagram are significant instances where collective living with ashramites was part and parcel of his experiments of truth concerning economic, political, moral, and spiritual growth of life. As Narayan Desai confirms to us, "Ashrams were the laboratories of Gandhi's way of life. They were also testing grounds for his inner quest" (1999: 23). The quest of Gandhi's life is spiritually oriented, as Suhrud elaborates this referring to Phoenix Settlement and Tolstoy Farm, "The ashram inmates viewed these spaces not as sites of material progress but of *sadhana*. For these communities' adolescent youth and children, the element of *sadhana* was not present as consciousness, but they lived a joyous life in harmony with nature, and their elders educated them. Both the communities respected labour. All activities, big and small, were equally valued. The other characteristics of the ashram that communal and inter-dependent living was present in both these communities. The ashram life was pious, moral, and spiritual. The communities in both Phoenix and Tolstoy are joined by the struggle for the self-respect of the Indian Community… Both the ashramas were training grounds for satyagrahis. Its experiments with food, emphasis on labour and other physical hardships were similar to what one would have to face in jail" (Suhrud, 2009: 428). Collective living in hardship and harmony represents an economic and political struggle of life and moral and spiritual struggle that eases one's understanding of self-respect and dignity of labour. Ashram exposed its members sharing limited resources and being content with receiving an equal share underlines justice and equality. Equality practised in every sphere of ashram life further highlight community life's duty, responsibility, and belongingness. Thus, the ashram is a space for nurturing a great sense of humanity, and thereby it unfolds a novel process of humanizing. Gandhi's ashramas were transparent institutions never deferred from this collective endeavour of the making of a man.

Gandhi on the Very Idea of Making of a Man

According to Gandhi, 'Man is the maker of his destiny'. It needs to be conceived beyond the theoretical understanding of the culture of technoscience that represents man in the mode of digitalization and quantification. No doubt, the twenty-first century major portion of everyday life activities are performed using technology. This proliferation of culture of technoscience has opened the scope for humanizing technology. However, that should not jeopardise human thinking, which would reduce man to a machine. Such a reductionism will always put him down in the hands of power. "Gandhi had warned against the technological determinism in which world seems to have already landed itself. He had no use for technological innovations which dehumanizes man, alienated him from his work or his fellow workers, and created a civilization of robots in which one group of man could easily manipulate others" (Nanda, 1997: 130). The increasing mechanization of everyday life is growing faster than ever, which is a dangerous trend as human dependence on technology is concerned. This dependence on technology increases helplessness because one could see the malicious intention of the promoter of this technology. Such promotion of technology ultimately exposes us to coercion, manipulation, and dehumanization.

The reason for dehumanization is 'the predominance of selfish, brutish and impatient attitudes largely exposed to social situations that lack self-restraints' (Gandhi, 1927: 387). "Human civilization has become possible because of the control of the baser tendencies like hatred and selfishness, and it can flourish in so far as these are replaced by goodwill and love" (Datta, 1953: 71). The general tendency to respect each other and share values has become a tradeoff amongst individuals and nations. On the contrary, goodwill and love have been pushed behind, calling them unpragmatic as backwards. Essentially people love to earn money, no matter what short-cut or easy means they have to adopt, but that will not help us overcome this civilizational crisis. We must have faith in ourselves and must know our worth. Let us not measure ourselves in terms of money. Greed is not a human virtue to be cultivated as it destroys the natural self. The self, which is in principle for Gandhi, possesses goodwill and love. 'Materialism robs man; does not allow one to live in the true spirit of humanity as it is insensitive to goodness' (Doctor, 1992: 157). Recalling Gandhi's advice, Arun Gandhi reiterates to us that 'Materialism and morality have an inverse relationship when one increases other decreases' (Arun Gandhi, 2017: 91). The experience of the decline of civilization is due to this glamour of materialism.

The power of money and an unconditional attachment to it 'fosters the materialism which is a major hindrance to man's moral development and evolution towards non-violence' (Doctor, 1992: 157). Non-violence is the key component of Gandhi's philosophy of life. The goodness of human existence can be measured only through non-violence. Gandhi emphasized that an individual must be non-violent in thoughts, words, and deeds. As a seeker of truth or *satyagrahi*, it becomes essential to lead a life with non-violent means. 'That is the beauty of *satyagraha*. It comes to oneself; one not to out in search for it" (Attenborough, 2000: 35). It is there within and disclosed to the one when practised in all the affairs of life. The inner self is essentially non-violent; by putting it in practice, an individual is bound to embrace humanity with love. Looking at the contemporary crisis, Arun Gandhi points out that non-violence is based on 'five pillars: respect, understanding, acceptance, appreciation and compassion' (2017: 217–218).

If we need to put civilization on track, there is a necessity to respect other religions, caste, and races. We must not only learn to advise others but also *listen to* them with honour. Gandhi's *ashramas* were institutions built on collective intentionality. Each ashram member felt that it was *home* for them; there was no fear or inhibition; instead, they had accepted each other with respect. They trusted Gandhi's integrity because whatever he *said*, he *meant* it.[1] If there were an issue, Gandhi would immediately resolve it resorting to direct communication. Dialogues and conversations were part of the Gandhian way of understanding others. Gandhi exhibited tremendous patience in *listening to* the other, whether the other is his children or grandchildren or someone else; he respected the presence and time of everyone. Whilst living in a shared world, no one is superior to others; no religion, race, or caste are superior. Often, we do not mean what we say to our children in our everyday lives and share it with our friends and colleagues. That is one of the issues in modern life where people lack transparency. We expect institutions to be transparent as the manufacture of knowledge or judgement, but when its members are not. Since we often do not speak the truth desirable in any institutional form of life, we will always find seeking truth challenging.

Lack of commitment leads to institutions' failure and a failure to develop oneself as a moral person. This is a matter of sheer negligence in oneself, as we are caught within a vicious circle of social reality that pays importance to material success and uses powers for vested interests; there is less care and appreciation for the integrity and, more importantly, *thinking*. As Martin Heidegger defines, "Thinking is not an act, but a way of living—way of life…It is gathering and focusing our whole selves on what lies before us and taking to heart and mind these particular things before us to discover in them their essential nature and truth. Learning how to think can add us to this discovery" (Heidegger, 1968: xxii). It is essential to be thoughtful about overcoming challenges and expressing commitment and responsibility towards others to grow as a person. As did one of Plato's prisoners who succeeded in freeing oneself from the personhood of the cave and returned to communicate the knowledge he gathered. Right from his childhood, Gandhi cultivated the courage of speaking the truth and *seeking* truth. As a seeker of truth, he demonstrates being an exemplar of a *thinking* person. He used his reason and, also in critical times, listened to his conscience. The voice of conscience, as he termed it, is the voice of God. There is a need to discover oneself, but a lack of integrity and *self-knowledge* can erode the moral foundation of one's being. "He can degrade himself by ignoring the truth, neglecting conscience, and pondering the animal passion and can turn himself into a brute. However, he can also follow the opposite path and become more and more like God, in love, goodness, and abiding joy, for 'the divine powers within us are

---

[1] I thank Tushar bhai Gandhi to highlight this point during a conversation.

infinite' (Datta, 1953: 71). Hence, it is essential to be thoughtful and morally strong to live in peace and harmony.

Home is a better space for living in harmony. It is not merely a space for the inhabitation of family members but a space for harmonious accommodation of thoughts and deeds. Hence, how we accommodate within it becomes sometimes challenging in the absence of reciprocity and respect. Each member of a family must be respected and cared for. Whether the members are young or old, whether they are earning or non-earning, such an understanding necessarily contributes to the happiness of a family. For Gandhi, *ashrams* were his home which offered him an opportunity to transcend and embrace the whole world as his family. Community life in the *ashrama* is better evidence of a committed space for sharing and caring which 'transcended bounds of blood, and economic or otherworldly interests' (Desai, 1999: 24). He could lead the community with the same love and affection as it was for his children. Hence everyone fondly addressed him *Bapu* or *Bapuji,* and he lovingly reciprocated. The joy of this reciprocity is evident in one of Gandhi's letters to Vinoba: "You seem almost to have met a long-felt wish of mine. In my view, a father is, in fact, a father only when he has a son who surpasses him in virtue. A real son, likewise, improves on what the father has done. If the father is truthful, firm of mind and compassionate, the son will be all this in a greater measure. This is what you have made yourself" (Gandhi, 2019: 207). This expresses Gandhi's spiritual intimacy concerning the virtue of parenting.

Good parenting is given importance not just to educate the children, but to make him/her a good person with morals. Moral education is learnt from home, and parents must set examples or be moral exemplars for their children. Parenting, no doubt, is a difficult job, particularly in the case of non-violent parenting. Whilst disciplining children, often we lose self-control and resort to physical violence. It affects the psyche of the child. Nowadays, even if we have declared our schools are by law free from physical punishment or violence, still our homes are not. Arun Gandhi writes, "Bapuji believed in teaching children using only non-violence mean, which is much subtler than just avoiding physical confrontation. To raise your children in the spirit of non-violence means filling your home with love and respect and a common purpose" (2017: 158). Non-violence brings joy by cultivating the spirit of oneness. This is one of the early experiments Gandhi did when he wrote about his confession to his father. For Gandhi, the rolling tears on his father's cheek were the first lesson of *ahimsa*. He writes, "Those pearl-drops of love cleansed the heart and washed my sin away. …This was, for me, an object lesson in *ahimsa*. Then I could read in it nothing more than a father's love, but today I know that it was pure *ahimsa*. When such ahimsa becomes all-embracing, it transforms everything it touches" (1927: 23–24). Thus, non-violence with its inherent power of love is transformative. A person's *sadhana* is inevitable to grasp the transformative content of a flourishing moral life. Gandhi could assert that 'all humanity is family' (Gandhi, 2017: 6) because he applied non-violence as his yardstick to seek the truth.

Whilst *seeking* truth, Gandhi experimented with food, cloth, health, gardening, walking, spinning, praying, discussing with colleagues, arguing with opponents, writing letters, addressing the public, going on a march/*padayatra*, being in silence, fasting, etc. He never saw them as discrete life activities, instead of integrated to understand what a simple, honest, and good life means. He followed the basic moral principle of a *satyagrahi*: *Satya, ahimsa, brahmacharya, astheya and aparigraha*— in English truth, non-violence, celibacy, non-stealing, and non-possession. It is not easy to elaborate on these experiments that Gandhi carried out as a lifelong mission; they are not truth centric but guided by truth as, for him, the truth was God. Whilst illustrating the relationship between truth and morality, Gandhi writes, "But one thing took deep root in me—the conviction that morality is the basis of all things, and the truth is the substance of all morality. Truth becomes my sole objective. It began to grow in magnitude every day, and my definition of it also has been ever-widening" (1927: 29). In brief, all actions should be grounded on morality and cannot be divorced from seeking truth.

To conclude, this integration of action, morality, and truth contributes immensely to freeing oneself from the prison-house of materialism and succeeding in making a man. Gandhi's staunch criticism against the modern industrial civilization stands valid to date, as the world encounters a new technoscience culture that yields advanced high-tech capitalism, which enforces several crises concerning humanity. In this connection, Gandhi's call for the denunciation of materialism and the materialistic form of life is worth considering. Gandhi's experiments in ashram life, seeking truth, and most essentially his adherence to non-violence are some of the glowing examples that any thoughtful person can use in his *tapasya* and *sadhana* to make oneself a better person. Thus, an *agraha* to renew oneself in the path of Gandhian principles of life would unfold an irrefutable commitment and responsibility for humanity.

References

Attenborough, R. (2000). *The worlds of Gandhi*. New Market Press.
Bilgrami, A. (2003). Gandhi, the philosopher. *Economic and Political Weekly, 38*(39), 4159–4165.
Bilgrami, A. (2006). *Self-knowledge and resentment*. Harvard University Press.
Brannen, S., Ahmed, H., & Newton, H. (2020). Covid-19 Reshapes the Future. *Centre for Strategic and International Studies*, July 28.
Cooper, D. E. (1999). Humanism and scientific worldview. *Theoria: A Journal of Social and Political Theory, Special issue: Science and Civilization, 93*, 1–17.
Datta, D. M. (1953). *The philosophy of Mahatma Gandhi*. University of Wisconsin Press.
Desai, N. (1999). *My Gandhi*. Navjivan Publishing House.
Devy, G. N. (2017). *The Crisis Within*. New Delhi: Aleph
Devy, G. N. (2019). *Countering Violence*. New Delhi: Orient BlackSwan
Doctor, A. (1992). The man in Gandhian philosophy. *The Indian Journal of Political Science, 52*(2), 152–167.
Easterlin, R. A. (2001). Income and happiness: Towards a unified theory. *The Economic Journal, 111*(473), 465–486.
Fuchs, C. (2020). *Communication and capitalism: A critical theory*. University of Westminster.
Gandhi, M. K. (1927). *The story of my experiments with truth*. Navjivan Publishing Press.
Gandhi, M. K. (2010). *Hind Swaraj*, ed. Suresh Sharma and Tridip Suhrud, New Delhi: Orient BlackSwan.
Gandhi, M. K. (2019). *Letters of Mahatma Gandhi*, New Delhi: Rupa.

Gandhi, A. (2017). *The Gift of Anger: Ten spiritual lessons for the modern world from my grandfather, Mahatma Gandhi*. Michel Joseph/ Penguin House.
Giri, A. (2002). *Conversations and Transformations: Towards a New Ethics of Self and Society*. Lexington Books.
Heidegger, M. (1968). *What is called thinking?* Trans and Intro Glenn Gracy, New York: Harper & Raw.
Jahenbegloo, R. (2017). *The decline of civilization*, New Delhi: Aleph.
Jahenbegloo, R. (2020). *The courage to exist: A philosophy of life and death in the age of corona virus*, New Delhi: Orient BlackSwan.
Jonas, H. (1979). Towards a philosophy of technology. *The Hastings Center Report, 9*(1), 34–43.
Lawrence, P. (2021). The global and national inequality Faultline: The economic dimension of In(security). *Journal of Global Faultlines, 8*(1), 23–33.
McDowell, J. (1994). *Mind and World*. Harvard University Press.
Mylthyntaus, T. (2010). Prologue: Constructing technology for everyday life. *ICON: Technology in Everyday Life, 16*, 2–21.
Nanda, B. R. (1997). *Gandhi and his Critics*. Oxford University Press.
Peters, M. (2020). *Critical philosophy of technological convergence education and Nano-bio-info-Cogno paradigms*. Helsinki University Press.
Pradhan, R. C. (2020). *The Metaphysics of Consciousness: The Indian Vedantic Perspective*. Springer.
Ratulea, G. (2015). *From the natural man to the political: Machine, sovereignty and power in the works of Thomas Hobbes*. Frankfurt: Peterlang.
Sandel, M. J. (2012). *What money cannot buy: The moral limits of markets*. Farrar, Straus & Giroux.
Sirgy, J. M. (1998). Materialism and quality of life. *Social Indicator Research, 43*(3), 227–260.
Sirgy, J. M., et al. (2013). Is Materialism Bad? *Social Indicator Research, 110*(1), 349–366
Sitze, A. S., Sarat, A., & Wolfson, B. (2015). The humanities in question. *College Literature, Special Issue: The Humanities Crisis: Beyond and Defense, 42*(2), 191–220.
Spadaro, A. P. (2020). Climate change, environmental terrorism, eco-terrorism and emerging threats. *Journal of Strategic Security, 13*(4), 58–80.
Suhrud, T. (2009). "Two Ashrams", *My Life is My Message*, (*Sadhana* 1936–1915), by Narayanan Desai. New Delhi: Orient BlackSwan.
Suhrud, T. (2010). Interrogating Ashram. *Indian Express*, March 19.
Teggert, F. J. (1919). The approach to the study of man. *Journal of Philosophy, Psychology and Scientific Methods, 16*(6), 151–156.

Ranjan Kumar Panda is a Professor of Philosophy at the Department of Humanities and Social Sciences, Indian Institute of Technology Bombay, Mumbai.

Chapter 7
Between Fact and Value: Locating Gandhian Science

Subhasis Sahoo

Abstract The paper draws on the influential ideas of M. K. Gandhi to examine the character and depiction of science in modern India. The predicament posed by Gandhian Science (GS)— the quandary of neither being an 'unmixed' enthusiast of science nor a 'sentimental' advocate of tradition—lies at the heart of contemporary contestations about what science means for the oriental societies, for instance, India. This paper thus attempts to conceptualize GS and to propose how it might advance ideas of postcolonial science, in general. There are broadly four filaments to this argument. First, to Gandhi, science was not only a legendary vocation, but also a commonplace of understanding things that does not bow to the dichotomies of 'the expert' and 'the layperson', of 'the elite' and 'the subaltern'. Second, GS emphasized data collection (whether in Champaran or in the surveys undertaken by Kumarappa) to understand reality without being content with impressionistic contents/management. Third, GS challenges Western conjectures of control over science and positioned the anti-vivisectionist approach derived from the indigenous systems of medicine in India's cultural traditions. Fourth, GS argued the social responsibility of science which was not just concerned with fact alone, but in the creation of meanings (value) in all activities in terms of reconciling science and ethics.

Keywords Gandhi · Gandhian science · Fact and value · India

A Search

In South Asia, the search for science and technology (S&T) has always been accompanied by ambivalence which witnessed the need to preserve useful elements of its past. India occupies a significant place in South Asia in terms of its long history of civilization and philosophical traditions. This is seen not only in Nehru's 'discovery of India', but also in Gandhi's reactionary modern Science and Technology package. Much has been written (Unnithan, 1956; Tendulkar, 1960; Erikson, 1969; Rudolph & Rudolph, 1967; Nanda, 1968; Iyer, 1973; Brown, 1989; Parekh, 1989; Panthan, 1995;

S. Sahoo (✉)
Department of Sociology, Central University of Allahabad, Prayagraj, India

Madan, 2011; Jahanbegloo, 2013)[1] about how Gandhi can be read in multiple ways, apart from his politics and his public life. My interest in Gandhi can be attributed to the time when I was working on people's science movement in India[2] for my doctoral dissertation at the Indian Institute of Technology (IIT) Kanpur; partly due to the present drift of global affairs, for which Gandhian ideas appear as both relevant and revolutionary as well.

History of science policy writings in India has largely marginalized Gandhi. There is also a lack of focus on science in Gandhian studies. The Gandhian project of science, what I call Gandhian Science[3] (hereafter GS) was treated as an ancillary to history and sociology of science in contemporary India. One can glean the actors behind GS from insightful historical records, memoirs, letters, speeches of Gandhi, and biographical sketches written by his close associates—J. C. Kumarappa,[4] Vinoba Bhave,[5] and Nirmal Kumar Bose.[6] Biography ought to be a pertinent source for understanding an individual's life and experiences. Further, Gandhi's autobiography[7] is a [successfully] constructed self outside the narrative which bears its testimony and judges the scripted self. Ideally, one would have liked to write the present account after going through all the volumes of Gandhi's writings. However, the benefit of accessing several volumes (if not all) of Gandhi's writings indicates the importance of the voice of science in India.

Against this backdrop, I call into question the fact-value distinction on which it is based. Then, I illustrate the fracas between fact and value to grasp Gandhi's stance on science; and third, to explicate Gandhi's association with one of the important methods of science, i.e. experimentation. Fourth, I present the pragmatic pursuit of Gandhian science and finally, discuss Gandhi's urge for social responsibility of scientists hoping to bring about social change.

---

[1] Each scholar floats his/her own Gandhi, i.e. his/her version of the recorded or remembered testimony of Gandhi. All were influenced by Gandhi's version of Gandhi, since he/she was the selector source of much which is known about him.

[2] It is contended that people's science movements have an affinity for Gandhi and consider modern science to be radical. For further details; see Sahoo (2010).

[3] The term Gandhian science is used here not to refer to a fixed set of meanings, but the larger lived experience of Gandhi.

[4] J. C. Kumarappa (1892–1960), trained in accountancy and economics, was a colleague of Gandhi. He was a Green Gandhian and one of the pioneers of the contemporary environmental movement (Guha, 2001).

[5] Vinoba Bhave (1895–1982), the leading Gandhian disciple who had elucidated the principles of *Sarvodaya* (uplift of all). For further details; see Del Vasto (1956).

[6] Nirmal Kumar Bose (1901–1971), an Indian anthropologist and better known as a close aide of Gandhi. Bidding farewell to Gandhi, he once said, 'Bapuji, I have always been a wanderer like this in life'. For further details see Bose (1953: 181).

[7] For details see M. K. Gandhi. 1927. *The Story of My Experiments with Truth.*

Fact Versus Value: The Fracas

Fact produces things as they are. Fact must be free from personal prejudices (biases) and prejudgements (values) for giving a balanced result. Hence, fact connotes an ability to see the empirical world as it is. The very aim of fact is to see reality. Pattnaik (2015) argues that fact is fixated with exactitude and not immune to any kind of digression, for instance, a monotheistic order. Connotations, however, change across time and space, with the facade of the reader, and with contexts. Value tests the postulation of whether ideas are undeviating and can be guarded. Therefore, value rejoices in fluidity. Contemporary global discourse views fact qualitatively in terms of true or false. In other words, fact gives objective truth. Value is subjective and its ultimate basis is personal prejudice or belief and not reason. Therefore, value is personal; but fact is communicable and open to all who wish to see. The ultimate basis of fact is by examination of evidence, not through coercion, personal argument, or appeal to authority.

It was German social thinker Max Weber (1949), who gave us a sophisticated understanding of the term value. Weber has called the term 'value' as the "unfortunate child of misery'. For him, the term 'value' has two meanings. Firstly, it refers to the standards or principles of worth that make something have value, and secondly, it refers to the worthy things themselves, the valuable. In this paper, the term 'value' shall be concerned only in the first sense. To explain it further, science land up with conclusions based on keen observation, experimentation, and verification (OEV). This rule of the game is universally valid and based on this tacit rule of the game, science becomes objective. By OEV, one should not simply mean the knowledge or the practice of science, but the capacity to separate the factual and verifiable from the more emotional and conventional sentiments. In a sense, scientific behaviour is autonomous, and therefore, it does not brook any interference within its realm whether from the human or the divine.

The essentially positivist[8] of science, on which the fact-value distinction is based, is overly restrictive in limiting explanations of scientific controversies to factors 'extrinsic' to science: values, bias, and the like. When science is examined as a form of organized, intellectual production, a much more complex relationship between scientific concepts, theories, and methodologies, on the one hand, and ideological and value commitments, on the other, emerges, which also allows explanations of controversies in terms of factors 'intrinsic' to scientific development (Johnston & Robbins, 1977; Robbins & Johnston, 1976).

Sahoo (2020: 187) points out that the binary understanding of fact/value stems from European modernity. Following the way of Dilthey and Rickert, he further argues that science can be viewed as *Naturwissenschaft or Geisteswissenschaft*. For him, although there are longstanding methodological issues related to the fact/value

---

[8] According to Redner (1986), the germs of positivism were born out of the nineteenth century sociology (e.g. Auguste Comte, Joseph Renan, Emile Durkheim, John Stuart Mill, and Herbert Spencer) and the nineteenth century scientific philosophy (e.g. Ernst Mach, Gottlob Frege, Max Weber, David Hilbert, Thomas Young, Albert Einstein, and Vilfred Pareto).

distinction, the notion of value is a subject of concern in liberal arts, social sciences, or natural sciences that needs to be addressed. He has illustrated this point through three traditions: (a) values be eliminated for establishing truth and prevent its collapse (e.g. Durkheimian camp).[9] (b) values are predestined and fundamentally a tool-kit[10] for problem-formulation, which is endowed with inquisitiveness and a strong desire to explore, to question, and to discover (e.g. Weberian camp); (c) values are vital for the knowledge claims in different contexts (Sahoo & Mohanty, 2019), that is the ability to sustain arguments and appeal to common experiences (e.g. Feminist and Marxist camp).

Whether truly or as it is held popularly, science is greatly responsible for the value crisis. The technologies which science has produced the great changes that threaten our assets, and the ways of thinking which science has engendered, have undermined the very values themselves. Therefore, often protagonists of the anti-modern science movement have been said to be 'Hands off' about values. Positivist science has done enough harm already, and the scientists should be grateful that he/she can go on about his/her business. If we wish to support science with values in this way, we are giving up on the possibility of supporting values by science. Thus, by limiting reason, we will make room for faith and close the door to enrich our lives. Hence, we must reason our way out of the formidable problem of science in favour of values.

An underlying conflict between what Weber calls the 'ethics[11] of conviction', can be defined as a commitment to ideas and ideals, despite the consequences, against the 'ethics of responsibility', where scientists may anticipate the consequences of their actions. Values and not just the act of making choices determine what constitutes a fact. Swanson (1978) says that nature might be spoken of as an obedient child rather than as a protective mother. She speaks only when spoken to; she is often seen but hardly ever heard of speaking by herself. For Swanson, data come to us only in answer to questions, and it is we who decide not only whether to ask, but also how the question is to be asked. As a result, every question has its premise. Messick (1980) indicated that how we put the question reflects our values on the one hand and on the other hand it helps us determine the answer. Hence, data are naïve, and we attach meaning to data with our values.

The celebration of modern science[12] is due to the exploding of the traditional fact-value relationship. Divorcing fact from value lifts the traditional constraint and creates conditions for far more general formulations in understanding the realm of facts. However, modern science does not merely divorce fact from absolute value but all values. The founding figures can be said to be conspicuous of the involvement of the value factor in selecting the new mechanistic, atomistic, and deductivistic conceptual scheme. But once a scheme is accepted, the rest of science essentially

---

[9] The French sociologist Emile Durkheim (1858–1917) was a follower of positivist tradition.

[10] Humans are said to be the only tool-using animals. I think we should not necessarily feel cramped by this 'essentialist' definition in one's exploration of the scientific aspects or paradigms of humans as tool-using animals. Tool seemingly produces a dual culture of 'E': enlargement and estrangement.

[11] Ethics entail a code of behaviour.

[12] For the celebration of modern science, see Alfred Russell Wallace's (1898) *Wonderful Century*.

develops as a value-free enterprise. Divorcing fact from absolute value can be merely a conceptual exercise because no absolute value may correspond to reality at all. But divorcing fact from all values is not merely a theoretical exercise since value is as much a part of the world as fact is. In fact, such a divorce limits the universality of scientific formulations.

Gandhi's Stance on Science

Science brought with it the possibility of transforming individual lives and landscapes, of overcoming the accretions of ossified habits and outdated customs, of becoming economically powerful through industrialization (Abraham, 2000). Gandhi's attitude to science is very far from being hostile, as perceived by many. He rather welcomes science and takes advantage of it in a variety of ways, and often people, wilfully misunderstanding him, accuse him of inconsistency because he does so, for instance, when he submits to an operation, or rides a motor car, or uses a printing machine, or telegraphs or telephones. In fact, he tended to seek the truth inside him, rather than externally by the methods of science. Therefore, the general impression many people have regarding Gandhi is that he was anti-modern science[13] or a Luddite[14] in contrast to Nehru.

Though he did not like the idea of large-scale machine production,[15] Gandhi never suggested that it should be scrapped (Gandhi, 1925). Gandhi disliked the machinery just because it was an ally of capitalism.[16] A fierce defender of individual freedom, he wanted that human beings should chiefly depend upon moral impulses. He did not endorse the Protestant view of the managerial craze for work and considered that extra work is not what humans should accept as his/her ideal. Such work culture is calculated to make humans more and more acquisitive, not self-reliant. Gandhi believed that humans can exercise their freedom to work in such a way that they will be able to retain effectively their control over the means or technology of productive work and will not be devoured or determined by the technology. In other words, Gandhi's disenchantment to technological determinism puts S&T in context.

Gandhi wanted to grow efficiency using the machine as one would, for instance, with a sewing machine that one can possess to create and repair goods. His views on work are substantially inconsistent with the autonomy claim of technology. Autonomous technology not only interferes with the ideal of individual freedom

---

[13] Aldous Huxley (1894–1963) wrote: "…. If we abolish science and "return to Nature" the population will revert to what it was-and revert, not in hundred years, but in as many weeks. Famine and pestilence do their work with exemplary celerity". For further details see *Selected Works of Jawaharlal Nehru*, 1973, First Series, Vol. 5, pp. 510–514. New Delhi: Orient Longman Ltd.

[14] Visvanathan (1998) argues that Gandhi has been portrayed as a 'Luddite, as the technocrats of the Nehruvian era did, is superficial'.

[15] In Sahasrabudhey's (2002) work Gandhi is seen to be moving from critique of technological determinism to construction of self-reliance.

[16] *Young India*, 13 November 1924.

and dignity of labour, but also cuts into the very possibility of internal development of human beings.[17] For him, the predicament in India was how to turn those idle hours into productivity. According to Gandhi, the sewing machine was one of the few useful things ever invented. Therefore, Gandhi was rather at war with industrial capitalism and was never overtaken or over-awed by it.

The dominant trend of anarchism is evident in Gandhi's thought and also proves inconsistent with autonomous and high-tech views of culture. Gandhi's sense of technology is somewhat akin to Karl Marx. Marx, also, believed that industrial capitalism had the tendency of becoming increasingly capital-intensive which led not only to the substitution of competition by monopoly, but also the misery of the millions of the working class. However, Marx believed that the inner contradictions between the capitalist class and the working class of industrial capitalism and the working-class organizations ultimately led to the inevitable revolution. The revolution would replace capitalism with a different kind of society, i.e. communism where the means of production are held in common. But Gandhi's view was different.[18] He wanted to avoid the ill effects of industrialization. Moreover, he criticized the West for specifically those characteristics in which it took pride, i.e. modernization and industrialization.

Gandhi's stance on science and industrialization has been a sceptical approach and the imperative of historical and cultural contextualization. But it does not mean a negation of science or destruction of the machine industry; rather one can find him as a reactionary what historian of science Prakash (1999) calls 'a different modernity'. For Gandhi, modernity has its own overarching logic. Not all his political contemporaries were happy with such an idea. At the individual level, Nehru did not endorse it, and he was highly critical of Gandhi's stance on science in the meetings of the Indian Congress. In his message to Silver Jubilee Session, Science Congress, Calcutta, Nehru (1936) remarks,

> It was [modern] science alone that could solve these problems of hunger and poverty, of insanitation and illiteracy, of superstition and deadening custom and tradition, of vast resources to waste of a rich country inhabited by starving people.

An advocate of big machinery,[19] Nehru (1933) said,

> I would like India to have socialism and wider spread industrialization. Believing all this, would it be possible for me, or the large number s who is like me, to cooperate closely for years with a person who stands for a policy which is inimical to science and industry and which might lead to a dreadful holocaust? And is it for this that we spend long years of our life in prison?

---

[17] He dismisses machinery as it ceases to assist the individual at times (*Young India*, 20 November 1924).

[18] The differences between Gandhism and communism are fundamental. But whatever differences there might be between Gandhism and communism, they converge at certain points. The cause of the have-nots is the basic sentiment running through both. Both Gandhism and communism regard the well-being of the poor and the oppressed.

[19] Big machinery brought the idea of 'Big Science' in big laboratories e.g. nuclear science, space science, electronics and communication, biotechnology, nanotechnology, etc. Big machinery is the eventual outcome of what Ravetz (1971: 31) calls 'the industrializing science'.

It is noted that the idea of science varies from one person to another, subject to their socio-cultural milieu. To Gandhi, born in a caste associated with trading and commerce, science was an instrument of social change. It had a positive role to play in human progress. He centres on the concepts of agency and creativity as formulated differently—scientist in his/her own right—in his attempts to frame his/her life. The agency of the scientist occupies a central place in Gandhi's schema (Prasad, 2001). Therefore, Gandhi emphasized that scientists should not be concerned with fact alone, rather with the creation of meanings (value) in their activities. Gandhi acknowledges that the process of technological development is very much relevant to the large sphere of society. His contention, however, is that the individual should not succumb to the temptation of imitative consumerism. The question can be posed as to whether the Gandhian ideal of self-controlled consumerism is viable in a technology-driven market situation? Further, he never saw the dichotomy between science and religion/spirituality and tried to fuse them, an enterprise that has since caught up in recent years.

GS as Experimentation

Experimentation means the ability to experiment and predict on a basis. The great power of science lies in the fact that its results can be proved by experiment. In physical sciences, experiments are carried out in realistic settings of laboratories. For Gandhi, the self and society are a laboratory. All through his life, Gandhi experimented with [him] self whether it was celibacy, diet, asceticism, medicine, personal hygiene, public sanitation, social customs, etc. He became the 'subject' of his own experiments. Through his autobiography, i.e. *The Story of My Experiments with Truth* (Gandhi, 1927) he narrated his experiments. His methodology and desire to directly engage with the act and activity was something far ahead of his time. His ethnographic eye looked deep into the contours of the physicality of a place and perceived the inner arrangements that shaped it, whether cultural or economic.

Gandhi was in search of truth throughout his life. For him, truth comes only from direct experience, what is otherwise known as empiricism. For example, we believe what we see, hear; know by touch, smell or taste. We believe whatever we know through our sense organs. In search of truth, he gave primacy to the experience over cognition (Bilgrami, 2003). Gandhi feels, like others that the growth of knowledge can be plausible through experiences. Therefore, GS is embedded in the rationalizing discourse of Baconian epistemology.[20]

Gandhi's idea of non-violence has been drawn from his strong pantheistic leaning and religious practices. The idea of non-violence was truth in itself that Gandhi had

---

[20] Francis Bacon (1561–1626) emphasized that knowledge can be generated through sense-experiences. He insisted that to understand sense-experiences one must consult nature. This act of consultation and understanding brings in observations, which form the basis of scientific knowledge. For Bacon, collecting materials, carrying out experiments, on a large scale, and find the results from a sheer of evidence is a scientific method.

learnt not from the text; rather from the context—in South Africa. Gandhi considered *satyagraha* as a technique of action for seeking truth (Jahanbegloo, 2013). *Satyagraha*[21] as conceived by Gandhi is a science in the making. In 1917, a *satyagraha* campaign was organized in order to secure the rights of workers in the indigo plantations at Champaran in the then Bihar. In February 1918, Gandhi led a millworkers' protest at Ahmedabad, in then Gujarat, followed by a tax relief campaign for cultivators of Kheda. All these protests and demonstrations were revolving around local issues but attracted the larger interests of the workers at the national level. As a result, the spring of 1918 witnessed the first all-India *satyagraha* campaign led by Gandhi against the Rowlatt Bills.

The Pragmatic Pursuit of GS

Being a pragmatist, Gandhi constructed science in terms of practice. For him, the practice of *charkha* (the spinning wheel), was one of the foremost [appropriate] technological tools, which got an in-built value component which Parel (1969) terms to be 'economic self-sufficiency, mastery over machinery, social and political harmony between the rich and the poor, and the value of *swaraj*'. The *charkha* amplifies the power of organization and relates people with each other. It recognizes the dignity of labour. Non-violence, humility, independence, and service are the characteristics of *charkha*. In addition, it is a product of locally available resources. It is a hand-woven technology. Gandhi (1920) wrote,

> Round the *charkha*, that is, amidst the people who have shed their idleness and who have understood the value of cooperation, a national servant would build up a programme of anti malaria campaign, improved sanitation, settlement of village industries, conservation and breeding of cattle and hundreds of other beneficial activities. Wherever the *charkha* work is fairly established all such ameliorative activity is going on according to the capacity of the villages and the workers concerned.

Gandhi emphasizes that the *charkha* practice is a kind of equivalent to the existence of certain values in society. What is that value? The value of 'cooperation' is the very idea of the *Charkha*. The *charkha* would be meaningless if it is practised by people who do not value cooperation and by the same symbol once people learn to value cooperation, the ameliorative consequences would follow with or without the *charkha*. The *charkha* not only exemplifies the 'science of spinning', but also a value-based technology with strong connections to the social movement of nation-making. Gandhi, however, was criticized for his attempt to revive the tradition which was a reaction to an alien tradition. His revivalist attempt was politically radical. Gandhi (1923) argued that:

> Needle has not yet given place to sewing-machine, nor has the hand lost its cunning in spite of the typewriter. Spinning mills and spinning wheels may co-exist. Spinning wheel could

---

[21] The credit of coining this term goes to Gandhi, which literally translated into 'holding on to truth'.

be made universal and could reach interior villagers; a mill cannot reach a fraction of the population.

Khadi (hand spun and hand-woven cloth)[22] is another pursuit in this regard which implies no violence, no deceit, and no impurity (Gandhi, 1938: 105–106). *Khadi* was a new technology for Gandhi, having twin objectives of self-reliance through local production of all, elite and the subaltern, in the struggle for independence from the other. It is in this context Gandhi (1920) wrote that:

> I feel convinced that the revival of hand-spinning and hand-weaving will make the largest contribution to the economic and the moral regeneration of India. The millions must have a simple industry to supplement agriculture. Spinning was the cottage industry years ago, and if the millions are to be saved from starvation, they must be enabled to reintroduce spinning in their homes and every village must repossess its own weaver.

The *khadi* along with the *charkha* formed the foremost amongst the pragmatic pursuits of GS. Gandhi's narratives of science through such symbols led to the formation of nationalist imagination.

In addition to *khadi*, and the *charkha* the practice of vivisection[23] was snubbed out by Gandhi. He condemned modern science as the defender of vivisection and advocated alternative practices in terms of change of diet and use of herbs.[24] The concept of macrocosm and microcosm was an expression of this totality of interactive systems in which human beings live. One has to come back to it with the knowledge and capabilities which have developed, but in doing so, pre-eminence to the sanctity of humans should be given, not merely technology. However, the empirical aspect of Gandhi's practice on health and body is quite juxtaposed. For instance, on the one hand, he was derisive of the modern medicines which he considered were the devil's disciples consisting of the concentrated essence of black magic. On the other hand, he deplored the Ayurvedic practitioners' apathy to new experiments. In this connection, Prasad (2001) writes that Gandhi was deeply appreciative of modern scientists' humility and spirit of inquiry, a spirit that he felt traditional practice solely lacked.

Gandhi's Urge for Social Responsibility of Scientists

Science is characterized by a spirit of 2R's: realism and rationalism. Because it is the 2R that analyses and critiques social reality. Thus, the spirit has always been

---

[22] During the freedom movement, hand spinning on *charkha* rather than hand weaving was given prime importance.

[23] Vivisection can be defined as the practice of performing surgery on live animals for the purpose of experimentation or scientific research, let's say preparing injections and serums, etc.

[24] Jainism and its philosophy was a strong influence on Gandhi for being sentimental about the notion of 'body'. Gandhi views the body as a microcosm of the universe where harmony can be attained at two levels: (1) the harmony of the body and its constituent parts and (2) the body and its environment such as earth, water, light, and air (Visvanathan, 2006).

the guiding light of capitalist entrepreneurs and their expansionist dreams of new markets and new commercial outlets, which would leave all competitors far behind. So it is not surprising that most scientists are willing to collaborate with industry, military or the government. When the social movements of the 1960s and 1970s gave rise to mounting criticism of all forms of domination at work, or between the sexes, races, and nations—it is not surprising either, that science should be criticized (Sahoo, 2010). Several groups have developed a deeper critique of S&T. Groups and individuals like the British Society for Social Responsibility of Science (BSSRS) and similar such organizations in other countries have argued that the entire programme of modern science is not neutral (Ibid.).

The critique of science that Gandhi offered can also be interpreted through the notions of ethics of responsibility. For Gandhi, a scientific world looks for the realm of ultimate values what leading sociologist Madan (2008) calls instrumental values. Gandhi was not against the spirit of research of the scientists, rather the direction that the spirit had taken. He sought interweaving of social justice and science/technology.

Jairath (1984) argues that the modern [Western] science was implanted in India by the Reformists; however, the Indian scientists were influenced by the Revivalist tradition and the Radical ideologies, especially in the national movement of the early twentieth century. For instance, P. C. Ray (1861–1944)[25] and J. C. Bose (1858–1937)[26] were both influenced by Gandhian ideas regarding science. Ray reckoned the relevance of Gandhi's indigenous values and he began the Bengal Chemical and Pharmaceutical Works in 1901 with the aim of economic and scientific self-reliance. Ray sought solutions for the country from the swadeshi movement. Ray's magnum opus *The History of Hindu Chemistry* in two volumes during 1902 and 1907 produced the ideological legitimacy of science in India (Sahoo, 2009). Residing within the Western scientific paradigm, Bose attempted to Indianize modern science. M. N. Saha (1893–1955),[27] a scientist with a social mission, played a staunch critique on GS. Saha was against the swadeshi movement based on Gandhian philosophy, which was gaining popularity amongst the Congress leadership and the masses before the Independence of India. He felt that this movement would do nothing else but bring back *Vedas, Khadi, Charkha,* and bullock carts to the country. He was keen on modernizing India and so believed that the country should go ahead with aggressive industrialization following the Soviet model of scientific development.

The positivist inspired views of science, which incorporate the fact-value distinction in their analysis, are thus inherently limited by their failure to examine the context of scientific advice and the way in which it can transmit social commitments. Speaking to students at Trivandrum in 1925, Gandhi argued that.

> How will you infect the people of villages with your scientific knowledge? Are you then learning science in terms of the villages and will you be so handy and so practical that the

---

[25] See the works of Sen Gupta (1972) and Sahoo (2009).

[26] See the work of Nandy (1995).

[27] A leading astrophysicist, who not only initiated the creation of several scientific institutions in the country, but also went on to become a Member of the Parliament to serve people through science.

7 Between Fact and Value: Locating Gandhian Science

knowledge that you derive in a college so magnificently put and I believe equally magnificently equipped – you will be able to use the benefit of the villagers? (Collected Works, 1967)

With such hunches, Gandhi introduced the notion of social responsibility of scientists.[28] Further, he said that.

The employment of the atom bomb for the wholesale destruction of men, women, and children was the most diabolical use of science. The moral to be drawn from the supreme tragedy of the bomb [following Hiroshima] is that it will not be destroyed by counter-bombs even as violence cannot be ended by counter-violence. Mankind has to get out of violence only through non-violence. Otherwise, counter-hatred only increases the surface as well as the depth of hatred. (Collected Works, 1967)

Such narrative implies the abuses of [modern] science and risk assessment that Gandhi was concerned with. This supports the view that the traditional division of labour between science and public policy, or at least the way it is usually perceived, is breaking down in complex areas of decision-making like risk assessment. Scientists do not operate in an exclusively factual arena, and decision-makers play a more active role than is usually realized in determining what is to count as a fact. If both parties are to operate effectively, and in good faith, they shall have to face up to this and adjust their roles accordingly. Gandhi would argue that the minimum requirements for this are for scientists to accept [social] responsibility for the commitments they inevitably make when devising approaches for the study of poorly understood phenomena. Moreover, they should be prepared to elaborate and clarify the implications of those commitments, especially in relation to the ethical and political considerations that arise in risk assessment. Lay participants in risk decision-making, in their turn, shall need to develop a more subtle understanding of both the strengths and limitations of the contributions that science can make to the clarification of these difficult issues. If it doesn't happen, then the social control of scientific and technological change shall continue to be blighted by the manipulation of passé ideologies of science by competing or dominant social groups.

Later, on a trip to the Indian Institute of Science at Bangalore in 1927, Gandhi said that.

all research will be useless if it is not allied to internal research, which can link your heart with those millions [of poor]. Unless all the discoveries that you make have the welfare of the poor as the end in view, all your workshops will be really not better than Satan's workshops. (Young India, 1927)

He was more interested in that form of science, i.e. science for rural development and science for the nation. Gandhi favours the idea of a cooperative state wherein the role of the state would be minimal and most of its activities would be delegated to the Farmers' Cooperatives, Traders' Guild, *Panchayat*, etc. To prevent the rise of

---

[28] Bertolt Brecht (1898–1956), a German playwright, who refashioned his play *Galileo* in a post-Hiroshima world, to criticize the egotistical scientist who sought to overturn an established authority which provided for the general good. Brecht clearly changed his mind about scientists and social responsibility.

the cult of State and technological culture therewith, Gandhi expects the citizens to take upon themselves the task of controlling their runway needs and greed. Without transforming human nature, it is argued, we cannot free ourselves from the dominance of technology and 'technological intimacy'.

He appealed to Indian scientists to pursue research on Indian diets under Indian conditions and in general to seek solutions to problems of development within the locally available human and material resources. Gandhi believed that sustainable development and the protection, as well as the preservation of natural resources, are neither a simple 'technological fix' nor a mere substitution of one set of materials with another. They involve, in their fullest form, changes in lifestyle and basic values. It is in this context, Gandhi proposed an alternative model of education, i.e. *Nai Talim* (Basic Education), through which science is not alien, but organically linked to children's experiments such as art, craft, handicraft, carpentry, etc. For Gandhi, these are the productive skills that relate ideas to practice as well as arouse children's curiosity and enthusiasm in learning. As a scientist in practical terms, Gandhi emphasized popularization of his scientific practices through organizations such as All India Spinners Association (AISA), All India Village Industries Association (AIVIA).[29]

A Final Remark

The late nineteenth and early twentieth century were enmeshed with the formation of [independent] nations worldwide. Indians, too, were busy with creating an independent nation. The connection between Gandhi and science remained unrecognized during this period in spite of all the writings on the national movement and Gandhi. The reason could be attributed to the subtleness of the connection, however, imperative in understanding the national movement of India that a group of nationalists was fighting for a scientific and technological India.

Gandhi had a deft touch with science and scientists through the metaphors, the narratives, and the symbols. GS had a dissenting voice that was against colonialism and modern [Western] science. In his distinctive way, Gandhi offers a critique to modern science in terms of spinning, *satyagraha*, *khadi*, anti-vivisection,[30] indigenous medicines, social responsibility of the scientists, and *Nai Talim*. By doing so, he produced alternative views of science and an array of alternative scientific practices as well. His alternative views of science layout the inter-relationship between individual and society. Furthermore, he outlines an alternative that emphasizes an individual's doings, his/her capacity for invention and progress, and the value of novelty and of intimacy with the things being probed. Here, science does not serve as a suspicious watchdog, but trusts an individual's imagination and intuition as

---

[29] The AIVIA was formed in November 1934, having the objective of encouraging the existing industries and reviving, where it is possible and desirable, the dying or dead industries of villages according to the village methods (Gandhi, 1934).

[30] Further details, see "Frog and Cyberfrog are friends" by Ken Fleischmann (2003).

contributively to knowledge. This view of science also corresponds to an image of both individual and society; individuals are felt to be content, and it is the satisfaction of their individual needs and the promotion of their welfare that is deemed the most important function of government. The alternative stream of scientific practices may have remained 'subaltern' (Guha, 1998); but rooted in concern for people, they are strong and widespread in postcolonial India.

In modern science, stress is placed upon the value of science in separating truth from falsity, and reality from fantasy. Such a view focuses on an individual's vulnerability to error, the significance of error-freeness, the value of thought in keeping individuals on the straight and narrow, the necessity of objectivity and detachment, and the importance of discipline and correction by facts. But Gandhi suggests that in this conception of science, the individual is, regarded at the bottom, seen as evil, and therefore, the government's first duty is superintendence. In this view, science is something above individuals, controlling and rectifying their native, untrustworthy impulses, and austerely maintaining a safe distance from those who are studied. So, GS falls in the intersection of fact and value (a local tradition) which makes Gandhi an autonomous person. Both fact and value question the social relevance of S&T through people's science movements (PSMs) in contemporary India (Sahoo & Pattnaik, 2012). Gandhi's attitude to science and scientific method is guided by diversity and plurality rather than uniformity. His notion of plurality allows the individuals to go for constant scrutiny, defiance, and conformity.

The biggest challenge before Gandhi was to reconstruct the disintegrated and colonized Indian society. He believed that science can be used as a repository of moral inspiration to reconstruct society. He understood that, on the one hand, science (and technology) can discover and produce things that indigenous knowledge cannot. On the other hand, he was equally concerned about the abuses of science and called attention for scientists to have social responsibility for their actions. Social responsibility, as Gandhi illustrates, involves making difficult judgements. Nonetheless, it has now become part of scientific culture. This can be seen formally in the codes of ethics adopted by many scientific organizations and informally by the diverse views articulated by scientists and in their actions (Sahoo, 2013).

Further, the GS finds a place in postcolonial India through the establishment of Khadi and Village Industries Commission (KVIC) (1956), the Handicraft Development Corporation (HDC) (1962), the Office of the Development Commissioner, Handlooms (1976), All India Handicrafts Board (AIHB) (1981), Centre for Application of Science and Technology for Rural Areas[31] (1974), Council for Advancement of People's Action and Rural Technology (CAPART) (1986). GS is less discernible, closer to the ground realities and connected to rural and cottage industry, remains

---

[31] In August 1974, a Centre for ASTRA (Application of Science and Technology for Rural Areas) was formed under the aegis of the prestigious Indian Institute of Science (IISc.), Bangalore under the leadership of Professor Satish Dhawan and the function of ASTRA is to correct the strong urban bias in research and development in science and engineering. Since then, ASTRA has been working with local communities of Karnataka state in areas such as alternative and low-cost buildings, fuel-efficient stoves and agro-processing driers, water purification, renewable energy, etc. In the later years, ASTRA has been renamed as the CST (Centre for Sustainable Technologies).

dispersed and outside the consideration of high-level decision-making bodies. His concern for integrating humanistic values and social concerns with science education through which society can be informed regarding the impact of research and development may have on them in the future.

Acknowledgements The author is grateful to Prof. B. K. Pattnaik, for his teaching on 'values in social science research' as part of the doctoral degree coursework at IIT Kanpur. Much of this article was written while the author was a Visiting Fellow to the National Institute of Science Education and Research (NISER), Bhubaneswar. The author expresses his gratitude to Dr. P. K. Swain at NISER for the invitation and hospitality; owes special thanks to Dr. Amarjeet Nayak and Dr. Sital Mohanty at NISER for fruitful discussions. Subsequent discussions with Prof. A. K. Giri at the Madras Institute of Development Studies (MIDS) are duly acknowledged. Special thanks are due to Dr. Anshuman Behera at the National Institute of Advanced Studies (NIAS), Bengaluru for his warmth and enthusiasm for this project, subsequent comments, and pressing the author to think harder. Dr. Pragyan and Dr. Niharika Tiwari very kindly gave me the much-coveted opportunity of presenting an earlier version of this paper at the seminar on Gandhi they organize at the State Institute of Educational Management and Training (SIEMAT), Allahabad, in March 2020. The anonymous reviewers massacred early drafts of the paper and are in part responsible for its present state. The author wishes to thank Dr. Akhaya Kumar Nayak at IIM Indore for making available a few pertinent papers on Gandhi; the staff of Nehru Memorial Museum & Library (NMML) and The Energy and Resources Institute (TERI) Library, New Delhi for their assistance. The usual disclaimers apply.

References

Abraham, I. (2000). Landscape and postcolonial science. *Contributions to Indian Sociology, 34*(2), 163–187.
Bilgrami, A. (2003). Gandhi, the philosopher. *Economic and Political Weekly, 38*(39), 4159–4165.
Bose, N. K. (1953) *My days with Gandhi*. Calcutta: Orient Longman Limited.
Brown, J. (1989). *Gandhi: Prisoner of hope*. New Haven, CT: Yale University Press.
Erikson, E. H. (1969). *Gandhi's truth: On the origins of militant violence*. New York: Norton.
Fleischmann, K. R. (2003). Frog and cyberfrog are friends: Dissection simulation and animal advocacy. *Society and Animals, 11*(2): 123–143.
Gandhi, M. K. (1920). *Young India*. 21 July.
Gandhi, M. K. (1923). *Young India*. 27 December.
Gandhi, M. K. (1925). *Young India*. 13 August.
Gandhi, M. K. (1927). *Young India*. 21 July.
Gandhi, M. K. (1934). *Harijan*. 16 November.
Gandhi, M. K. (1938). *Cent percent swadeshi*. Ahmedabad: Navajivan Press.
Gandhi, M. K. (1967). *Collected works of Mahatma Gandhi*. New Delhi: Publications Division, Government of India.
Guha, R. (2001). The green Gandhian: J. C. Kumarappa'. In R. Guha (Ed.), *An anthropologist among the marxists and other essays* (pp. 81–86). Delhi: Permanent Black.
Guha, R. (1998). *A subaltern studies reader*. Delhi: Oxford University Press.
Iyer, R. (1973). *The moral and political thought of Mahatma Gandhi*. New York: Oxford University Press.
Jahanbegloo, R. (2013). *The Gandhian moment*. Harvard University Press.
Jairath, V. (1984). In search of roots–the Indian scientific community. *Contributions to Indian Sociology (n.s.), 18*(1), 109–130.

Johnston, R., & Robbins, D. (1977) The development of specialties in industrialized science. *Sociological Review, 25,* 87–108.
Madan, T. N. (2008). Whither Indian secularism? *Modern Asian Studies, 27*(3), 667–697.
Madan, T. N. (2011). *Sociological traditions: Methods and perspectives in the sociology of India* (pp. 101–115). New Delhi: Sage Publications.
Messick, S. (1980). Test validity and the ethics of assessment. *American Psychologist, 35*(11), 1012–1027.
Nanda, B. R. (1968). *Mahatma Gandhi: A biography.* New Delhi: Allied Publishers.
Nandy, A. (1995). *Alternative sciences: Creativity and authenticity in Two Indian Scientists.* Delhi: Oxford University Press.
Nehru, J. L. (1933). *Letter to Aldous Huxley refuting to his characterization of Congress as anti-Science.* 1 September.
Nehru, J. L. (1936 [1989]). Jawaharlal Nehru: An autobiography. Oxford University Press.
Panthan, T. (1995). Gandhi, Nehru, and modernity. In U. Baxi, B. Parekh (Eds.), *Crisis and change in contemporary India.* New Delhi: Sage Publications.
Parekh, B. (1989). *Gandhi's political philosophy: A critical examination.* New York: Springer.
Parel, A. (1969). Symbolism in Gandhian politics. *Canadian Journal of Politcal Science, 2*(4), 513–527.
Pattnaik, D. (2015). *My Gita.* New Delhi: Rupa Publications.
Prakash, G. (1999). *Science and the imagination of modern India.* New Delhi: Oxford University Press.
Prasad, C. S. (2001). Towards an understanding of Gandhi's view on science. *Economic and Political Weekly, 36*(39), 3721–3732.
Ravetz, J. R. (1971). *Scientific knowledge and its social problems.* Oxford: Clarendon Press.
Redner, H. (1986). *Ends of philosophy: An essay in the sociology of philosophy and rationality.* London: Croom Helm.
Robbins, D., & Johnston, R. (1976). The role of cognitive and occupational differentiation in scientific controversies. *Social Studies of Science, 6,* 349–368.
Rupolph, S. H., & Rudoph, L. (1967). *Gandhi: The traditional roots of Charisma.* Chicago IL: University Chicago Press.
Sahoo, S. (2009). The emergence of modern science and the national movement in Colonial India. *Science and Culture, 75*(6), 394–398.
Sahoo, S. (2010). *Mobilizing people for science: Empirical studies of people's science movements in late XXth century of India.* Unpublished PhD Dissertation, Indian Institute of Technology Kanpur.
Sahoo, S. (2013). Would you mind, if we record this? perceptions on regulation and responsibility of Indian Nanoscientists. *NanoEthics: Studies of New and Emerging Technologies, 7,* 231–249.
Sahoo, S. (2020). Recast(e)ing scientific temper in a democracy: The eccentricities of Ambedkarian science. *Sociological Bulletin, 69*(2), 174–190.
Sahoo, S., & Mohanty, S. (2019). Knowledge in context: Production and practices of indigenous mode of knowledge. *The Eastern Anthropologist, 72*(3 & 4), 319–336.
Sahoo, S., & Pattnaik, B. K. (2012). Understanding people's science movement in India: From the vantage of social movement perspective. *International Journal of Sociology of Science and Technology, 3*(4), 8–72.
Sahasrabudhey, S. (2002). *Gandhi's Challenge to Modern Science.* Goa: Other India Press.
Sen Gupta, J. (1972). *Prafulla Chandra Ray.* New Delhi: National Book Trust.
Swanson, E. B. (1978). On the nature of a data base and its use in inquiry–a tutorial. *Information & Management* 35–43.
Tendulkar, D. G. (1960). *Mahatma: Life of Mohandas Gandhi* (Revised). Delhi: Publications Division, Government of India.
Unnithan, T. K. N. (1956). *Gandhi and free India.* Groningen: J. B. Walters, Bombay: Vora.
Del Vasto, L. (1956). *Gandhi to Vinoba.* London: Rider and Company.

Visvanathan, S. (1998). A celebration of difference: Science and democracy in India. *Science, 3*, 42–43.
Visvanathan, S. (2006). Reinventing Gandhi. In R. Raju (Ed.), *Debating Gandhi* (pp. 195–222). New Delhi: Oxford University Press.
Wallace, A. R. (1898). *The wonderful century*. New York: Dodd, Mead and Co.
Weber, M. (1949). *The methodology of the social sciences*. Free Press.

Dr. Subhasis Sahoo is an Assistant Professor at the Department of Sociology, Central University of Allahabad. He was previously a Visiting Fellow at the National Institute of Science Education and Research, Bhubaneswar.

Chapter 8
Education for Un-Alienated Life: Gandhian Principles

Satyabrata Kar

Abstract As overarching social transformations are underway, one can find an increasingly palpable sense of the extent and intensity of 'alienation' as a psychological and social phenomenon involving the perceived loss or the 'problematic separation' of 'self' from 'itself' or 'other'. The paper contends that Gandhi's ideas on education are worth revisiting at this juncture to find out if we live any answer to this crisis. The centrality of education in achieving full human potential and bringing about economic and social change is commonplace in development discourse across global, national, and local levels. While the current policy impetus is focused on equitable, inclusive, affordable, flexible, and quality education, it is reckoned that Gandhi's ideas of 'basic education' and *'nai talim'* can be revived to influence our spontaneous concern for education in its varied forms in such a way that we 'learn to know', 'learn to do', 'learn to live together', and 'learn to be' for realizing the ideal of un-alienated life, without getting into the trap of the never-ending inherent contradictions between the central ideals of the western political enlightenment such as 'liberty', 'equality', and 'rights'.

Keywords Gandhi · Un-alienated life · *Nai-talim* · National Education Policy (NEP) · Quality education

Introduction

Although Gandhi was not a formal educationist, he developed firm views on education that are consistent with his key socio-political ideals such as *swaraj, satyagrah, sarvoday,* and *ahimsa*. His philosophy of education as articulated through the ideas of *'Nai Talim'* and 'Basic Education' offers a robust and comprehensive framework characterized by a harmonious blending of idealism, naturalism, and pragmatism. Gandhi's educational thought was holistic and transformational. It underscored the importance of both the intrinsic and the instrumental value of education while transcending the individual/society and liberal/vocational divides in education. His ideas

S. Kar (✉)
New Statesman Media LLP, Hyderabad, India

© National Institute of Advanced Studies 2022
A. Behera and S. Nayak (eds.), *Gandhi in the Twenty First Century*,
https://doi.org/10.1007/978-981-16-8476-0_8

on education were developed in reaction to the prevalent colonial English education system as well as the western modernity at large. Several political leaders and social reformers were critical of the education system prevalent in colonial India. 'But no one rejected colonial education as sharply and as completely as Gandhi did, nor did anyone else put forward an alternative as radical as the one he proposed' (Kumar, 1999:1).

The Rise and Fall of Gandhi's *Nai Talim*

An All-India Educational Conference to develop the first blueprint of a national system of education for India was convened by Gandhi at Wardha, Maharashtra, in October 1937. A scheme of basic national education was initiated by a committee under the chairmanship of Zakir Husain that led to the formation of the Hindustani Talimi Sangh for developing the programme and running experimental schools. *Nai Talim* or New Education was envisioned as a comprehensive education system encompassing three stages of education, namely Pre-Basic, Basic, and Post-Basic, of which the basic education programme was the first to be defined in a clear manner, whereas the 'post-basic' secondary school programme or the higher education programme was yet to be worked out fully.

The major tenets of basic education included seven years of free, compulsory, and universal education for all children of the nation; the mother tongue as medium of instruction; the centrality of productive and manual work; and self-financed schools. Contrary to the prevalent primary education system that was homonized only with the sole focus on numeracy and literary skills, the new basic education scheme promoted by Gandhi was characterized by its assertion of activity-centric knowledge emphasizing the importance of practical experience and observation. Therefore, the curriculum content and the pedagogy were intelligently designed around three main axes of interrelationships between craftwork, and the natural and social environment.

The basic national education policy of 1937 was envisioned as a silent social revolution to prepare Indian children to assume their responsibilities as adults in a transformed social order (Sykes, 1988).

However, in post-independent India, although several basic schools were set up with a mandate to promote Nai Talim, these schools gradually lost relevance and vitality as the government-led by Nehru adopted a development ideology that emphasized on 'economic regeneration' through centralized planning and large-scale industrialisation. The Ministry of Education relegated basic education in the form of craftwork alone to be covered through the socially useful productive work (SUPW) in 1978. Although the importance of experiential learning and the vocational aspects of education has been mentioned in subsequent policy documents including the National Curriculum Framework 2005, Nai Talim has been subjected to a subordinate and peripheral status till recently.

Gandhian Thrust in India's National Education Policy (NEP) 2020

The fact that the relevance of Gandh's ideas was not confined to the historical specificity of India's colonial experience is probably best exemplified by the striking resemblances of some of the core aspects of Gandhi's educational philosophy in the country's recent National Education Policy (NEP) 2020. The resonance of Gandhi's ideas of education is especially evident from the changes in school education that the NEP 2020 envisages in terms of the emphasis on practical knowledge, dismantling the distinctions between academic and vocational streams, encouraging multilingualism, providing greater flexibility to study courses of one's choice, and the encouragement of local community participation.

The policy recognizes the need to incorporate the practical and vocational elements into the mainstream education with greater rigour.

> While learning by rote can be beneficial in specific contexts, pedagogy must evolve to make education more experiential, holistic, integrated, discovery-oriented, learner-centred, discussion-based, flexible, and, of course, enjoyable. The curriculum must include basic arts, crafts, humanities, games, sports and fitness, languages, literature, culture, and values, in addition to science and mathematics, to develop all aspects of learners' brains and make education more well-rounded, useful, and fulfilling to the learner. Education must build character, enable learners to be ethical, rational, compassionate, and caring, while at the same time prepare them for gainful, fulfilling employment. (National Education Policy, 2020:3)

The policy also marks a significant break from the previous vision documents as it talks about 'multiple pathways' in education promoting open schooling even at elementary level. Instead of restricting school education within the formal legal strictures of the Right to Education (RTE), it envisages education as a responsibility of the society and allows home schooling as well as 'public philanthropic partnerships' in education. Apart from introducing vocational course and internship in middle school, the policy includes extra-curricular activities and sports within school education. Furthermore, it encourages the initial education to be in mother tongue which was emphasized by Gandhi.

The Global Imperative

Gandhi's observations of the alienating effect of western liberal education and the alternatives he offered to alter the symbolic meaning of 'education' by way of 'Nai Talim' and 'basic education' stand the test of time not only in the Indian social milieu but also in the global context. The problem of 'alienation through education' or 'alienation because of education' that was historically articulated mainly in response to the colonial imposition of western liberal education has found renewed attention in the western developed countries including the USA and the UK.

Worth mentioning, in this regard are the two of the recently published seminal books during the COVID-19 pandemic in 2020- *Tyranny of Merit: What's Become of The Common Good?* by Michael Sandel (2020), and *HeadHand Heart: The Struggle for Dignity and Status in the 21st Century* by David Goodhart (2020).

Sandel (2020) argues that the popular resentment and discontent of the American youth over the last four decades is not only because of the deepening economic inequality but also because of the stalled social mobility and the attitude towards winners and losers created by the hubris of meritocracy that has contributed to hollowing out the social recognition and esteem in work that the multitude do.

> But economic hardship is not the only source of their distress. The meritocratic age has also inflicted a more insidious injury on working people: eroding the dignity of work. By valorizing the "brains" it takes to score well on college admission tests, the sorting machine disparages those without meritocratic credentials. It tells them that the work they do, less valued by the market than the work of well-paid professionals, is a lesser contribution to the common good, and so less worthy of social recognition and esteem. It legitimates the lavish rewards the market bestows on the winners and the meager pay it offers workers without a college degree. This way of thinking about who deserves what is not morally defensible…….it is a mistake to assume that the market value of this or that job is the measure of its contribution to the common good. (Sandel, 2020: Chap. 7).

Like Hegel and Durkheim, Sandel (2020) argues that work is not only 'a way of making a living' but also a 'socially integrating activity', a source of social recognition, and 'a way of honouring our obligation to contribute to the common good'. In a similar vein, Goodhart (2020) is overwhelmed by the sudden realization of the importance of 'key' or 'essential' manual works and the caring and emotional support services involving hand and heart in the society during the coronavirus pandemic that are otherwise undervalued compared to the work of head (cognitive), which alone has been found to be constituting the ultimate yardstick of human esteem. He takes this opportunity to suggest that it is time for a radical rethink to value the works of head, hand, and heart equally.

Both of the above accounts call for the resurrection of the dignity of work in the society which entails, for its actualization, a reconstructed and equal emphasis on relevant vocational education and training in the discourse and practice of education. The social philosophy and the pedagogic strength of Gandhi's craft-centric basic education are in the offer for re-imagination and reconstruction to derive vital lessons and insights to overcome this crisis. Gandhi's *Nai-Talim* was a scheme of un-alienated education that favoured ordinary children belonging to lower strata of the society. Rather than mere accumulation of informative knowledge, it focused on character building in terms of the development of virtues including strength, courage, fearlessness, and the capability to immerse in selfless work, and to awaken in children the sense of duty to society, nation, and humanity.

Gandhi's Authority as an Educator

Gandhi's ideas on education ensued from his decades-long experiments with educational institutions both in India and abroad. Gandhi experimented his idea of education for the first time in South Africa. Ruskin's book *Unto this Last* had a profound impact in shaping his experiment called Phoenix Settlement in South Africa. Gandhi was immensely captured by the following seminal ideas of Ruskin that had a direct bearing on some of his own experiments with truth as well:

(1) That the good of the individual is contained in the good of all. (2) That a lawyer's work has the same value as the barber's in as much as all have the same right of earning their livelihood from their work. (3) That a life of labour, i.e. the life of the tiller of the soil and the handicraftsman, is the life worth living (Gandhi, 1966: 224).

Gandhi saw a great opportunity in experimenting these new ideas, as he was utterly dissatisfied with the prevalent system of education. Phoenix Settlement was started around these ideas by a handful of Indian and European idealists in 1904 which evolved into a tiny village in due course. The key thrust behind the experiment was to realize the extent to which harmonious co-living of a group of people with a conviction for simplicity of life can be practiced effectively and joyfully. Tolstoy Farm was Gandhi's next venture which was envisioned as a school involving no use of textbook, as the 'culture of the heart' and 'the building of character' constituted the top priority.

'For there were no servants on the Farm, and all the work, from cooking down to scavenging, was done by the inmates. There were many fruit-trees to be looked after and enough gardening to be done as well' (Kumarappa, 1953:14).

After returning to India, Gandhi later set up several educational institutions including the Gujarat Vidyapith in Ahmedabad and a polytechnic for women at Wardha. The distinctiveness of Gandhi's educational philosophy can probably be best understood by relating it to that of Dewey and Tagore. Both Gandhi's and Tagore's idea of education can be seen consistent with Dewey's definition of education 'as a process of the continuous reconstruction of experience, with the purpose of widening and deepening its social content, while at the same time the individual gains control of the methods involved' (Dewey, 1957). Both tend to believe that education was an expression of life as well as a preparation for it, and a system of education should not alienate man from his environment, because knowledge has organic connection with his surroundings.

But what brings Dewey much closer to Gandhi is the fact that 'Gandhi wanted the whole education to be activity-centred, based on crafts suiting the genius of the local people and at the same time wanted it to be self-supporting. But in Tagore's conception, utility yields place to aesthetic pleasure as the criterion of value'. Both Dewey and Gandhi emphasized on the inseparability between school and society, the importance of vocational element in education, the usefulness of 'learning by doing', and the character building and social transformation through education. Dewey criticized educational practices that appealed only to our intellectual faculties instead of stimulating our instincts and impulses to make and create things in the form of utility or art. (Dewey, 1965: 26).

Dewey (1966: 306) denounced the 'antithesis of vocational and cultural education' by challenging the dichotomies of labour/leisure, theory/practice, and body/ mind as superficial and bogus.

His proposal for the reconstruction of the vocational education emphasized on a holistic conception of education incorporating the intellectual and social significance of a vocation (Dewey, 1966: 318). According to Pring (1995: 189), Dewey was not convinced the way 'liberal' is counter posed with 'vocational' as if the vocational education, appropriately administered, doesn't have any liberating effect by itself. He contended that vocational education, infused with liberal values, can unlock new imaginations and possibilities; the craftsman can relish the aesthetic joy in the object of his creation; a technician can appreciate the science behind the artefact; and a reflective teacher can make robust theoretical sense of the live practice. Building on Arendt's distinction between 'work' and 'labour', one can argue neither Gandhi nor Dewey reduced work in education to mere labour or toil purely on utilitarian ground, but both saw work as possessing intrinsic value and a meaningful purpose that the individual can associate.

While Dewey's proposition of educational reform sought to protect a special space for children during unbridled capitalist expansion that threatened to dehumanize people, Gandhi's educational proposal is seen as a plea to delay the capitalist advancement so that the men and women could find ample time to strengthen their capacities to live with machines without falling prey to the dehumanizing effects of industrial capitalism. (Kumar, 1999:4).

Re-Vitalizing Gandhi

Gandhi is relevant for the current discourses and practice of education at a very basic yet deeper level. His ideas of education provide the much-needed yardstick to identify whether and to what extent the nature and purpose of our learning practices are related to actual conditions of life. Whether and how education, as a human practice and a social process, can be holistic, experiential, and rooted in the organic linkages with the immediate physical and social environment to meet the immediate local needs.

Troubleshooting such basic missing links in the discourse and practice of education is of utmost importance, especially considering the ways a benign and innocuous image of education has come to play itself out unfettered in our time. Although the concept and certain practices of 'schooling' have been criticized on different ideological or philosophical grounds, the importance of education and the values it entails for individuals and the society are beyond any doubt or question.

The centrality of education in bringing about economic and social change is commonplace in development discourse across global, national, and local levels. Education, for its intrinsic worth and powerful instrumental value, is being regarded as one of the strongest pillars for future development in policy thinking as well as in public sphere at large.

The constitutional commitment as well as the moral responsibility of the state to ensure education to all members of society is a common feature among all the nation-states, let alone India. 'Everyone has the right to education. Education shall be free at least in the elementary and fundamental stages. Elementary education shall be compulsory. Technical and professional education shall be made generally available and higher education shall be equally accessible to all based on merit'—reads the Article 26 (1) of the Universal Declaration of Human Rights (United Nations, 1948).

Thanks to this benign image, it has been rooted in our popular belief that any educational programme is good for the society. One also notices a kind of fixity in the way we are measuring the standard and effectiveness of education of education in terms of certain numbers such as the gross-enrolment ratios, attendance rates, the number of schools, the number of enrolled children, and the number of teachers. Even though the issue of quality in education is emphasized, it is limited to infrastructure facilities, qualification of teacher, and reading ability of children.

While our education discourse is predominantly couched on the languages of quantity, quality, and equality, these three concepts are seen as constituting an 'elusive triangle' for explaining 'the contrary pulls working on educational policy in the shape of demands and resistance' (Naik, 1975: 4).

It is observed; the issues of quality and equality have come to be treated in such a fragmented manner in our education discourse that the discussion of one often tends to obscure the other. While discussing issues of quality, the questions of socio-cultural equality often tend to be bracketed off. Conversely, the issue of (in)equality is assumed to be settled through an overwhelming focus on the language of access, inclusion, and rights without elaborating the implications for quality (Pappu & Vasanta, 2010).

At a time when quality talks regarding education have proliferated significantly, one finds ample reasons to resist the very modalities of inscription of the term quality on fundamental grounds. The meanings attached to the term quality in the context of education are found to have locus not in education itself but in things either related or external to education. The quality talks are hardly seen to be engaged with any fundamental sense of quality in education that would involve the conception of education and its aims, according to (Kumar, 2010).

It's rightly pointed out that given a situation of 'vacuousness' pertaining to diverse perceptions about the aim of education, it is hardly surprising that the popular mode of understanding quality has been in terms of 'input' or 'output', which risks short-circuiting the worth of traditional categories such as aims, standards, curriculum, and pedagogy in the pursuit of quality in education (Winch, 2010). The dominant socio-economic ideology of our time such as global capitalism, knowledge society, and neoliberalism are also alleged to have affected our frequent use of the term quality and equality despite their thin characterization.

This is evident from our association of quality with an array of factors lying away from the very concept of education such as the idea of competitive edge in global economy, the preference for a differentiated product of (English) education by private institutions, and the vision that ICT will ensure quality to universal access of education. On the other hand, although a concern for quality is invoked as a moral imperative of equality, the language of 'universal access' and 'inclusion' in mechanical sense essentially distorts and dilutes the concern for equality. 'Universality' cannot be translated as 'uniformity'. Nor 'access' or 'inclusion' can provide for quality given a background of socio-cultural inequality (Kumar, 2010).

In India, the ambitious goal of education for all children has been reiterated time and again since Independence. This culminated in the milestone legislation of the 'Right of Children to Free and compulsory Education (RTE) Act, 2009' that empowers all children to demand eight years of schooling. The RTE Act entails eight years of free and compulsory education by obliging the government to provide elementary education guaranteeing compulsory admission, attendance, and completion of schooling to every child in the age group of six to fourteen. 'Free' means that no child shall be liable to pay any kind of fee or charges or expenses which may prevent him or her from pursuing and completing elementary education.

Our policies, discourse, and practices of education appear to be more concerned about the access and coverage of education as if education is an external good that must trickle down, than about the nature, purpose, and process of education. 'Access to school' seems to be equated with 'Right to Education'.

One cannot solely rely on an 'institution provisioning approach' alone to bring substantive reforms in education. The National Curricular Framework 2005, for example, pointed several deeper issues in the Indian education system, such as— (a) learning has become a detached activity, instead of encouraging children to forge organic linkages between knowledge and their lives in any meaningful manner; (b) schools tend to endorse a regime of thought that dampens original thinking and insights; (c) what is imparted in the name of learning in schools fails to trigger the inherent capacity of children to create new knowledge; (d) the 'future' of the child is given so much prominence at the cost of the child's 'present' that it quietly endangers the well-being of children and the society at large, without much notice.

At a time, the prevalent discourse of education is couched on the languages of rights, access, justice, equity, quality, affordability, freedom (choices), and accountability, that are often found to be mutually contradicting with each other, Gandhi offers an important corrective to focus instead on only one basic and primordial condition, i.e. 'un-alienation', which is presupposed by all these ideals. And when education becomes 'un-alienated', the above ideals are automatically achieved and the inherent contradictions among them also dissolve automatically.

The Gandhian Ideal of 'Un-Alienated Life'

Un-alienated life is the most coveted goal of politics for Gandhi, and it is a necessary precondition for his other integrated ideals such as *swaraj, satyagrah, sarvoday, and ahimsa*. Like Marx, Gandhi showed concern for the increased loss of 'genuine subjectivity' and 'subjective engagement' in the wake of changes brought about by imperialism, capitalism, and western modernity. While Marx located the source of alienation in class and economic formation of capitalism, Gandhi associated alienation with the 'cultural and cognitive effects' of western modernity (Bilgrami, 2012).

Gandhi sought to avoid the effects of capitalism and modernity through 're-enchantment' of a world that is characterized by an undifferentiated unity between humanity and nature in which individuals' agency and engagement are identified in terms of their perceptual experience of a value-laden world and their response to the normative demands of the world upon themselves (Bilgrami, 2009).

Although his stress on harmony and connectedness between individuals and the social/natural world is commonly attributed to a mere 'sacralized' visualization of the relationship between humanity and nature, one finds secular credentials of his ideal of 'un-alienated life', which is a prerequisite for the meaningful realization of the major political ideals of enlightenment, such as liberty, equality, and rights.

Gandhi is not essentially a conservative thinker who blindly believes in the continuity of tradition and rejects everything new as alien to the prevalent social and cultural milieu. He rather believed in epistemological pluralism and recognized reason, intuition, faith, traditions, collective wisdom accumulated over generations, and emotions as valuable sources of knowledge that help us in practical understanding and dealing with the complex realities of human life.

His appeal to swadeshi or indigenous traditions, thus, is not so much about preserving or asserting the uniqueness of indigenous identity as much it is about forging communities that reflect man's participation in a reality that transcends the realms of ethics, aesthetics, and responsibility. His principles of *satyagraha* and *swaraj*, for instance, go beyond the dualism of 'self' and 'other' to realize *advaita* (non-duality), illuminating a conception of freedom and self-determination in terms of man's search for the transcendental ground of being.

For Gandhi, 'truth' was much more than what could be grasped by science or reason. His critique of western modernity, however, does not target science as such, but the 'mentality' and 'outlook' created by the 'dominant status' of modern science that gives rise to the forms of detachment causing alienation by 'undermining our subjectivity and moral engagement with which we would otherwise inhabit the world' (Bilgrami, 2012:9).

Gandhi was critical, at a deeper level, of the genealogical disruption regarding the conception of world/nature brought about by the 'metaphysics' of modern science which is marked by a crude characterization of nature as a detached object, and the opportunistic tendencies it garnered in 'systematically extractive forms of political economy'. Gandhi is seen to be perplexed as to when and how the 'world' underwent conceptual transformation 'to cease to be a place merely to live in and become instead a place to master and control' (Ibid:10) and how nature got reduced to mere natural resource bereft of any other values?

He did not oppose the defining principles of the enlightenment, such as liberty, equality, and fraternity, but what he showed indifference to as the deeper 'underlying commitment' of the enlightenment that reinforced these ideals—the conviction that 'though we are capable of bad things, the bad in us can be constrained by good politics' (Ibid:21).

According to Bilgrami, Gandhi diagnosed a distinctive trait of modernity, characterized by a conceptual linkage of 'the metaphysical transformation of the concept of nature and the political transformation of the concept of humanity', as the root cause of alienation (Bilgrami, 2009).

For Gandhi, a 'relaxed ideal' of 'merely living', along with the 'perceptible experience of values' in a world that normatively and seamlessly demands our moral sentiments and agency as responses, is the necessary precondition for un-alienated life.

Unlike Hume and Adam Smith, Gandhi did not see 'values' as something created or projected by individuals that they are reducible to mere desires, rather he held values to be suffused in the world we live in, and our desires are nothing more than our responses to the 'desirabilities' or values already present within the world. For example, in *Hind Swaraj* (Chap. 3), Gandhi maintains that 'civilisation is that mode of conduct which points out to man the path of duty'.

If un-alienation involves undetached relaxed living, as well as seeing and responding to the world rightly, his idea of *swaraj* refers to a situation wherein individuals, morally in command of themselves (the rule of the mind over itself), do what is right, and resolve their differences and conflicts themselves without depending on the state or any other external agency to discipline them and regulate their social relations. It presupposes the disposition by individuals neither to dominate nor be dominated by others' (Parekh, 1997:93).

While it is widely believed that the whole edifice of Gandhian thought ultimately collapses into *dharma* and some mere religious strictures, there is a growing recognition of Gandhi's contribution outside the realm of religion. Parel (2016) announces Gandhi's political philosophy as is his most valuable contribution to India and the world, and the most distinctive characteristic of his political philosophy is a framework based on a radical reinterpretation of the four great aims of life (*purusharthas*) of the Indic tradition that include *dharma* (ethics and righteousness), *artha* (political power and economic means), *kama* (longing and pleasure), and *moksha* (spiritual salvation or ultimate liberation).

Parel believes Gandhi was successful in re-articulating these goals of life in such a way that there is internal coordination between them, and they do not become antithetical to each other. His idea of *swaraj*, for example, is intended to enable one to pursue *artha* and *kama* within the bounds of *dharma*, and his idea of *sarvodaya* envisions spiritual, economic and political well-being in unison. He did not see *moksha* as essentially divorced from worldly pursuits, as he did not see secularity and spirituality as antithetical to each other.

Relevant Educational Principles for an Un-Alienated Life

Holistic Education and Experiential Learning

Gandhi was a firm believer of wholesome development of mind, body, and heart through education. He wrote in an influential article in *Harijan*, 31 July 1937:

> Man is neither mere intellect, nor the gross animal body, nor the heart or soul alone. A proper and harmonious combination of all the three is required for making of the whole man and constitutes the true economics of education…By education I mean an all-round drawing out of the best in child and man–body mind and spirit. Literacy is not the end of education not even the beginning. It is one of the means whereby man and women can be educated. Literacy in itself is no educationI would therefore begin the child's education by teaching it a useful handicraft and enabling it to produce from the moment it begins its training. (Gandhi 2008:151).

Gandhi reckoned manual training as the principal means of stimulating the intellect. The highest development of the mind could occur only through a scientific cultivation of the faculties of the mind and body. Hence, education of a child should be accomplished through teaching the child a constructive handicraft and enabling its production right from the beginning of training. Children should be given the opportunity of making things on their own, however imperfect the products of their making be. They should also be led to analyse the 'whys and wherefores' of everything in their immediate environment. The reflexive learning of a craft, along with literary training and physical exercises, constituted the heart of the basic education system. Gandhi, however, opposed literary training without vocational training, and physical exercises for purely body beautification purposes.

In Gandhi's view, the participatory productive work under conditions similar to real-life situations is pedagogically linked to the organic learning process, as it represents a vital medium of knowledge acquisition, values internalization, and skill formation, at the same time. Learning while working is helpful in harnessing the cognitive, affective, and psycho-motor dimensions of a child in a holistic manner by fully integrating 'head, hand and heart'.

He emphasized work experience as an essential component of education, as, through work experience, the children start deriving observations and predictions to form intuitive knowledge from their own spontaneous explanations of things, based on which they further explore and keenly improvise the work they do. Through work, they also learn to meaningfully relate themselves with the world and with people. Like the ancient Indic *Mimamsa* School of Thought, Gandhi decried 'knowledge without action' as meaningless. He believed in knowledge creation and meaning making through practical engagement in a stimulating learning environment, instead of mere memorization and the development of an abstract intellect outside its existential context.

Character Building and Life-Skills

The prime goal of education, for Gandhi, was character building in terms of the development of moral strength, fearlessness, righteousness, and the ability and enthusiasm to engage in altruistic work, while awakening in children the sense of duty to society, nation, and humanity.

'My definition of NaiTalim is that if the person who has received Nai-Talim, is enthroned, he would not feel vanity of power; on the other hand, if he is given a broom, he will not feel ashamed. For him, both the jobs will be of equal importance.' (Bapuni Chaayaman, pp. 157–158 (Translated from Gujarati) as cited in Gandhi on Education (1998).

Gandhi also intended the process of basic education to be productive in real material sense as it will instil self-confidence and boldness in children as they manage to pay for their education through their own labour.

Through education, Gandhi aspired everyone to wholeheartedly appreciate the delight of personal worth, dignity, and efficiency and to cultivate a keen desire for self-improvement and social service in a cooperative community' (Shrimali, 1949: 87–88).

Hi scheme of basic education was designed to produce self-made workers who would not necessarily depend on state and society for a living.

Gandhi championed the cause of relating education to society so that the student would feel a sense of belongingness and gratitude not only to his parents but also to the village and the larger society, and hence, would realize the importance of making some return to them in his/her capacity. Instead of clinging to a rights-based approach to everything, he foregrounded the due performance of 'duties' as the fulcrum of 'rights'.

His ideal of an educated man is best summarized in the below quotation from Huxley in his book Hind Swaraj. 'His body is the servant of his will and does its work with ease and pleasure.... his mind is stored with knowledge of the fundamental truths of nature; his passions are under the control of a vigorous will and a tender conscience; he has learned to hate all vileness and to respect others as himself. Such a man and no other has had a liberal education' (Sykes, 1988).

Openness to Learning

Although Gandhi alluded to the ideals of swadeshi or indigenous culture and tradition, he did not show any hatred for foreign languages and cultures as such. It is best evident from his reply to Tagore in an article in Young India.

> I do not want my house to be walled in on all sides and my windows to be stuffed. I want the cultures of all the lands to be blown about my house as freely as possible. But I refuse to be blown off my feet by any. I refuse to live in other peoples' houses as an interloper, a beggar, or a slave. I refuse to put the unnecessary strain of learning English upon my sisters for the sake of false pride or questionable social advantage. (Kumarappa, 1953:9).

Secular Pedagogy

Although one can easily discern Gandhi's religious bearings in almost all spheres of his thought and action, his basic education plan provided no room for religious teaching. He apprehended that religions, if not taught and practiced properly, can potentially breed conflict rather than forging unity. Gandhi, however, insisted that the common truths shared by all religions be taught to each and every child, but not through sermonizing or book readings, as he wanted the children internalize these truths only through a teacher's day to day conduct.

'Why do I not lay stress on religious instruction? Because this system is to be common to all, Hindu, Muslim, Parsee, Christian, and I am teaching them all practical religion, the religion of self-help. The whole plan springs out of non-violence, it is an integral part of the discipline of non-violence and truth' (Sykes, 1988).

Student Teacher Relationship

Gandhi was a votary of teacher's autonomy with regard to the school's daily curriculum. His basic education plan was intended to bring an end to the teacher's subservience to the stipulated textbooks and curricula (Kumar, 1999:3).

At the same time, he envisaged a non-hierarchical relationship between teachers and student.

> A teacher who establishes rapport with the taught, becomes one with them, learns more from them than he teaches them. He who learns nothing from his disciples is, in my opinion, worthless. Whenever I talk with someone, I learn from him. I take from him more than I give him. In this way, a true teacher regards himself as a student of his students. If you teach your pupils with this attitude, you will benefit much from them. (Talk to Khadi Vidyalaya Students, Sevagram, Sevak, 15 February 1942 CW 75, p. 269).

Peace Education

Gandhi's Nai Talim bore a resolute expression of non-violent principles in the sphere of education, as, in essence, it was meant to prepare for, and practise the peaceful and cooperative community life. Although 'peace education', as it is taught as an academic subject, has value in terms of information and analysis pertaining to some global and national issues such as terrorism, nuclear race, the significance of the UN, etc. such kind of information are meaningless if these are seen as something to be merely memorized for an examination and forgotten thereafter.

Peace education is as relevant at the personal, school and village level, as at the international level, and it becomes real and comes alive only when it is related to an attitude of mind and spirit, which can be accrued through a system of education that teaches—there is no way to peace, but peace is the way.

'Education for peace means learning to live peace, daily and hourly, wherever one happens to be, learning to tackle and resolve the tensions and conflicts of outlook and interest which are a necessary and valuable part of human experience' (Sykes, 1988).

On Higher Education

Higher education, according to Gandhi, was to be left to private enterprises and ought to fulfil national needs. He suggested universities to be the custodian of the whole field of education by preparing and approving fit-for-purpose courses suitable for the Indian context. His proposal of higher education, therefore, can be seen as an extension and continuation of his scheme of Basic Education.

He insisted the aim of university education should be to produce true servants of the people for meeting the immediate local needs.

Taking cue from Gandhi and Tagore, the University Commission 1949 in independent India, under the Chairmanship of Dr. Radhakrishnan, gave serious thought to the problem of higher education being disconnected to the reality and sounded a note of warning that.

> India must decide whether to aim at a widely distributed population making the villages such prosperous, interesting and culturally rich places with such a range of opportunity and adventure that young people will find more zest and interest in more cultural advantages and more opportunities for pioneering there, than in city or whether to run to vast centralized industries, with all labour taking direction either from the state or from the private corporations. (The Report of the University Commission, 1949).

The committee strongly advised a system of rural colleges and universities that could supply the required skills and training for the advancement of rural India. It recommended that rural education must be allowed to evolve with its own distinctive pattern without complying with traditional forms of educational administration. It pointed out that the existing colleges and universities of India were totally inadequate to undertake the responsibility of developing rural India.

While commenting on their drawbacks, the Commission observed the prevalent universities 'touch only the fringe of what is required in the way of higher education in the world's newest and most populous democracy. There is a vast field of pioneering before us in the process of evolving new institutions of higher learning which will answer to the needs and aspirations of this democracy' (The Report of the University Commission, 1949:555).

A significant recommendation of this commission was the 'Rural University Model' with the prime objective of injecting *'relevance'* into the Indian educational scene. The concept of 'Rural University' was an attempt to discover the 'higher educational version' of the idea of 'Basic Education' proposed by Mahatma Gandhi. The Dr. Radhakrishnan Committee Report is one of the acclaimed reports in India in terms of its vision. In this report, a chapter on 'Rural University' was incorporated, which was drafted by Dr. Arthor E Morgan, the President of the Tennessee River Valley Authority in the USA and one of the commission members.

In this chapter, he had envisaged a model university suited to Indian ethos by advancing an argument that the existing universities focused on cities and towns, without taking into account the villages where huge swathes of the Indian population lived, and that the whole educational system was devised to prepare personnel for Government jobs and not for social transformation. He pleaded that it was high time for India to have distinct, independent institutions in place to groom a leadership cadre to spearhead transformations in the Indian rural society.

He synthesized the system of learning from three historically important experiments; People's College Model (FolkeHojskole) of Scandinavia, Land Grant University system of USA, and the Sriniketan Experiment of Rabindranath Tagore.

Further, in 1954, the Government of India constituted a committee under the chairmanship of Dr. K.L. Shrimali to investigate the problems and prospects of rural higher education in the country and suggest necessary recommendations. The Committee, in its report, suggested an umbrella institutional body to oversee the academic activities of Rural Institutes. The National Council for Rural Higher Education (NCRHE) was established in accordance with the Committee's recommendation in 1955. In phase one, NCRHE identified ten institutions as Rural Institutes which would later be upgraded into rural universities.

The rural institutes were conceptualized as multi-disciplinary and broad-based institutions to play a characteristically distinctive role by way of a confluence of both 'top-down' and 'bottom-up' functions of education. While the 'top-down' function involves the application and extension of knowledge obtained from the higher level, the 'bottom-up' role refers to knowledge creation from within through a learning paradigm characterized by an orientation of solving local problems locally and the principle of experiential learning. The rural institutes were intended to create rural leadership and foster community participation for multifarious purposes, starting from sanitation, entrepreneurship development and promotion of rural livelihoods, to the protection of rural industries and the innovation of tailor-made technologies to serve the local needs.

By the year 1964, although 14 rural institutes were functioning in different parts of the country, the Rural Institute experiments became diluted as these institutes gradually became part of the mainstream higher education framework by coming under the rubric of the University Grant Commission (UGC). They eventually ended up functioning as any other colleges affiliated to conventional universities, without being able to register any visible impact in line with their original mandates.

Concluding Remarks

When it comes to the new possibilities of learning, knowledge, vocation, skills of our time in the twenty-first century, it is not surprising that Gandhi's principles of education appear outdated and impractical. At a time when 'software coding' or 'computer programming' is being talked about an essential skill that the children must learn (especially during the Coronavirus pandemic, online training programmes on coding languages such as Python became popular among parents for kids of even seven years old age), Gandhi's village craft-based basic education may appear not only adventurous but also regressive.

However, our life in the current epoch is being increasingly shaped by the transformative forces of globalization, neoliberalism, and technologies as well as the normative imperatives of sustainability and human rights, while the perceived crisis of the modern world are being increasingly sought to be resolved through techno-managerial solutions.

The modern society which is characterized by greater technological mediation and information revolution can be seen presenting a new alienating effect on the minds of children as they risk the loss of ability to see the obvious picture staring at them in the face, because their minds are increasingly cluttered with so many things, be it due to 'over analyses, or 'information overload'.

As the problem of alienation fuelling popular discontent looms large in the face of these overarching social transformations, it is worthwhile to revisit the Gandhian principles of education that transcend the liberal/vocal, rural/urban, and individual/social divides to influence our spontaneous concern for education in its varied forms in such a way that we 'learn to know', 'learn to do', 'learn to live together', 'learn to be' and live with dignity without compromising the ideal of 'un-alienated life.

In the Gandhian philosophical framework, 'un-alienated life' is treated as the most basic political ideal that ought to be secured instead of getting into the trap of the never-ending inherent contradictions between 'liberty', 'equality', and 'rights', the central ideals of the western political enlightenment.

Probably, Gandhi will not mind if a rural child learns 'coding', but he would certainly ensure that the child does this not at the cost of organic linkages with the local culture and environment, that the child knows what coding is and learns algorithm through real-life examples, and the child also knows how it is related to the life in the immediate physical and social surrounding.

References

Bilgrami, A. (2009). Value, enchantment, and the mentality of democracy: Some distant perspectives from Gandhi. *Economic and Political Weekly, 44*(51), 47–61.

Bilgrami, A. (2012). Gandhi and marx. *Social Scientist, 40*(9/10), 3–25.

Dewey, J. (1966). *Democracy and education.* New York: Free Press.

Gandhi on Education. (1998). Retrieved September 27, 2020, from http://www.schoolofeducators.com/wp-content/uploads/2012/02/GANDHI-ON-EDUCATION-BOOK-COMPLETE.pdf.

Gandhi, M. (2008). *India of my dreams.* Chandigarh: Abhishek Publications.

Gandhi, M. K. (1966). *An autobiography and the story: My experiments with truth.* Ahmedabad: Navajivan Publishing.

Kumar, K. (2010). Quality in education: Competing concepts. *Education Dialogue, 7*(1), 7–18.

Kumar, K. (1999). *Mohandas Karamchand Gandhi (1869–1948).* Retrieved September 28, 2020, from http://www.ibe.unesco.org/sites/default/files/gandhie.PDF.

Kumarappa, B. (Ed.). (1953). *Towards new education.* Ahmedabad: Navajivan Publishing House.

Naik, J. P. (1975). *Equality, 'quality and quantity: The elusive triangle of Indian education.'* New Delhi: Allied Publisher.

National Education Policy. (2020). Ministry of Human Resource Development, Government of India.

Pappu, R., & Vasanta, D. (2010). Educational quality and social inequality: Reflecting on the link. *Education Dialogue, 7*(1), 96–119.

Parekh, B. (1997). *Gandhi: A very short introduction.* Oxford: Oxford University Press.

Parel, A. J. (2016). *Pax Gandhiana: Essays on Gandhi's political philosophy.* New York: Oxford University Press.

Pring, R. (1995) *Closingthe gap: Liberal education and vocational preparation.* London, England: Hodder & Stoughton.

Sandel, M. J. (2020). *The Tyranny of merit: What's become of the common good?* UK: Penguin.

Shrimali, K. L. (1949). *The Wardha scheme: The Ghandhian plan of education for rural India.* Udaipur: Vidya Bhawan Society.

Sykes, M. (1988). *The story of Nai Talim: Fifty Years of education at sevagrram India (1937–1987).* Retrieved September 27, 2020, from http://home.iitk.ac.in/~amman/soc748/sykes_story_of_nai_talim.html.

The Report of the University Commission (1949),Ministry of Education Government of India, Availablehttp://www.academics-india.com/Radhakrishnan%20Commission%20Report%20of%201948-49.pdf (Accessed on 27.09.2020)

United Nations, Universal Declaration of Human Rights. (1948). Retrieved October 26, 2020, from https://www.un.org/en/about-us/universal-declaration-of-human-rights.

Winch, C. (2010). Search for educational quality: The dialectic of inputs and outputs. *Education Dialogue, 7*(1), 19–40.

Satyabrata Kar is a Senior Editor (Energy Projects) for the London-based New Statesman Media Group.

Part IV
Environment and Public Health

Chapter 9
Resolving Environmental Crises: A Gandhian Approach

Nibedita Priyadarshini Jena

Abstract This chapter reasons with Gandhian ideas to offer possible resolutions for the environmental crises. The chapter argues that, for Gandhi, the steppingstone of the process of self-realization is self-restraint that involves certain virtues like *ahimsā*, *aparigraha* (non-possession), *asteya* (non-stealing), *brahmacharya* (celibacy), braid labour, etc. The very process of self-realization does not confine merely to the inner perfection of humans, yet it encompasses the safety and security of every living creature and the environment as a collective. This chapter goes on to highlight that though Gandhi's ideas for the protection of the environment are premodern it is not impossible provided someone peruses her desire. The major objectives of the chapter are to analyse certain relevant proposed virtues like *ahimsā, aparigraha,* etc. which makes a philosophical foundation to the protection of the environment and to demonstrate how Gandhi's different moral principles can be harmlessly employed in resolving environmental crises.

Keywords Gandhi · Environmental Crises · *Ahimsā* · *Aparigraha* · *Asteya* · *Brahmacharya* · Vegetarianism

Introduction

Environmental crisis, that includes pollution, overpopulation, waste disposal, deforestation, climate change, loss of biodiversity, public health issues, etc. is the greatest challenge for humanity today. Most of these issues emerged from modern technology and its lifestyle. Modern technology no doubt makes human life easier and comfortable but at the cost of most vulnerable environmental problems. Emission of harmful gases and release of hazardous wastages from the industries and factories pollute air as well as all water bodies, respectively. Industrialization causes deforestation and a loss of biodiversity resulting in instability of climate and imbalance in ecosystem, respectively. Modern technological products like non-biodegradable plastic waste disposal damage the environment in a direct and an extensive way. Post-industrial

---

N. P. Jena (✉)
Department of Philosophy, Bengaluru Central University, Bengaluru, India

© National Institute of Advanced Studies 2022
A. Behera and S. Nayak (eds.), *Gandhi in the Twenty First Century*,
https://doi.org/10.1007/978-981-16-8476-0_9

society has changed the lifestyle of human beings from their sleeping time to food habits that cause many incurable diseases. And the list is endless. So, all sections of society, including scientists, social workers, and governments, try hard to restore the damage. Nonetheless, retracing premodern society cannot be the solution. In addition, it is impossible since humans have been entangled in modern technology. However, an attempt can be made to minimize its effect if humans can realize the actual potentiality of itself as Mahatma Gandhi has proposed. Gandhi at large is a pragmatic, moral, and environmental philosopher. He tried to reconcile all these three components in theorizing the ultimate purpose of human life and other related concepts. To Gandhi, the potentiality of humans is to achieve self-realization—identifying oneself with the transcendental/universal ego. For him, every human should strive to seek truth. The process of knowing truth is natural since humans are the natural seeker of it. The steppingstone of the process of self-realization is self-restraint that, for Gandhi, necessarily involves certain virtues like *ahiṃsā, aparigraha* (non-possession), *asteya* (non-stealing), *brahmacharya* (celibacy), braid labour, etc. The very process of self-realization does not confine merely to the inner perfection of humans, but also encompasses the safety and security of every living creature. For example, humans restrain themselves from eating meat through *ahiṃsā* and thus many innocent animals are saved. Similarly, they can restrain themselves from having more unnecessary possessions following the principle of *aparigraha* and hence can prevent deforestation and pollution. Gandhi's technique for the protection of the environment is premodern but possible if someone meditates on her desire. This paper aims to (1) analyse certain relevant proposed virtues such as *ahiṃsā, and aparigraha, which constitute* a philosophical foundation for the protection of the environment, and (2) demonstrate how his different moral principles can be tactfully employed in saving the environment.

Gandhi on *Ahiṃsā*

Any theorization of Gandhi's explorations is incomplete without raising his concept of *ahiṃsā*. He was a pragmatic moral philosopher and accordingly, he theorized his notion of *ahiṃsā* centering on practical considerations. His understanding of *ahiṃsā* goes farther than what the term denotes generally, i.e. not-killing or not-hurting and involves a spiritual dimension: 'Not to hurt any living thing is no doubt a part of *ahiṃsā*. But it is its least expression. The principle of *ahiṃsā* is hurt by every evil thought, by undue haste, by lying, by hatred, by wishing ill to anybody.' (Gandhi, 1968, V. 4, 218). It implies that *ahiṃsā* needs to be practised in thought, word, and deed. This broader notion of *ahiṃsā* is the outcome of the influence of Indian and Western religions such as Hinduism, Jainism, and Christianity; philosophical schools *Sānkhya,* and *Yoga*; and the personalities like Leo Tolstoy. His idea of *ahiṃsā* can be divided into two aspects based on Indian and Western influence. From the Indian perspective, based on three *guṇas* of *Sānkhya* and the Gītā, his notion of *ahiṃsā* stands in contrast to *hiṃsā* as well as inaction. The three guṇas *sattva*, *rajas* and *tamas* correspond to illumination and goodness, activity and passion, and inertia and ignorance, respectively (Refer Raghuramaraju, 2016 and Jena, 2017). However, he prefers *rajas* to *tamas* because he prefers actions to inactions (Raghuramaraju, 2016: 346–47). More fairly, for him, violent action is superior to inaction and this idea is underpinned on the fundamental principle of the Gītā, i.e. non-attachment towards fruits of the actions or any beings (*niskāmakarma*). In other words, one should refrain from being attached to either fruit of the action or any person otherwise one 'may lag spiritually in two respects': primarily, one may be reluctant to perform one's duty which could be inappropriate. For instance, Arjuna was reluctant to fight against his kin, whereas in this situation not fighting would have been an incorrect decision. Secondarily by completely ignoring any action one may enter inertia (*tamas*), 'which is more dangerous, according to Gandhi, because *tamas* promotes ignorance and sloth both of which drag humans down into a grimy world' (Jena, 2017: 399). Therefore, Gandhi's complex tenet of *ahimsā* avows that morality lies in performing a relevant action, be it *ahimsā* or *himsā*, thereby concentrating only on duty (Jena, 2017: 399).

Another aspect of Gandhi's notion of *ahimsā*, *a later addition,* involved Western influence and it was reflected in his unique conceptualization of *ahimsā*. Considering it as a duty to add something novel to the existing concept of *ahimsā*, he attached another element to *it* such as love, and compassion that emerged from his understanding of Christianity. Gandhi's understanding of the New Testament deepened through the reading of Tolstoy's *The Kingdom of God is Within You*. He was influenced by Tolstoy's interpretation that the kingdom is the regnant of 'inward perfection, truth, and love' (Chatterjee, 1983: 50–51). And this 'inward perfection' is possible through non-violence in expressing one's boundless love. Gandhi reinterpreted *ahimsā* as 'an ocean of love, whose vastness no one has ever been able to measure. If it fills us, we would be so large-hearted that we would have room in it for the whole world' (Gandhi, 1999: V.43, 11). This definition of *ahimsā* also involves 'duty' as a primary step in practicing morality as it expands its purview (including entire humanity/universe) beyond interpersonal relations. Therefore, 'he greatly valued even the lives of his enemies, those opposed to non-violence and peace' (Johnson, 2006: 228–236; McLaughlin, 2012: 681).

However, the uniqueness of Gandhi's tenet of *ahimsā* does not stop here because his notion stands asymmetrical to Jainism's theory of *ahimsā*. Although Gandhi was deeply influenced by Jainism since he was brought up in a neighbouring Jain culture, he was unwilling to accept absolute *ahimsā* viewing it as highly impractical. His theoretical structure of *ahimsā* is grounded on the belief in the impossibility of absolute *ahimsā*. Accordingly, there are two reasons for which he discarded absolute *ahimsā*: 1. his doctrine of *ahimsā* follows the principles of the Gītā 'which justifies violence in some conditions since it encourages the performance of duty and chooses violence (action), over inertia' (Jena, 2017: 401); 2. there is a central difference between the conceptualization of both the theories, i.e. Jainism's *ahimsā* is rooted in its metaphysics (Soni, 2013), whereas Gandhi's doctrine is embedded on duty. Gandhi's precept is free from the unified relationship between ethics and metaphysics and that is why 'he is hardly obliged to accept absolute non-violence' (Jena, 2017: 401).

Self-realization and Environment

Gandhi's denial of absolute *ahimsā* may seem human-centric but it is practically significant. Violence is a part of the very existence of society. Humanity is impossible without external *himsā* (Gandhi, 1968: V.II, 521–22). For example, millions of lives in the ecosystem (organisms) are killed while eating, sleeping, drinking, etc. It is important to discuss his stance on humans compared to other beings, though his argument is contextual, while crediting him as a pragmatic philosopher. Showing his absolute bias towards humanity he states, 'I have no feeling to save the lives of animals which devour, or cause hurt to man …I will never sacrifice a man's life to save theirs' (Gandhi, 1960: V. II, 65). He consciously favoured to kill menacing monkeys and rabid dogs because 'such killing becomes a duty' (Gandhi, 1960: V. II, 65) to protect humanity. This argument has direct implication on happenings in the world regarding the human-animal conflict. For example, the killing of hundreds of wild camels in Australia becomes a duty to save humanity and the environment, in general, from water scarcity due to wildfire. The current situation does not strongly demand to find out the reason why the fire broke out in the forest; rather search for ways to protect human society including the environment. Hence, killing camels is not an act of filth since it is one of the important solutions to minimize water scarcity.

However, Gandhi's emphasis on the human species is not one-sided as he demands more responsibility from humans towards nature. Rationalizing that the human species is a superior species he says, '[man] is higher than the brute in his moral instincts and moral institutions' (Gandhi, 1999: V.35, 144). Unlike animals, human beings are provided with a power of reason and can distinguish between virtues and vice, good and evil. So, 'what distinguishes him from the brute is his ceaseless striving to rise above the brute on the moral plane' (Gandhi, 1968: V.6, 110–111). And the final objective of the lives of humans is to achieve 'self-realisation': 'what I want to achieve,—what I have been striving and pining to achieve … is self-realisation, to see God face to face, to attain moksha' (Gandhi, 1968: V.1, xix). Here, Gandhi does not refer to a narrow, ordinary 'self' or 'ego'; instead, he talks about universal Self that encompasses not merely humans but all living creatures. The universal Self identifies itself with every living creature. This approach contradicts his other writings (mentioned above), still that contradiction is contextual. Most of his writings and his moral practices harmonize with his conceptualization of self-realization. His ideal of self-realization through moral means offers a holistic approach towards every living being including the environment. This introspective environmentalism has been better recognized by the environmentalist Arne Naess (1987). He initially identifies the nature of Gandhi's self-realization and then establishes an ecological theory (deep ecology) subscribing to his notions of self-realization and *ahimsā*. Gandhi's universal benevolence is explicit when he says, 'I believe in *advaita*. I believe in the essential unity of man and for that matter of all that lives...' (Gandhi, 1999: V.29, 408). Naess, the founder of deep ecology, uses this credence of Gandhi to distinguish 'deep ecology' from 'shallow ecology'. Identifying oneself with every other being (keeping a healthy relationship with nature) is incomplete without non-violence as Gandhi says: 'We cannot have ecological movement designed to prevent violence against Nature unless the principle of non-violence becomes central to the ethics of human culture' (Quoted in Moolakkattu, 2010: 155). It seems self-realization and non-violence complement each other, and one is incomplete without the other. Naess rightly says: 'the rock bottom foundation of the technique for achieving the power of non-violence is belief in the essential oneness of all life' (Naess, 1987: 39). To him, environmental degradation is caused by the consideration of narrow isolated 'self' or 'ego' of human beings. This narrow self is considered separate from nature which is wedged in anthropocentric approach (shallow ecology). He has proposed a new and broader understanding of self what he calls as 'ecological self' (self-realization). In the framework of the ecological self, the self needs to be understood as inseparate from nature as both are interwoven. The ecological self supposes that humans' actions must align and harmonize with nature. And once this harmony is attained, the exploitation of nature will end. This leads to a practice of 'biocentric egalitarianism' in which every natural being is considered as intrinsically equal being.

However, **Naess's deep ecology has been ridiculed by Ramachandra** Guha (1989) **at various levels. One of his criticisms finds the absence of radicalness involved in deep ecology favouring environmentalism. As claimed by some exponents, the preservation of wild is very much a vital element of contemporary American consumer society, though it's ironic that in the guise of conserving environment it promotes more consumerism. In his words,**

> the enjoyment of nature is an integral part of the consumer society. The private automobile (and the lifestyle it has spawned) is in many respects the ultimate ecological villain, and an untouched wilderness the prototype of ecological harmony; yet, for most Americans it is perfectly consistent to drive a thousand miles to spend a holiday in a national park... by virtue of their economic and political dominance (Guha, 1989: 79).

Complimenting Guha's claim, it can be argued that even prior to Naess's theoretical articulation of deep ecology, Gandhi was already explicit about the idea of humans' connectivity with nature and it 'must be inferred from an overall reading of the Mahatma's writings' (Weber, 1999: 351).

Gandhi's concept of self-realization asserts the well-being of all beings (*sarvodaya*) in the ecosystem. Gandhi's notion of *Sarvodaya* takes a significant place in the domain of ecology. In the ecological framework, Gandhi appeals to maintain an unexploited sensible relation towards the entire nature. Much of his writings have been directly dedicated to saving animals (More on this see Jena, 2017), whereas his sensitiveness to trees and plants can also not be undermined. It is reflected in his writings as well as the incident that once happened in his life. He asked for some strands of leaves at night, but he was given more than his request. So, he bemoaned, 'Trees are living beings just like us... It is a wretched thing to go and tear the leaves of a tree at night when it is resting! And why have you brought such a huge quantity? Only a few leaves were necessary.... We should feel a more living bond between ourselves and the rest of the animate creation' (Gandhi, 1961: V.1, 303). This passage 'shows his commitment to environmental protection' (Joseph & Bharat, 2011: 6) which is reinforced through the principles of non-violence and non-possession. Gandhi's commitment towards environmental protection asserts an ecological relation in which 'ecological citizenship' is assigned to humans 'requiring the scrutiny of one's bodily consumptive behaviors, ...' (Godrej, 2012: 438).

Being a deontic philosopher, Gandhi states that humans have certain duties towards the environment. Their performance of duty towards the environment requires, above all, self-restraint and humans are capable of that as Gandhi says, '[man] is man because he is capable of and only so far as he exercises self-restraint' (Gandhi, 1957: 317). It seems self-restraint has been overemphasized by him in certain cases. For instance, Gandhi realized the requirement of birth control, but on the contrary, he was against the modern technique of contraceptive that was proposed to be adopted (Gandhi, 1999: V.30, 390–91). For him using modern contraceptives has double side effects: 1. It causes other health issues since it is not natural, and 2. It prevents humans to practice self-restraint (*brahmacharya*). Nonetheless, ignoring his overemphasized *brahmacharya* part, Gandhi's credibility on population control is valued on the account of his defense of preventing the birth of unwanted children, which is highly significant in the present scenario since the world is facing the issue of overpopulation.

The purpose of raising the concept of 'self-restraint' is to show its significance in achieving self-realization. The notion of 'self-restraint' is a part of ethics arising from the Indian Philosophy of Yoga system and Tolstoy.[1] In ordinary language, Yoga that refers to controlling over the mind aims at self-purification through physical practices (*Hat Yoga*) as well as moral code of action (*Raj Yoga*). Gandhi prefers *Yama*, one of the restraints of *Raj yoga*, since it encompasses five fundamental commandments meant for right living and one must avoid hurting (*ahimsā*) and not telling false (*satya*); one must embrace non-stealing (*asteya*); celibacy (*brahmacarya*); and not being acquisitive (*aparigraha*) (Patanjali, 2003, Yoga Sūtra II: 30). In the contemporary context, *ahimsā* and *aparigraha* (non-possession) have direct implications.

---

[1] Gandhi in the speech on Tolstoy's birth centenary mentioned that in Patanjali's treatise on yoga the first step prescribed for the student of yoga, for one aspiring after self-realisation, is the observance of the disciplines of yamaniyama. There is no path but that of self-control for you or me or others. Tolstoy showed this by leading along with the life of self-control. I wish...we shall earn the lesson of self-control from Tolstoy's life (Gandhi 1999 V.43, 11). Gandhi prescribes 11 vows i.e., non-violence, truth, non-stealing, non-possession, celibacy, control of the palate, fearlessness, bread labour, removal of untouchability equality of religions, and humility (Gandhi 1999 V.43, 4–11, 1932).

Ahimsā and *Aparigraha* (Non-possession): Relevance in Current Environmental Crisis

The non-possession is significant from micro- to macro-level concerning the contemporary environmental crisis. The philosophical meaning of non-possession is that an individual should limit herself only to necessary possessions. Keeping this definition in his mind, Gandhi correlates non-possession with the other commandment, i.e. non-stealing. It is considered theft if any individual accumulates goods more than what is required for her (Gandhi, 1932: 16). If Gandhi's principle of non-possession is true, then it would not be wrong to say that the three fourth part of the world is filled with thieves since most people want to have things far beyond their necessity that causes environmental degradation. For instance, buying unnecessary items from the e-market and the wrappers or poly bags accrued from this process creates a new challenge to the environment. Gandhi offers a broader meaning of *aparigraha*: it 'is a principle applicable to thoughts, as well as to things' (Gandhi, 1932: 17). This wider definition deeply involves two important principles, i.e. non-attachment principle of the Gitā and non-violence. Non-possession and non-attachment go hand-in-hand since an individual follows non-attachment to abide by the principle of non-possession. Unless we subdue our desires to get unnecessary things such as dresses, mobiles, and laptops, we cannot follow non-possession. In addition, making an internal connection between non-violence and non-possession, he says that the individual who fairly follows the principle of non-violence diminishes the desire to claim anything in this world his or her own (non-possession). She should try to merge herself with nature (Gandhi, 1999: V.32, 228). At this juncture, non-possession seems to be a necessary condition for non-violence and therefore both are essential for self-realization. Since non-possession and non-violence are interwoven, he claims that non-violence presupposes non-possession because superfluous acquisition leads to unnecessary violence: 'today we only desire possession of a thing; tomorrow we shall begin to adopt measures, straight, if possible, crooked when thought necessary, to acquire its possession' (Gandhi, 1932: 15). For instance, clearing a small part of the forest for one's dwelling may not be wrong but destroying a large part of the forest to construct an apartment and earn money is immoral that leads to wildlife destruction and an imbalance in nature.

Gandhi's role as an environmentalist or his idea of environmentalism is indisputable. But then, whether he has predicted about the environmental disaster, caused by modern technological society in *Hind Swaraj*, is debatable. Ramachandra Guha (1995) may have correctly analysed that Gandhi has not directly predicted environmental crises in *Hind Swaraj but* in other writings, he has certainly examined the dire consequences of modern technology including environmental devastation. If we subscribe to Naess-Gandhian ecology, then it would be right to say that Gandhi's rejection of technology fundamentally presupposes the preservation of nature, considering humans as part of nature itself. Since they are a part of nature, let us discuss his points against modernity at the individual level. The reason behind introducing modern technology is to remove poverty in giving an opportunity to sustain the livelihood of individuals. However, he believes that any profession which is not done for its own sake, is merely done for the livelihood that is not ideal and thus he analyses the drawbacks of the professions pertaining to the industrial society. The most important thing he points out, that has high relevance to the contemporary world, is the lack of freedom in the industrial professions. The real meaning of freedom is not to gain ordinary material needs but to enhance a higher intellectual level. According to him:

> [it] is at least debatable whether the profession of a clerk or bookkeeper is better or more respectable than that of a [vegetable] hawker. A hawker is an independent man. He has opportunity of studying human nature which a clerk slaving away for a few pounds per month can never have. A hawker is master of his own time. A clerk has practically no time he can call his own. A hawker, if he chooses, has opportunity for expansion of his intellect which a clerk cannot dream of (Gandhi, 1999: V.10, 388).

In line with this argument, he further says industrialism is underpinned on the principle of exploitation. So, a country like India should desist embracing industrialization:

> Industrialism depends entirely on your capacity to exploit... a vast country like India cannot expect to benefit by industrialisation. In fact, India, when it begins to exploit other nations-as it must do if it becomes industrialized-will be a curse for other nations, a menace to the world (Gandhi, 1999: V.54, 84-85).

The relevance of Gandhi's comment cannot be ignored because modern industrial society causes unhealthy living conditions due to lack of freedom and physical activity, unnecessary exploitation, competition, conflict, work stress, and so on. All these together harm individuals both at personal as well as social levels. Health issue causes mayhem in modern society and that leads to a chain of undesirable activities which affect environment explicitly or implicitly: for example, physical and mental suffering of humans, demand for the opening of more hospitals, exploitations by the private hospitals, more research on Medical Sciences that involves the suffering of animals, and last but not the least, non-degradable disposals of the hospitals. Gandhi's grave anticipation of modern industrial society is under the scope of environmental as well as personal degradation. Being an environmental philosopher, he expects humans' co-operation with nature for their bread and butter. His polemics against technological artefact as a source of livelihood can be summed up as.

> the great nature has intended us to earn our bread by manual labour- the sweat of our brows- and intended him to dedicate his intellect not towards multiplying his material wants and surrounding himself with enervating and soul-destroying luxuries, but towards uplifting his moral being— towards knowing the will of the Creator— towards serving humanity and thus truly serving himself (Gandhi, 1999: V.10, 388).

His rejection of technology is very much involved in the process of self-realization. The process of self-realization is more viable in ancient society rather than the modern one. And thus, the lacuna between ancient and modern society was highlighted by him. The ancient society teaches us how to control our wants through self-restraint, whereas the modern society teaches us how to progress by multiplying our wants, leading to overconsumption. Significantly, the fundamental difference Gandhi holds between self-restraint and self-indulgence is that the former is *dharma*, and the latter is *adharma* because 'the ideal of self-restraint attaches less importance to the outward life than to the inner' (Gandhi, 1999: V.19, 430–31). Farah Godrej correctly points out that Gandhi's antagonism against industrial society shows that the latter obstructs the conditions for the awakening of humans' inner selves than showing its destructiveness towards nature (Godrej, 2012: 440). Moreover, the actual need of humans and what they desire may not often complement each other. For example, a diabetic may desire to have delicious, sugary, and greasy food, but such type of food should be avoided to keep oneself healthy and therefore is not one's need. For Gandhi, the actual human need is spiritual in nature governed by the higher-order reason, whereas ordinary desire of piling wealth is governed by the instrumental reasoning. Thus, his rejection of modern technology entails internalizing one's desires for the well-being of oneself as well as the environment. In addition, his notion of human's inward development is underpinned in his other philosophically substantial notion, i.e. *Swaraj* which warrants universal welfare. He says, '[the] first step to Swaraj lies in the individual. The great truth: 'As with the individual so with the universe', is applicable here as elsewhere. Even if he has not predicted about environmental degradation in his phenomenal work *Hind Swaraj*, his idea of sustainable economic development includes the quality of life of humans and the environment in general.

In the dialogue of denying modern technology, he states how technology directly affects the environment by polluting the air. Emphasizing the importance of fresh air for human life and how humans are deprived of it he says, 'air is the most essential. Consequently, Nature has provided it to such extent that we can have it at no cost. But modern civilization has put a price even on air. In these times, one has to go off to distant places to take the air, and this costs money' (Gandhi, 1999: V.12, 395–96). The price of modern technology is paid by the manner by which many humans suffer from diseases like allergy/asthma, mostly caused by polluted air. Observing Gandhi's characterization of modern society, one can say that the existing environmental crisis is an impact of materialistic practice of life. The excessive desire to have things leads to more accumulation of non-degradable garbage and the pollution of the environment. Production factories are the major root causes of environmental depletion. Appealing to curtail one's unnecessary greediness, he claims that nature has provided us with sufficient natural resources and he utters the famous maxim: 'it is the fundamental law of Nature, without exception, that Nature produces enough for our wants from day to day, and if only everybody took enough for himself and nothing more, there would be no pauperism in this world, there would be no man dying of starvation in this world' (Gandhi, 1999: V.15, 171).

Gandhi's romanticism against technology is closer to other well-known philosophers' anti-technology ideas. For instance, Martin Heidegger. The Heideggerian theory explains that technology is itself a mode of disclosedness and the essence of it is 'enframing' the objects considering those as 'stock' or resource (source of energy) (Malpas, 2003: 159; Dusek, 2006: 75). For example, the river becomes 'hydroelectric power', and human beings become human resources. Although he said that crafts were better than modern technology, he acknowledged that it is impossible to keep us away from technology and humans need to put a check on its use. However, Gandhi's rejection of modern technology seems more stringent and practicable because his rejection involved a cluster of issues that emerged from technology like pollution, exploitation, and physical labour. Considering the stringent part, he was even against modern medical studies because (1) this study process necessarily involves the killing of innocent animals which is against the principle of *ahimsā*, and (2) there is another alternative to get rid of diseases, i.e. 'nature cure' (Gandhi, 2003: 38–43). How far Gandhi's 'nature cure' method is acceptable in the present scenario is a matter of doubt. The world is facing a certain type of disease that cannot be cured through the nature cure process even though those diseases exist because of modern technology and humans' unnatural way of life.

Heidegger might have correctly said humans cannot come out of technology. Implicatively Medical Science is needed to save humanity and Gandhi would not have denied it since saving humanity is the prime duty for him. Though humans are entangled with the technology, for Heidegger, humans should strive to minimize its use that might go in favour of Gandhi's absolute denial of the same. Less use of technology may open the door for the 'nature cure' method and can be considered as a major technique to cure diseases. It is beneficial in protecting the environment in two respects: (1) many animals can be saved from their ruin (since less diseases need less of experimentations) and (2) purity of nature (pollution-free) can be maintained.

The entire world is concerned about the non-degradable plastics, global warming, hole in the ozone layer, etc. caused by modern technology. Nations are spending crores of rupees to get rid of these problems. At this juncture, it would not be wrong to say that Gandhi had predicted this scenario years ago and hence discarded modern technology underlining the principle of non-possession. His assessment, keeping a watertight relation, characterizes village with handicrafts and town with modern mills/machines. Both are excluded from each other. And he believes that any trespass is harmful for villages as well as villagers. So, he says, '[it] is a process of double drain from the villages. Urbanization in India is a slow but sure death for her villages and villagers.' (Gandhi, 1999: V.64, 409). It is undeniable that modernization has influenced the rustic environment. Villages have lost their natural beauty in a chain of transition from mud house to concrete house, muddy road to concrete road, simplicity to corrupt-complex mental attitude, peace-loving to violence preference, hard labour to idleness, and so on. All these lead to the loss of the village and thus the destruction of the natural environment.

Nonetheless, for Gandhi technology is not the only source that pollutes the environment but also the incorrect way of living. Spitting everywhere, excreting, and urinating at open space, etc. cause foul smell and pollute the air. He appealed to stop all these completely by giving examples of other non-human animals. Some animals, like cats and dogs, naturally learned to cover their defecation with mud. We humans should consciously learn to cover our defecation and should educate our children to follow the same. According to Gandhi there must be separate spaces for urinating and as per his guideline, urinating space must be far away from the living space and the place should be sprinkled with soil after urination. Intriguingly, he did not suggest burying the urine, unlike defecating, too deep because 1. natural evaporation process

9 Resolving Environmental Crises: A Gandhian Approach 143

(through the heat of the sun) cannot be done and 2. urine might pollute neighbouring underground water springs (Gandhi, 1999: V.12, 403–405).

Believing in 'cleanliness is godliness' and preserving good health are the primary necessary conditions for being happy, he says, '[no] one should spit or clean his nose on the streets. In some cases, the sputum is so harmful that germs are carried from it, and they infect others...' (Gandhi, 1999: V.19, 98). The significance of the argument is highly relevant, particularly during this pandemic period, where masking our faces and maintaining social distance are the norms of the day. Thus, two things can be abstracted from the above-mentioned discussion, and both are interlinked. First, keeping our healthiness presupposes an essential condition, i.e. healthy environment that precludes defiled air and water, flies, winged insects, etc. Second, keeping a healthy environment presupposes a disciplined lifestyle that includes good habits. Together it brings out the good health of humans as well as a healthy environment. After more than a hundred years of his appeal, Gandhi's reformative idea has been implemented formally by the government of India starting with the project named *Swachh Bharat Mission (2014). It includes helping poor villagers financially to build a latrine for their personal use. This prevents them from having a latrine outside as well as to save them from social shamefulness (from latrine outside) and keeping common garbage bins for the cleanliness of the individual houses and environment too. The governmental mission to implement Gandhi's village reformation plan takes a broader scope including urban places/slums as well.*

Gandhi also appeals to keep water clean: a basic requirement for good health. The water used for drinking or cooking must be kept clean. Accordingly, he suggests reserving the wells and ponds clean by taking various steps—not to take bath, not to wash clothes, etc., in the ponds (Gandhi, 1999: V.19, 98). Implementation of his reformative idea on clean water is practiced to some extent both at individual as well as governmental level. Families use their borewells or tube wells and the government, instead of fostering to keep ponds or wells clean, supplies centralized clean water, and dig tube well in villages and in urban areas too. However, absolute reformation is yet to be done.

The fundamental 3 R principles (refuse, reuse, and recycle) are best reflected in Gandhi's campaign to protect the environment. The concept of 'refuse' is very much included in his notions of non-possession and non-stealing. He talks about reusing and recycling in a different context, explaining the process of making organic manure and its benefit to keep the village clean and healthy. It is highly relevant when the current environmental concern is taken into an account. He says.

> It is scarcely necessary to enlarge upon the rule that dirt must not be thrown on the street. Disposal of refuse is also a science. Glass, iron, etc., should be buried deep. Twigs and sticks used for cleaning teeth should be washed, dried, and used for fuel. Rags may be sold. Leftover food, peelings, etc., should be buried and turned into manure. I have seen many a heap of manure prepared in this way. Paper can be made from rags. It should not be necessary to employ anyone to remove refuse in a village, because there is very little of it and most of it can be converted into manure. (Gandhi, 1999: V.19, 99).

This small quote is excerpted from his article titled 'Father of the World (IV)' published in *Navajivan* on February 11, 1919. The entire article is dedicated to the health and hygienic issues of the village people concerning the quality of water they drink, the type of food they eat, the quality of the air they inhale, etc. and how these can be executed. This quote expresses multiple ideas including environmental cleanliness as well as himself comprising how his astuteness was undisturbed by the outcome (modernization) of the instrumental reasoning. Gandhi's vision of keeping villages clean not only involves the apparent cleaning, but it also fosters extensive purity, and maintenance of the environment. It encompasses air, water, soil, and so on. His idea of garbage segregation including reuse and recycle has a pragmatic value in terms of current environmental concerns.

The above discussion shows (1) Gandhi's proposed idea to take initiatives to maintain hygiene around the village and environment in general and (2) undisguisedly he took the responsibility of showing how the fertility of the soil can be improved using natural compost which is now highly encouraged by agricultural scientists and the government of the country. The most important question that remains to be answered is whether the quality of life of poor villagers has been improved by the technology or not. This question has been debated between Gandhi and Nehru (first prime minister) regarding introducing and advancing modern technology to remove poverty. Both have opposing views, in this regard, though their objective is same, i.e. well-being of the people of India (especially village people).

Conclusion

This paper has done a comprehensive study of Gandhi's environmentalism. His vantage point on the protection of the environment is a unified concept of many other notions. Importantly, he endorses maximum practice of non-violence and violence in the inevitable situation. By constraining any strict rule against all violence, his tenet is praxis in the current mode of living. However, his supportive stance on humanity provides a broader horizon of protection to the environment. Human life is not confined to engage merely with her inner-outer development. Instead, it includes the protection of her surroundings. Gandhi assigns higher responsibility to humans, being a superior creature in nature. He, considering humans as part of nature, asserts that the real development of humans moves towards construction/protection of nature not towards the destruction of nature by adopting so-called modernity. Embracing modernity is the decadence of society and undisguisedly causes many complex issues, for example, poverty, pollution, and bad health. Gandhi plausibly did not question the progress of intellectual creativity of humans. He emphasized that human engagement should go together with nature and not with the orientation of creating artificial artifacts. This in turn puts nature to ruin. Thus, a Gandhian approach to preserve nature is indeed pragmatic and remarkable.

References

Chatterjee, M. (1983). *Gandhi's religious thought*. Macmillan Press.
Dusek, V. (2006). *Philosophy of technology: An introduction*. Oxford: Blackwell.
Gandhi, M. K. (1932). *From Yeravda Mandir: Ashram observances*. Ahmedabad: Navajivana Publishing House. Retrieved March 31, 2020, from https://www.mkgandhi.org/ebks/yeravda.pdf. (Translated by Valji Govindji Desai).
Gandhi, M. K. (1957). *An autobiography: The story of my experiments with truth*. Boston: Beacon Press. (Translated by Mahadev Haribhai Desai).
Gandhi, M.K. (1961). *In search of the supreme* (Vol. 1). Ahmedabad: Navajivana Publishing House.
Gandhi, M. K. (1960). *Non-violence in war and peace* (Vol. 2). Ahmedabad: Navajivana Publishing House. First Print 1942.
Gandhi, M. K. (1968). *The selected works of Mahatma Gandhi* (Vol.1–6). Ahmedabad: Navajivana Publishing House.
Gandhi, M. K. (1999). *The collected works of Mahatma Gandhi*. New Delhi: Publication Division, Ministry of Information and Broadcasting, Government of India.
Gandhi, M.K. (2003). *Gandhiji on environment*. Mumbai: Mani Bhavan Gandhi Samgrahalaya. (Selected and compiled with an introduction by Divya Joshi).
Godrej, F. (2012). Ascetics, warriors, and a gandhian ecological citizenship. *Political Theory, 40*(4), 437–465.
Guha, R. (1989). Radical American environmentalism and wilderness preservation: A third world critique. *Environmental Ethics, 11*, 71–83.
Guha, R. (1995). Mahatma Gandhi and the environmental movement in India. *Capitalism Nature Socialism, 6*(3), 47–61.
Jena, N. P. (2017). Gandhi's perspective on non-violence and animals: ethical theory and moral practice. *Journal of Global Ethics, 13*(3), 398–416.
Johnson, R. (2006). Satyagraha: The only way to stop terrorism. In L. Johnson (Ed.), *Gandhi's experiments with truth: Essential writings by and about Mahatma Gandhi* (pp. 228–236). New York: Lexington Books.
Joseph, K.S., & Bharat M. (Eds.). (2011). *Gandhi, environment and sustainable future*. New Delhi: Gandhi Peace Foundation.
Malpas, J. (2003). Martin heidegger. In R. C. Solomon & D. Sherman (Eds.), *The Blackwell guide to continental philosophy* (pp. 143–162). Oxford: Blackwell.
McLaughlin, R. P. (2012). Non-violence and nonhumans: Foundations for animal welfare in the thought of Mohandas Gandhi and Albert Schweitzer. *Journal of Religious Ethics, 40*(4), 678–704.
Moolakkattu, J. S. (2010). Gandhi as a human ecologist. *Journal of Human Ecology, 29*(3), 151–158.
Naess, A. (1987). Self-realisation: An ecological approach to being in the world. *The Trumpeter, 4*(3), 35–42.
Patanjali. (2003). The yoga sutra of Patanjali. Retrieved March 31, 2020, from http://www.arlingtoncenter.org/Sanskrit-English.pdf. Sanskrit-English Translation & Glossary, Chip Hartranft.
Raghuramaraju, A. (2016). Ethics of M. K. Gandhi: Nonviolence and Truth. In S. Ranganathan (Ed.), *The bloomsbury research handbook of Indian ethics* (pp. 341–356). London: Bloomsbury publishing Plc.
Soni, J. (2013). Philosophical justification of non-violence in Jainism. *Journal of International Philosophy, 2*, 192–197.
Weber, T. (1999). Gandhi, deep ecology, peace research. *Journal of Peace Research, 36*(3), 349–361.

Dr. Nibedita Priyadarshini Jena is an Assistant Professor in Department of Philosophy at Bengaluru Central University, Bengaluru. A PhD in philosophy from University of Hyderabad, Dr. Jena also worked in Delhi University and University of Hyderabad.

Chapter 10
Mahatma Gandhi's Insights on Air Pollution and Clean Air

S. N. Sahu

Abstract The issue of air pollution and its adverse effect on public health cannot be more direly felt and understood than during a period when the humanity is passing through an unprecedented pandemic of COVID-19. While the urgency of access to clean air and concerns against air pollution is a common challenge to the entire humanity, Gandhi recognized these issues in early twentieth century. The issues related to air pollution and access to clean air that Gandhi identified continue to have relevance in the twenty-first century. This paper revisits Gandhi's insights on air pollution and reasons with their relevance in present day context. Echoing prophetic ideas of Gandhi that in modern civilization clean air would not be available free of cost, the paper engages with Gandhi's ideas under four major themes. The paper begins engaging Gandhi's ideas on air pollution and clean air from spiritual perspectives. Subsequently, it highlights Gandhi's concerns over air pollution as a public health issue. The paper also engages with Gandhi's ideas linking air pollution with Swaraj, governance, and educational perspectives.

Keywords Mahatma Gandhi · Maganlal Gandhi · Air pollution · Sevagram · Public health · Swaraj

Introduction

The Age of Anthropocene marked by domination of human species in every sphere of planet earth has generated several crises and one of the foremost and existential crises is air pollution. The grave danger caused by air pollution worldwide has imperilled life and resulted in number of deaths surpassing the lives lost during many wars and conflicts in human history. Considering the graveness of the situation the World Health Organisation (WHO) in a conference (Global Conference on Air Pollution and Health-October 29 to November 1, 2018) discussed the urgency of the issue and made efforts to prepare a strategy to deal with it (WHO, 2018). It was the first such conference ever convened in the history of humanity to deal with a situation

---

S. N. Sahu (✉)
Special Duty and Press Secretary, New Delhi, India

© National Institute of Advanced Studies 2022
A. Behera and S. Nayak (eds.), *Gandhi in the Twenty First Century*,
https://doi.org/10.1007/978-981-16-8476-0_10

marked by prevalence of high levels of toxins in air we breathe for our very survival. It is said that India is the worst affected by air pollution in the world (Child, 2019) and the rising crises caused by such pollution are getting intensified on a day-to-day basis across the country. The lethal effects of air pollution combined with ever increasing and multiplying menace arising out of global warming and climate change are dangerously compromising the right to life which is the basis of all other rights and entitlements which humans enjoy and often expand to make life more meaningful and fulfilling. The sheer gravity of the situation can be gauzed from the critical observations highlighted by the WHO. The WHO warned that since the world is getting hotter and populated, the humanity continues to produce more dirty emissions. As a result of which, around a half of the world population has hardly any access to clean fuel and the air that people breathe is getting polluted by every day to extent of ninety percent of the population breathe polluted air which results in killing of seven million people every year. The WHO also highlighted the bad effects of polluted air in terms of causing serious health hazards such as stroke, lung cancer, and other heart-related diseases which can be equated to the health issues caused by smoking and tobacco consumption. The WHO also flagged the warning in terms of difficulty involved in escaping the air pollution that causes serious heath issues to the entire population (WHO, 2018).

The above passage is self-explanatory and constitutes a grim indication of the future shape and shock that would completely overwhelm humanity if appropriate measures were not taken to keep air free from pollution and contamination. The serious breathing crises confronting humanity because of the carbon economy created over several centuries is not amenable to easy solution. In this context, it is instructive to know that more than hundred years back Mahatma Gandhi had presciently reflected on air pollution and underlined the necessity of looking at the issue of clean air from integrated perspectives. He looked at it from the perspective of not only public health but also from the perspective of freedom and independence of India from colonial rule. He also located the issue of clean air as a categorical imperative in context of governance and economy of the country. Besides, he looked at it from the larger perspective of spirituality and education. Such integrated perspectives to deal with the deadly menace of air pollution are fundamental prerequisites to safeguard humanity from an existential crisis.

Gandhi Looked at Air Pollution as a Public Health Issue in Early Twentieth Century

The critical concerns relating to the effects of air pollution on human civilization highlighted by the WHO in 2018 resonates with Gandhi's understanding that he reflected on decades before. Articulating on the importance of clean air Gandhi wrote that, there could be possibility for humans to manage without water for a day, but it is hardly a possibility to live without air even for a minute. He mentioned that if polluted water can have serious health implications, similarly, the negative implications of polluted air on human's health are beyond anybody's imagination. Gandhi, while highlighting the importance of clean air, was certainly perplexed with the collective indifference people generally showed towards the issue of air pollution (Gandhi, 1994: CWMG, vol. 97).

A glance at those words would give the impression that someone well versed with the scale and magnitude of mounting air pollution in twenty-first century world would have authored that paragraph to convey the point that people have neglected the impact of air pollution on health for too long because they were not educated or made aware of its consequences. But that paragraph was written by Mahatma Gandhi in a letter to Maganlal Gandhi in 1914 (Ibid.) when air pollution was hardly an issue and possibly it was not even reckoned with by the leaders who played key roles in managing the affairs of statecraft and governance.

In twenty-first century world life adverse impact and threatening impact of air pollution on health has been well researched and documented in prestigious medical journals. For instance, the study published in Lancet journal (2021) reiterated the concerns of WHO that the air pollution has been an important factor causing many diseases, leading to premature deaths and, arguably, the largest global environmental health threat.

The pages of Collected Works of Mahatma Gandhi (CWMG) reveal that he made in-depth analysis of air pollution and outlined the critical necessity of clean air for a healthy life and transmitted the ideas and insights through his writings beginning from the first decade of twentieth century till his last days.

Gandhi founded Indian Opinion, a weekly newspaper, in 1903 in South Africa as a mouthpiece of Indians staying in that country. It was used by him to transmit news and views and educate Indians on diverse issues of public interest. It is illuminating to note that a few months before he started his first *Satyagaraha* in South Africa for the rights and dignity of Indians he authored a piece in the Indian Opinion on 5March 1906 and reflected on the indispensability of clean air for healthy living. He wrote that 'a man can do without food for several days and live a day altogether without waters, but it is impossible to carry on without air even for a minute. If a thing that is so very vital to life is not pure, the result cannot but be deleterious' (Gandhi, 1906).

The above passage was written by him in the context of the large cities of England where several factories had come up and labourers had to work in constricted spaces all day and lived in small houses where clean air for breathing was not adequately available. Gandhi observed that such harsh working and living conditions were responsible for deterioration of their health and even the death rate among people who lived in narrow space of small rooms was higher than those who were accommodated in spacious houses. He apprised that Cadbury brothers and Lever brothers appreciated those reasons and shifted their factories outside cities and went for construction of better accommodations with amenities such as gardens and libraries for the workers. He also flagged the point that despite such investments for workers the profits of those companies went up and other business concerns followed those examples (Ibid). Drawing from this experience, Gandhi suggested that the Indian leaders should have considered the importance of clean air and better living conditions for the people.

He asserted that it is because of the indifference to the value of pure air, diseases like plague continued to spread in India (Ibid.).

That point was reiterated by him in another article 'Plague in Sydney' published in the Indian Opinion on 24 March 1906. He stressed upon the continuous warnings that highlighted on uncleanliness and polluted air as causes of plague (Gandhi, 1906). Therefore, urged people to let 'plenty of fresh air flow into the house' (Ibid). Gandhi's sensitive observations in 1906 which highlighted on realizing the value of pure air sounds so contemporary in the context of the alarming levels of air pollution in several parts of the world. The severity of air pollution is making people conscious of the value clean air. Therefore, people getting suffocated by the sheer volume, scale, and magnitude of contaminated air are now speaking up and joining the movement for defending their inalienable right to breathe clean air.

There is a striking parallel between his explanation that a disease like plague occurred because of absence of clean air with the explanations offered by medical experts that growing pollution of air is now responsible for rapid spread of lungs, heart, and brain diseases. The COVID-19 pandemic has flattened the health, human and economic securities across the world. Its lethal second wave along with the variants of the novel coronavirus have caused deaths of people in India and rest of the world. It's devastating impact is continuing causing catastrophic consequences. It is evidenced by destruction as much of life as of livelihood of people. COVID-19 infected people and even leading hospitals in the capital of India, New Delhi, and other cities were desperately searching for medical oxygen which was frighteningly in short supply during April and May 2021. As a result, thousands died because they could not get access to oxygen to breathe and save their lives. Experts have identified air pollution prevailing in India as one of the factors behind faster spread of COVID-19 in several parts of India (Pandey, 2020).

A recent scientific study (Sahu et al., 2021) observes that the people who are living in and around highly polluted areas are found to be more vulnerable to getting infected with coronavirus. One of the major findings of the study is the correlation between the level of air pollution and the number of coronavirus infected cases. The consumption of fossil fuels and industrial activities that contribute to air pollution also substantially contribute to the rising number of COVID-19 cases. According to this study, the prolonged exposure to particulate matter (PM2.5) in the states of Delhi, Gujarat, Maharashtra, and Uttar Pradesh explains the high rises in the COVID-19 cases. Such scientific studies highlighting the strong correlations between impure air and the spread of diseases like the COVID-19 reminds us of Gandhi's attribution of plague to prevalence of unclean air. The linkages he established between air pollution and origin and spread of plague sounds contemporary for twenty-first century world grappling with enormous health crisis caused by air pollution.

We should be mindful of the fact that the situation as it prevailed in the England of 1906 and explained by Gandhi in his article has become a common place experience across large parts of the world in twenty-first century. Therefore, Mahatma Gandhi's concerns expressed about the absence of purity of air and the resultant morbidity assume critical relevance for our time. The understanding of Mahatma Gandhi on pollution of air caused by factories and the attendant disease burden and the health crises it generated then in the beginning of twentieth century constituted an approach which looked at the issue from the perspective of public health. Such an approach is now being underlined to grapple with the menace of air pollution which spares none.

Yet another articulation of Mahatma Gandhi found in his letter addressed to Harilal Gandhi on 25 July 1911 brought out his finer understanding of clean air and its correlation with healthy life. He observed that consumption of simple but nutritious food and access to open air could be a major remedy for tuberculosis patients (Gandhi, 1964: CWMG, vol. 11). It affirmed his approach to look at the issue of clean air from the perspective of public health. Again, in an article authored by him under the caption *Tuberculosis* (Gandhi, 1911) he referred to 'gospel of open air' (Ibid) preached by an English doctor Adam who said that the effective treatment of TB could be taken forward by breathing fresh air in open space. In the same article, he wrote that it would be difficult to persuade those who breathed in the 'contaminated, and carbon loaded atmosphere of a stuffy room' (Ibid) to believe that their salvation would be ensured by breathing fresh air and by drinking clean water rather than the polluted ones.

It is educative to note that Gandhi reflected continuously on this issue through his writings. While he was spearheading the *Satyagraha* in South Africa, he penned *General Knowledge about Health* (1913). Through these writings, he asserted the importance of clean air for a healthy life and the implications of polluted air on health in terms of causing diseases. He would say that there is no other *Vaidya* or *hakim* compared to fresh and clean air (Ibid).

More than a century later the pollution of air has been badly deepened and intensified and contributed to the spread of infectious diseases across the world. Epidemiologists have stated that several new viral infections including COVID-19 have become air borne. It is now proven beyond doubt that accelerated pace of air pollution remains at the root of several non-communicable diseases such as cardiovascular diseases and lung and brain disorders. In a letter to Sharda Chokhawala on 22 October 1941 Gandhi asked him the reason for falling ill. Answering his own question he would say that 'If your diet is correct and you have enough fresh air nothing should happen.' (Gandhi, 1979: CWMG, vol. 75).

Those observations of Gandhi bear special importance in the context of increasing crisis of morbidity caused by air pollution and the urgent necessity of effectively dealing with it by detoxifying air. Those observations are worth quoting to understand the gravity of air pollution which is acting as a slow poison and imperceptibly impairing health. While addressing a prayer meeting in New Delhi on 21 April 1946 he said, 'nature is lenient. It often does not punish us for our sins immediately. Thus, we can go on breathing impure air and drinking impure water over long periods without any dramatic ill effects. But there is not the slightest doubt that such a thing lowers the vitality and makes one fall an easy prey to disease' (Gandhi, 1981: CWMG, vol. 84). Such nuanced understanding of Gandhi on the harmful impact of air pollution on health and well-being affirmed his vision to go into details of a problem and appreciate its deeper ramifications which do long-term damage to vigour and vitality of people.

Many of Gandhi's writings throw light on his idea of housing facilities which should provide people adequate access to fresh air. As early as 22nd October 1941 he reflected on housing issue in a prayer meeting in *Sevagram* and explained that one of the reasons behind high mortality rate in India was the clumsy dwelling places where large number of people shared space for sleeping (Gandhi, 1941). In fact, what Gandhi was indicating in his sensitive observations was the issue of indoor pollution which is now documented as a principal factor causing health complications and even death. Regretting that some people kept their cattle inside their houses and so they had very poor standard of sanitation he thoughtfully suggested them to construct their houses to admit the free flow of fresh air and sunlight (Ibid). He wanted the villages of India to have such houses. His emphasis on the architecture of house for villages providing free flow of fresh air signified the health dimension of housing facilities which he looked at from the perspective of adequate and quality ventilation which is now flagged as one of the measures to prevent COVID-19 and indoor pollution.

In Modern Civilisation Air Would not Be Available Free of Cost

Very insightfully Gandhi explained the phenomenon of air pollution by analysing the idea of economic progress prevalent in Europe in the beginning of the twentieth century. He authored an article *Sarvodaya* (Gandhi, 1908) in the *Indian Opinion* and stated that economists gave primacy to the accumulation of material wealth disregarding other human factors. So, he argued that such an approach paved the way for more generation and accumulation of wealth through more and more work in factories. He traced the establishment of multiple factories in England and elsewhere to such an approach to economic development which gave overwhelming importance to possession, acquisition, and multiplication of wealth. Gandhi persuasively explained that large number of men left their farms and moved to cities for working in those factories. He stated that these people were happy breathing the foul and contaminated air of the factories as they left their villages giving up the pure and fresh air (Ibid). Gandhi's analysis that the malaise of modern civilization characterized by more and more accumulation of wealth based on unhindered production process caused pollution of air is evocative of his critique of modern civilization as it evolved in the western world.

It is rather fascinating that while in 1908 he wrote about the movement of people from their farms to the cities for the purpose of working in factories despite the polluted air prevailing there, in 1913 he prophetically said that in modern civilization air would be polluted and people would prefer to leave cities and move to those far off places where they would get fresh air for inhalation. It is worthwhile to examine and appreciate those farsighted ideas of Gandhi and understand its context.

With rare farsightedness Mahatma Gandhi traced the cause of air pollution to many factors one of which was modern civilization the chief attribute of which, he said, is incessant multiplication of wants and desires. In his book *Hind Swaraj*, he described European civilization as 'a nine-day wonder' (Gandhi, 1938) and 'ephemeral'. In his article of 1913 on *General Knowledge About Health* he observed that nature provided air free of cost for humans to breathe (Gandhi, 1913) and noted with anguish that '…. civilization has put a price even on air' (Ibid). Then he wrote poignantly that to breathe fresh air people would go off to distant places and that would cost money. Gandhi, therefore, noted that it would not be wrong to say that 'air is free' in the modern times (Ibid).

How prescient was Gandhi indeed! What he wrote in 1913 has come true in twenty-first century world. To breathe fresh air people are rushing to far off and less crowded places free from air pollution. To get access to pollution-free air people are installing air purifiers at considerable cost at their residential and workplaces. Such developments in modern civilization of twenty-first century have put a price tag on air that is worth breathing. Like ill health which is seen as an industry by some unscrupulous members of medical fraternity, the purification and provision of clean air is now seen as a big business opportunity for many business houses and entrepreneurs to make enormous amount of money. As a result, provision of access to pollution-free air has become a business proposition with a huge cost attached to it. Therefore, Gandhi was right in saying that 'civilisation has put a price on air' (Ibid.).

While on the one hand, Gandhi's reflections on air pollution flowed from his critical assessment of modern civilization his understanding that even in villages people did not get fresh air brought out his rare sensitivity in exploring human activities which made air impure even in rural areas. He firmly believed that India lived in her villages and wanted Indians to cultivate rural mindedness. Yet he never hesitated to point out shortcomings of villagers which gave rise to pollution of air. As early as 6th December 1917 he wrote an article, *Some General Suggestions Concerning Plague* (Gandhi, 1965: CWMG, vol. 14) and wrote there that the unacceptable and harmful methods followed by Indians in terms of their daily sanitary habits in the open space polluted air all around. He observed that many people defecated in the open field and never cared to cover the excreta with earth (Ibid). He explained that the poisonous gasses generated by the uncovered excreta caused air pollution all around. He then thoughtfully observed that, 'it is obvious that when air, which is men's best food, is being thus continually polluted, they cannot maintain good health' (Ibid). He also wrote, 'the air gets polluted also by reason of people urinating or spitting or throwing litter and other rubbish anywhere on the roads. Doctors have discovered that germs spread even from the spittle of certain categories of patients, of tuberculosis patients for instance, and infect others' (Ibid.).

The air pollution which Gandhi traced to such defective ways of relieving in the open has been the source of uncleanness and infectious diseases in large parts of India and world. Such air pollution despite clean surroundings in the villages finds mention in numerous writings of Gandhi. One such reference he made in one of his speeches in 1935 when he observed that the people who live in the villages hardly get fresh air and fresh food despite, they being surrounded by freshest food and air (Gandhi, 1935). He, therefore, suggested that the villages should be turned into model villages. No wonder that while speaking at *Gujarati Sahitya Parishad* on 31 October 1936 Mahatma Gandhi had said, 'I must have pure air, pure water and pure food. That is my condition for living in a village' (Gandhi, 1936). That statement embodied his vision of model village where access to pure air would be a lived-in experience for anyone staying there.

The Government of India formulated to end open defecation. It has succeeded to some extent to provide toilet facilities to people in villages and dissuade them from relieving themselves in public spaces. The Swachh Bharat Mission (SBM), the biggest programme, for putting an end to open defecation was launched in 2014 supported by the UNICEF. At the completion of its five years on 150th birth anniversary of Gandhiji, the UNICEF (2019) observed that India has moved from 39 per cent to almost universal toilet coverage in five years. However, it also noted that a lot must be achieved to construct toilet in every household. To sustain the hard achieved gains of the SBM, the Government of India has launched the second phase. The major objective of the second phase of the programme is to ensure the communities remain hygienic and clean by preventing the faecal waste flowing and contaminating the surroundings. Moreover, the State of the World's Sanitation Report by UNICEF and WHO reveals that 4.2 billion people that amount to more than half of the world population continue to use services with human waste untreated. This process possesses serious threat to human health and environment. The children, across the countries, have been at the receiving end as such practices hinder social and economic progress and development of children. The absence of safe sanitation system contributes to the fulfilment of children's growth and their social well-being unattainable (Ibid.). The objectives outlined in the SBM were embodied in the vision of Mahatma Gandhi who had identified the irresponsible behaviour of people to answer calls of nature in open surroundings as a source of air pollution and pollution of larger environment.

The articulations of Gandhi on air pollution in the context of villages of India are quite significant for our time when polluted air apart from severely impacting cities and towns have affected village people and their dwelling units. Therefore, his advocacy for model villages free from pollution is quite pertinent for political regimes and public policy formulators who often ignore the air pollution in villages of India. Existing literature on air pollution in India (Dey, 2021) observe that the issue of air pollution is often seen as an urban phenomenon. Accordingly, the initiatives taken to deal with the air pollution issue, quite predictably, continue to be urban centric. In this process, we hardly witness any efforts made to address this issue for the rural poor. Gandhi by focusing attention on pollution in villages and sensitively explaining it by analysing the harmful way in which people relieve themselves in open surroundings in complete disregard of the severely ill effects of their activities on the environment had emerged as a doyen of environmental protection.

He traced the problem of air pollution to modern civilization and flawed ways of people for answering calls of nature. But it is worthwhile to note that he asked himself and the fellow inmates of Sabarmati Ashram to examine if any of the activities they were engaged in resulted in pollution of air. In a letter to Naran Das Gandhi written on 3rd April 1932 (Gandhi, 1972: CWMG, vol. 49) he pointed out that some inmates of *Ashram* underwent suffering due to ill health and, therefore, requested all the inmates to ascertain if because of their deficiencies such sufferings were caused. In this regard, he wrote that 'we should find out if we are polluting the air in any way. For this, we should examine whether the arrangements for the disposal of night soil and the excreta of cattle are satisfactory' (Ibid). That letter of Gandhi was a fine example of turning search light inwards to critically assess one's own conduct which could have been a factor behind the pollution of air in the place or premises where one stayed.

The example set by Gandhi for ascertaining if one's own conduct caused pollution of air deserves to be followed seriously during our time when many self-righteous proclamations have been made by people and several organizations that their actions were not responsible for any environmental degradation, whereas their actions completely negated what they said or proclaimed.

Gandhi Saw the Issue of Air Pollution and Clean Air from the Perspective of Spirituality

Gandhi had an uncanny ability to look at everything from a spiritual perspective. The way he saw the issue of pure air from the perspective of spirituality is indeed noteworthy and admirable. It was evident from a message he issued to Verrier Elwin on 13 November 1932 (Gandhi, 1972: CWMG, vol. 51). Gandhiji identified four important laws for the 'communion with God': cleanest air, cleanest water, simplest food, and cleanest thinking (Idid.). According to Gandhi, the first three laws flow from the fourth one.

Yet another splendid example of Gandhi correlating air pollution with spirituality was evidenced in his speech delivered in a prayer meeting on 24 March 1946. He said, 'anyone who fouls the air by spitting about carelessly, throwing refuse and rubbish, or otherwise dirtying the ground, sins against man and nature. Man's body is the temple of God. Anyone who fouls the air that is to enter that temple desecrates it' (Gandhi, 1981: CWMG, vol. 83).

In saying that access to cleanest air and cleanest water would mean communion with God and anyone who fouled the air was desecrating body, temple of God, Mahatma Gandhi was elevating the issue of air pollution beyond the material domain and integrating it with a lifestyle associated with cleanness and clean thinking associated with higher consciousness. Such an understanding of air pollution is also seen in the writings and commentaries of other spiritual leaders who look at the contamination of air as a spiritual issue. For example, the Archbishop of Canterbury had described the environmental pollution of which air pollution is a major component as a spiritual issue of our time (As quoted by Narayanan, 1993). What was stated by the Archbishop of Canterbury in the late twentieth century was stated by Gandhi in the beginning of 1930s.

Yet another example of Gandhiji looking at the air pollution from the spiritual perspective was demonstrated from his indicting remarks on those who defecated on the banks of rivers, lakes and places of pilgrimage and caused contamination of air and the surroundings. In his article 'Does a Village mean a Dunghill' (Gandhi, 1970: CWMG, vol. 41) written in 1929 he observed that the holy scriptures across the religions have provided suggestions regarding keeping our surroundings clean. However, despite these teachings, Gandhi regretfully adds, people continue to disregard these religious teachings. What pained more to Gandhi was people contributing to rising filth in and around the religious places too (Ibid). Dismayed by the activities of the pilgrims which caused air pollution in some places regarded as holy and sacred he wrote with pain:

> I have seen thousands of men and women dirtying the banks of the Ganga at Hardwar. Pilgrims defecate at the very spot where people sit, wash their faces, etc., in the Ganga and then again fill their pots at the very same spot. I have come across pilgrims defiling lakes in the same manner at places of pilgrimage. In doing this we destroy the dharma of compassion and disregard our duty to society. Such recklessness leads to pollution of air and water. Is it surprising then that cholera, typhoid and other infectious diseases follow because of this? (Ibid.)

Gandhi's usage of the words 'Dharma of compassion' in the context of air pollution due to the activities of pilgrims and the need to prevent the violation of such Dharma for the cause of clean air and good health brought out his sensitivity for a spiritual approach for dealing with the problem of air pollution. It is worthwhile to note that in the article he invoked sacred texts of Hinduism, Islam, Christianity, and Zoroastrianism in the context of cleanliness. In doing so he was adopting a confluential approach embracing the scriptures of major faiths which are integral to the spiritual ethos of India.

Gandhi Understood Clean Air from the Perspectives of Swaraj and Governance

It is well known that Gandhi looked at Swaraj or independence of India from colonial rule from the perspectives of Hindu-Muslim unity, abolition of untouchability, economic equality, women's empowerment, etc. It is lesser known that he also looked at the issue of clean air and clean water from the perspective of independence and governance. In doing so, he, more than hundred years back, set a refreshing trend in understanding liberty, freedom, and independence from the environmental perspective.

On 1 January 1918 while addressing a meeting organized in Ahmedabad to protest irregular and insufficient water supply by the Ahmedabad Municipality Gandhi talked about air, water and grain and described them as aspects of Swaraj (Gandhi, 1965: CWMG, vol. 14). He also said that those three issues had a critical influence on public health (Ibid). He observed that 'air, water and grains are the three chief kinds of food' (Ibid.).

Slightly more than hundred years ago Gandhi reflected on air pollution and linked the issue of clean air as one aspect of Swaraj and independence. It is tragic that almost a century later clean air and water is getting increasingly polluted. So, if Gandhi considered air as one aspect of Swaraj, then it means that increasing pollution of air in India would mean deficiency or pollution of Swaraj or independence. As has been discussed elsewhere he also said that air got defiled because the way in which toilets were kept unclean and unhygienic practices were followed by people to answer the calls of nature. It is noteworthy that he located the issue of a clean toilet, free from pollution, in the context of Swaraj. For instance, while speaking at the Gujarat Political Conference on 3rd November 1917 (Ibid) he referred to unpolluted air in the cantonments because of wide and clean roads, detached houses and sanitary habits of the residents (Ibid) and indicted the unhygienic habits of people in rest of the cities. In that context he observed that the Swaraj would have very little meaning unless we get rid of the dirty habits that contribute to pollution and change the conditions in the cities (Ibid). On another occasion he famously said that 'If we leave our courtyard stinking, then there is every chance of a foul stench arising from our swaraj' (Gandhi, 1970: CWMG, vol. 38). The stench representing foul smell with severe implications on pollution of air and that too in the context of cleanliness of the back yard was linked by Gandhi to measure the quality of Swaraj or independence of India.

In 1931 he reflected on just administration in his article 'Of Princes and Paupers' (Gandhi, 1931) Gandhi termed democracy (people' *raj*) as an era of truth (*Satya*). This was also used interchangeably with his concepts of *Swaraj, Dharmaraj,* and *Ramarajya*—a just administration. Under such administrative arrangement, Gandhi says, the administrator should be the protector or friend of the citizens. Accordingly, contrary to the British rule, there should not be any gulf between the poorest and the one who governs. Gandhi adds that *Swaraj* means when both enjoy pure water and air (Ibid). In other words, in Gandhi's conception of democracy, there would be equal access of the rulers and ruled to pure air and water. It is indeed illuminating to know that Gandhi understood democracy from the perspective of people's access to clean air and water much before India got independence. The Supreme Court of India has interpreted the fundamental right to life of persons as the right, among others, to clean environment which include pollution-free air for breathing.

Gandhi's interpretation of democracy in 1931 in terms of equal entitlement and access of both the ruler and ruled to pure air and water assumes contemporary significance for our time when mounting pollution of air has spelt harmful consequences for public health and the very right to life. It is a fact that due to pollution of air large sections of people have no choice but to breathe unclean air. In contrast, those among the ruling classes who have air purifiers installed in their places of work and residences have easy access to clean air. Such stark differences between people and the ruling classes for their access to clean air devalues democracy which Gandhi understood from the perspective of clean air.

Gandhi Saw Clean Air and Air Pollution from Educational Perspective

Mahatma Gandhi not only reflected on air pollution right since 1906 but also suggested some measures to find solutions to it. His most important suggestion was that students in schools and colleges should be educated about the value of clean air and the steps required to keep it clean. On 16 February 1916 while addressing the students in Madras he regretted that they 'knew nothing of fresh air or bright light' (Gandhi, 1964: CWMG, vol. 13).

Thirteen years later while delivering a speech at Gujaratis' meeting in London on 10 March 1929 he drew the attention of the audience to the fact that he did appreciate some good practices of Britishers despite his rejection of British rule and exploitation. In that context, he said that Britishers had established big schools in places like Darjeeling and Shimla and urged Gujaratis to establish a school where children would get good air and abject lesson in cleanliness (Gandhi, 1929).

On 28 March 1932 he wrote an article 'Some Reflections on Education' and quoted words of John Ruskin who suggested the need for every child to learn the important properties of clean air, water, and earth. Accordingly, he also suggested every child to know how to keep water, air, and earth clean and pure in order to know their benefits (Gandhi, 1972: CWMG, vol. 49). What Mahatma Gandhi wrote in 1916 and 1932 constituted some aspects of environmental education which are of critical necessity to address not only growing air pollution but also rising levels of ecological disaster the humanity is confronting in this Age of Anthropocene.

In one of his writings (Gandhi, 1945) about constructing programme, Gandhi highlighted eighteen themes.[1] Of these eighteen themes the one on education in health and hygiene is of relevance in the context of this article. In a well-ordered society, for Gandhi, the citizens are aware of the rules of health and cleanliness. It is the lack of awareness and indifference towards the rules of health and cleanliness that contribute to the outbreak and spread of diseases. Gandhi also maintained that apart from poverty, it is the lack of education on health and hygiene that contribute substantially to the high death rate (Ibid.). Therefore, as part of the exercise to learn the fundamental laws of health and hygiene, which he said could be easily learnt but difficult to put into practice, he prescribed breathing of the clean air. While stressing on the pure and clean air, water and food, Gandhi urged people to be take care of the hygiene of their surrounding along with personal cleanliness (Ibid.).

What is required in twenty-first century world to deal with air pollution is the overarching approach consisting of several perspectives woven around public health, spirituality, governance, and education. The present-day environmental activists and movements for sustainable development are in fact in favour of such an overarching approach to face the challenges posed by mounting air pollution.

---

[1] Communal Unity, Economic Equality, Removal of Untouchability, Prohibition, Khadi, Other Village Industries, Village Sanitation, New or Basic Education, Adult Education, Women, Education in Health and Hygiene, Provincial Languages, National Languages, Economic Equality, Kisans, Labour, Adivasis, Lepers and Students.

There is hardly any literature outlining the ideas and insights of Mahatma Gandhi on the issue of air pollution and clean air. Right from his South Africa days he started reflecting on air pollution and located it in the context of many issues including modern civilization which he said put a price on air for breathing. During the struggle for independence, he explained the idea of Swaraj or independence and interpreted democracy in terms of people's access to clean and unpolluted air. It brought out his sensitivities in locating the issue of air pollution in the larger context of freedom and liberation of India from colonial rule. Mahatma Gandhi's interrogation of modern civilization and his persuasive and prophetic words that people would travel to places located far away from cities to inhale clean air awakens consciousness to pursue the path of sustainable development which would safeguard purity of air. Such consciousness and the attendant practical measures are of critical significance for liberating human civilization from the bondage of pollution and ecological disaster.

References

Child, D. (March 5, 2019). India has the world's worst air pollution. *The Al Jazeeara.* Retrieved June 1, 2021, from https://www.aljazeera.com/news/2019/3/5/india-has-the-worlds-worst-air-pollution-report.
Dey, S. (February 3, 2021). Air pollution in rural India: ignored but not absent. *Down To Earth.* Retrieved June 15, 2021, from https://www.downtoearth.org.in/blog/pollution/air-pollution-in-rural-india-ignored-but-not-absent-75341.
Gandhi, M. (1906). *Indian opinion.* March 3 and 24, 1911-August 5, 1913-February 1, 1908-July 18, 1913- February 1.
Gandhi, M. (March 24, 1929). *Navajivan.* Ahmedabad.
Gandhi, M. (February 22, 1931). *Navajivan.* Ahmedabad.
Gandhi, M. (March 1, 1935). *Harijan.*
Gandhi, M. (November 22, 1936). *Harijan bandhu.*
Gandhi, M. K. (1938). *Hind Swaraj or Indian Home Rule.* Navajivan Publishing House.
Gandhi, M. (November 1941). *Sarvodaya.*
Gandhi, M. K. (1945). Constructive programme: its meaning and place. Ahmedabad: Navajivan Trust.
Gandhi, M. Collected works of Mahatma Gandhi (CWMG), Ahmedabad. Navajivan Trust, Vol.11–1964, p.130, Vol 13–1964, p. 235, Vol. 14, pp. 100, 103, 143, 48 &66, Vol. 38–1970, p. 430, Vol. 41–1970, pp.445–448, Vol.49–1972, pp. 259–61, Vol 51–1972, p. 416, Vol.75–1979, p.40, Vol. 83–1981, p. 316 Vol.84–1981, p.43, Vol. 97–1994, page- 9.
India State-Level Disease Burden Initiative Air Pollution Collaborators. (2021). Health and economic impact of air pollution in the states of India: The global burden of disease study 2019. *Lancet, 5*(1), e25–e38.
Narayanan, K. R. (May 26, 1993). The greening of development: problems and prospects Andrew Sermon Memorial Lecture.
Pandey, V. (2020, October 20). COVID19 and pollution: Delhi starring at coronavirus disaster. Retrieved June 15, 2021, from https://www.bbc.com/news/world-asia-india-54596245.
Sahu, S. K. et al. (2021). Establishing a link between fine particulate matter (PM2.5) zones and COVID-19 over India based on anthropogenic emission sources and air quality data. *Urban Climate, 38.* https://doi.org/10.1016/j.uclim.2021.100883.

UNICIEF. (2019). A clean (Swampoorna Swachh) India: Towards maintaining an open defecation free and clean environment and managing wastes efficiently. Retrieved June 10, 2021, from https://www.unicef.org/india/what-we-do/ending-open-defecation.

World Health Organization (WHO). (2018). WHO's first global conference on air pollution and health. Retrieved May 17, 2021, from https://www.who.int/news-room/events/detail/2018/10/30/default-calendar/who-s-first-global-conference-on-air-pollution-and-health.

Satya Narayan Sahu is a student of Collected Works of Mahatma Gandhi and served President of India, late K R Narayanan, as Officer on Special Duty and Press Secretary.

Chapter 11
Mahatma Gandhi and Public Health in India

Rajni Kant

Abstract This chapter provides a detailed account of Gandhi's experience and ideas on health-related issues. Regarding the seriousness and the immediacy of public health issues Gandhi realized the importance of addressing health and its association with poverty, socio-economic conditions, poor hygiene, and food habits of common Indians. For Gandhi, a simple but very effective solution for the individual health issues was to focus on cleanliness which he believed to be the direct cause of most health-related problems. The chapter starts with providing a brief description on Gandhi's major health conditions that he experienced in different stages of his life. The personal health experiences of Gandhi made him stress upon two important aspects for a healthy lifestyle: vegetarianism and physical fitness. The chapter subsequently discusses the medical legacies of Mahatma Gandhi. Gandhi's role in nursing patients, treating specific medical conditions like dog and scorpion bite, leprosy is discussed in detail. This chapter engages with Gandhi as someone who had suffered from health conditions, learned from his experiences, and used his experiences to serve people. The Chapter describes that Gandhi believed in Holistic Health with focus on prevention of diseases, adopting naturopathy, healthy lifestyle, balanced diet and ayurveda and in case required to go for the modern medicines. He emphasized that treatment should be affordable, accessible and within the reach of the community.

Keywords Gandhi · Public health · Gandhi and Col Maddock · Gandhi and ayurveda · Gandhi and his health seeking behaviour · Vegetarianism

Introduction

Mahatma Gandhi was born on 2nd October, 1869 in Porbandar, Gujarat—a small coastal town in western part of India. He later became known as Mahatma around the globe by his exemplary work and simple living. He was an ordinary man with extraordinary qualities. The man who led the freedom struggle following the path of

---

R. Kant (✉)
ICMR-Regional Medical Research Centre (RMRC), Gorakhpur & ICMR Hqrs, New Delhi, India

truth and non-violence. A leader, motivator, researcher, crusader, visionary, apostle of peace, Gandhi was an institution in himself. He was also an environmentalist, a seasoned economist, and an experimental scientist. In fact, it would not be much of an exaggeration to mention that he was one of the first thinkers who attempted to integrate socio-political movements with public health in India. Gandhi's lifestyle and teachings, arguably, resonate with what George Bernard Shaw's philosophy of 'life is all about creating oneself' (As cited in Dietrich, 2008). This holds true for Gandhi because he preached what he practiced and for him, change started with himself. His charisma ensured that his presence was felt so far and wide that there were hardly any socio-political and economic issues which remained untouched by him. He nursed and took care of the ill throughout his life. In fact, it would be of great interest for the readers to know that he wanted to pursue study in medicine and become a doctor, but when he came to know it involves dissection of animals, he abandoned the idea and became a barrister instead. But his passion for caring for the ill and downtrodden continued throughout his lifetime. Accounts suggest that he was an able clinician and would always be approached for advice on health- related matters by those around him.

Gandhi's Vision for Health

Regarding public health, Gandhi was extremely concerned about the lifestyles of the common people. During the early twentieth century under British colonial rule, India was vulnerable to diseases such as tuberculosis, malaria, leprosy, cholera, plague, infections, and malnutrition. Gandhi realized the importance of health and its association with poverty, socio-economic conditions, poor living, and food habits. He focused on cleanliness as this was directly the source of many problems. A public leader with an unprecedented mass following, he himself started cleaning his surroundings and advised people to keep their houses clean. Along with stressing on cleanliness, another area where he focused on is availability and consumption of the right kind of food and diet. Accordingly, he experimented on his own diet and advised people to have a balanced diet, which he thought was very important to fight malnutrition. He also advocated on prevention of diseases like malaria and tuberculosis and worked towards caring for those suffering from diseases like leprosy which ostracized the sufferer. His awareness over public health issues suggests that he practiced what he preached and believed it was important to keep one's body fit and healthy with physical activities. Beside physical fitness he also advocated for good mental health which can be attained by following a disciplined life and observing a strict routine for sleep, food and avoiding tobacco and alcohol. He emphasized the role of compassion to keep balance between mind and soul. He believed in holistic health and his philosophy of good health was quite simple but equally effective, which is so relevant today when we are struggling to combat lifestyle-related non-communicable diseases.

Gandhi's ability to link the role of physical and mental well-being for a healthy life reflects upon his good understanding of public health. His insights on public health can be derived from his private health file and his health-seeking behaviour. The next section explains these aspects in detail.

Health File of Mahatma Gandhi and His Health Seeking Behaviour

To get a sense of Mahatma Gandhi's health file, I highlight his major health conditions. During his stay in Durban, South Africa, there were two major health issues Gandhi suffered from, debility and rheumatic inflammation. In Durban, he used to be treated by Dr. P. J Mehta. Again, in Johannesburg, he was prone to constipation for which he would go for laxative and follow a regulated diet. However, not fully convinced with laxative as a remedy, he also tried Kuhne's hip bath. (Kuhne's hip bath involves sitting in cold water and rubbing one's body from waist down with a piece of cloth). During his Johannesburg days, he also suffered from frequent headaches. It was during his stay in South Africa Gandhi familiarized himself with the importance of earth treatment and natural diets which mostly consisted of fresh fruits and nuts. Adolf Just's book *Return to Nature* (1903) influenced Gandhi to experiment with earth treatments. However, it is important to mention that Gandhi did not practice an exclusive fruit diet contrary to what was otherwise an important prescription of the book. For the earth treatment, Gandhi would apply a piece of cloth moistened with clean earth and cold water on the lower abdomen which brought substantial relief against the health issues mentioned above.

Gandhi's experiments with his diet to get rid of his frequent headaches deserves a mention here. Once he got to know about the *'No Breakfast Association'* of Manchester, Gandhi experimented with skipping his breakfast to get rid of frequent headaches. Though the initial days of this dietary practice of skipping breakfast was tough for Gandhi, he would gradually find himself relaxed from the headache. Through this dietary practice of skipping breakfast, Gandhi would realize that an individual should not eat more than what he or she needs. Gandhi's experiments with dietary changes in curing diseases helped him greatly when he suffered from pleurisy in 1914 while he was touring London. Pleurisy caused inflammation of the lung lining and anxiety. A British doctor, Thomas Allinson, who Gandhi had met in 1890 advised him to go for dietetic changes along with external remedies. Following the prescribed diet changes and external remedies, Gandhi could overcome this health issue.

Gandhi's commitment to strict vegetarian dietary habits and natural treatment were exemplary. He would never compromise on these principles of healthy living even during critical health conditions. One of such incidents was when Gandhi suffered from diarrhoea in Nadiad, Gujarat, in 1918. Following the prescriptions of Nature Cure, Gandhi stopped eating and was against taking any medicine. Though resorting to hydrotherapy brought him some relief, still his body was very weak. To get rid of prolonged weakness of body, Gandhi was advised by his doctors to go for meat broth in the place of milk to regain strength. Even though such advice had support from the Ayurveda, Gandhi declined the prescription to have any meat products. Moreover, he even rejected the advice of consuming eggs to come out of the weakness as suggested by one of the doctors. This reflects upon his commitment to not harming the animals as a principle which he never wanted to dilute even for his own health reasons and even when prescribed by the doctors. This prolonged illness led him to examine and test his principles. In fact, Gandhi had strong faith in nature therapy. On one occasion, Gandhi suffered from acute illness induced by nervous breakdown due to extreme weakness. Though the doctors who examined him found no major issues as his pulse was strong and he was in no danger, Gandhi would still find himself uneasy as the weakness persisted. In this situation, Gandhi was advised for a nature therapy treatment by doctor Kelkar (Gandhi used to call him 'Ice Doctor'). Accordingly, he was advised by the doctor to rub his back with ice as a method to regain the vigour back. A hesitant Gandhi, initially though, would go for this ice-based treatment once it was endorsed by Doctor Talwalkar. As claimed by doctor Kelkar, adherence to this nature therapy helped Gandhi regain his vigour in a fortnight (Bhargava & Kant, 2019).

While Gandhi was particularly supportive of nature therapy and practiced a strict vegetarian diet, he was never averse to modern medical practices. For example, when he was imprisoned in the Yeravda jail in Pune, a British doctor Col. Maddock following the urine and blood investigation of Gandhi (as he complained of high fever and acute stomach pain) suspected appendicitis. Following a thorough investigation, Gandhi was advised to go for a surgery, while Gandhi wanted to consult Dr. Dalal before taking any decision. As Gandhi was intending to take a decision after the consultation with Dr. Dalal, Col Maddock warned him that if Gandhi did not go for the surgery, he could develop peritonitis. However, on Gandhi's consent, Col. Maddock did the operations on 12 January 1924, in the presence of Doctor Pathak from Pune. It is important to mention that the operation was conducted on a rainy day with disruption of electricity supply and the surgery was completed with the help of a hurricane lamp. He later thanked Dr Maddock and two became very god friends. The available literature on Gandhiji's health revealed that he suffered from acute dysentery twice, 1918 and 1929, from malaria in 1925, 1936, and 1944 and was operated on for piles in 1919 and for acute appendicitis in 1924 (Bhargava & Kant, 2019). He also suffered from gastric flu in 1939 and from influenza in 1945. It is important to mention that every time, through his strong will power, strict diet regimen and adhering to desired therapies he got back on his feet and re-started his work as early as possible.

Gandhi's commitment to nature therapy continued during the latter part of his life as well. While he was suffering from high blood pressure (His blood pressure readings were on the higher side. The blood pressure count was 194/130 and 220/110 on 26.10. 1937 and 19.02.1940 respectively) Gandhi would go for nature therapy treatments to bring down the high blood pressure. In this practice, he would place mud poultice on his abdomen to keep his high blood pressure down. Additionally, he also used Sarpagandha, an ayurvedic medicine to help him reduce the blood pressure. As an additional measure, he would place a mud bandage on his head, during the summer season, to control fluctuations in his blood pressure and to get relief from the heat as well. From the accounts of Doctor Talwalkar (1935), it can be found that Gandhiji started to take raw garlic regularly as a remedy for his blood pressure with the advice from a friend. It is important to mention that with an open mind in terms of following health tips, Gandhi would religiously follow the advice once he was convinced by the prescriptions. However, available literature also highlights his initial hesitancy in going for newer forms of treatment and health practices. A great mind that he was, Gandhi believed in all forms of medicine. An ardent practitioner of nature cure and nature therapy, Gandhi also consulted the doctors of modern medicines such as Jiv Raj Mehta, P.J. Mehta, Sushila Nayyar, and others for his health-related issues.

Guha (2016), in an article, The Mahatma on Medicine, writes that during the early part of his life in the 1920s, '30s and '40s, Gandhiji was a strong believer in nature cure, the ayurvedic system of medicine, and learnt yoga as well. His experiments with nature and herbal cure were always on himself; he also advised his friends and disciples to follow these remedies. Later, in the 1950s, his interest in the modern system of medicine grew. As mentioned before, he was successfully operated on by Dr. Dalal for piles in 1919 and by Dr. Maddock in Pune in 1924 for appendicitis. This further enhanced his faith in modern medicine. While he was not averse to modern medical practices, his inclination for traditional and natural medicines was very much evident. This was evident through his food and dietary habits of vegetarianism.

Gandhi and Vegetarianism

Gandhi's experiments with vegetarianism go back to his student days in London, 1888–91. A book that influenced Gandhi a lot for adherence to vegetarianism was that of Henry Salt's 'A Plea for Vegetarianism' (1886). Deeply influenced by Henry Salt's writings on vegetarianism and its effects, Gandhi would state that 'It was Mr. Salt's book, which showed me why, apart from hereditary habit, and apart from my adherence to a vow administered to me by my mother, it was right to be a vegetarian. He showed me why it was a moral duty incumbent on vegetarians not to live upon fellow-animals' (Gandhi, 1931). This position of Gandhi on vegetarianism was in honouring Henry Salt at one of the meetings of Vegetarian Society on 20 November 1931. His adherence to a vegetarian diet also influenced his close friends to go for the same. While in Africa, Kallenbach, a close friend of Mahatma Gandhi, also adopted vegetarianism. Kallenbach was observed to be closely following Gandhi's practices of vegetarianism in terms of fasting and other dietary changes. As Gandhi derived pleasure in changing to new diets, he would passionately discuss the advantages and benefits of dietary changes with his close friends like Kallenbach. As mentioned before, Gandhi would suggest that one should not eat to please the palate but for the requirements of the body. Speaking of keeping the body going, Gandhi also stressed on the aspect of physical fitness.

In terms of keeping the body fit, Gandhi, as a student, maintained a habit of daily walking up to eight miles a day. Of many important factors, one can attribute adherence to vegetarian diet and daily exercise in open air which contributed substantially to his good fitness. Accordingly, Gandhi stressed upon good food and regular exercises for a healthy mind and body. Commenting on the importance of physical exercise, Gandhi would suggest regular physical exercises for the people engaged mostly in intellectual professions for better intellectual output. On an average throughout his political career Gandhi would walk almost 18 kms every day for nearly 40 years. It is important to highlight here that between the duration of 1913 and 1948 Gandhi walked 79,000 kms for his political activities of fighting for independence. With these brief reflections on the health file of Gandhi, the next section highlights his medical legacy.

Medical Legacy of Mahatma Gandhi

Nursing Patients

Apart from his dietary practices and adherence to vegetarianism, Gandhi also offered his services as a nurse to many of his friends and people. As a nurse he was very gentle and extremely compassionate to the patients he served. We get the accounts in this regard from the accounts of Dr. Suhila Nayyar's writing, 'Medicine for Masses' (Nayyar, 1944 as cited in Bhargava & Kant, 2019). This writing of Sushila Nayyar also reveals the subtle desire of Gandhi to be a doctor when he was asked about the same by the former. However, despite his busy schedule as a lawyer and, later, a freedom fighter, Gandhi devoted a substantial amount of his time in practicing nature therapy, vegetarianism, and nursing patients. It was this devotion which inspired Gandhi to establish the Tolstoy Farm and the Phoenix Colony in South Africa where he and his co-workers lived lives of self-discipline and service. He dispensed medicine, dressed wounds, and rendered help whenever possible to the patients. There are examples of several instances where Gandhiji treated people with conditions such as rheumatism and arthritis by suggesting them a proper diet, nursing them, and telling them to adopt simple nature cure practices. Some of the patients Gandhiji treated in 1912 were Raojibhai Manibahi Patel at the Phoenix Ashram for rheumatism and Dattoba for arthritis. Gandhiji would personally take care of the patients by nursing them and keeping a watchful eye on their diet. Gandhi's efforts in nursing his wife Kasturba also needs a mention in this regard.

Thrice during his lifetime, Gandhiji saw his wife, Kasturba, fall seriously ill. Each time she was cured through household remedies. The first time this happened, the Satyagraha movement was about to commence. During this time, Kasturba Gandhi was frequently haemorrhaging. A doctor suggested surgery, to which she agreed. Her condition deteriorated and the doctor advised her to take brandy. This upset Gandhiji and with Kasturba and their son's permission, he decided to take his wife out of treatment. Gandhiji knew he was taking a huge risk. An advance message was communicated to Phoenix with instructions which enabled the presence of a bed, hot milk, and water along with six volunteers to carry Kasturba. Gandhi also joined the volunteers carrying Kasturba. She was very weak and undernourished, but she slowly picked up strength following hydropathic treatment.

Plague Dilemma/Scorpion Bite

During an outbreak of pneumonic plague (black plague) while he was in South Africa at Johannesburg, Gandhiji's colleague Madanjit was so shaken to see the effect the disease was having on people that he sent a note to Gandhiji requesting him to come immediately to help. Gandhiji covered the distance to the location by cycle and from there wrote the town clerk, asking him to give him details of the circumstances. With the help of three colleagues, Gandhiji put all the patients in a vacant house and took on the role of both doctor and nurse.

Gandhiji's ability to treat people who had been stung by scorpions was narrated by a person who witnessed an incident during one of his prison terms in South Africa. A native attendant of the prison was stung by a scorpion and approached Gandhi for help. The spontaneous Gandhi helped the person by washing the stung area with water and drying it. Once it was dry, Gandhi sucked out the poison which offered the person much relief. Back in India, Gandhi also followed the same method to help Pyrelal, who was stung by a scorpion, in Sevagram.

Concern for Leprosy

Parchure Shastri, a renowned Sanskrit Scholar was suffering from a severe form of leprosy and had been going from hospital to hospital and came to Sevagram to see Gandhi one last time. One evening while Gandhi was going on his routine evening walk, he found him outside the gate of Sevagram Ashram. Gandhi asked Kanu Gandhi to provide food to Parchure Shastri and continued with his walk. But Gandhi was not at ease, and he felt conflicted. His body rested; mind rested but his soul was in revolt. The battle within continued and at last a great soul won the struggle. He woke up at 2 AM knowing he had to listen to what his heart was trying to tell him. After the morning prayers that day, he addressed the inmates of the Ashram and told them, God had sent Parchure Shastri to test his sincerity. After discussing the matter with the Ashram inmates, Gandhiji ensured a neat cottage was set up close to his own. He started nursing him regularly and gradually he started improving. Gandhiji's medical help in terms of nursing was not limited to the humans only. He was also against cruelty towards animals. He considered it an inhuman practice and maintained his express position of not sending any monkey abroad for vivisection. As mentioned before, this was, perhaps, the only reason he did not pursue medical science as it involved dissection.

Experiments with Diet and Dietetics

For Gandhi, one can observe that his experiments with diet were very much linked to the adherence of principles of *Ahimsa*. That was the reason he was always troubled by consumption of goat milk as he felt it was against the pledge that he had taken against the cruelty of animals. That said, Gandhi's experiments with dietetics had always been based on personal observations. For example, as he started living in Sevagram, he was not familiar with the local food. Taking the help of the local people Gandhi advised them to try different foods and accordingly he observed the good and bad effects of them. And that was the process through which he curated his diet during his stay in Sevagram. Gandhi used to have regular conversation with Robert Mac Carrison, then Director of Nutrition Research Laboratories (now ICMR-NIN), for the nutritive values of different kinds of foods. Based on his extensive experiments on food and dietary practices, Gandhi would suggest going for fasting for a healthy body and mind. Speaking of Gandhi's experiments with diet, fasting was always an important component. He believed in fasting as an important activity for keeping oneself healthy and fit. Based on his personal experiences and observations Gandhi suggested that one should keep fast to get relief from the following health-related issues such as constipation; anaemia; fever; indigestion; headache; depression; rheumatic; gouty; fretting; and fuming.

An important aspect of Gandhi's understanding of health was bringing the mind and the body together. Contrary to the binary that is often created to separate the body and mind, Gandhi believed that a healthy mind contribute to a healthy body. On his own health, he would state that the reason for his high blood pressure is his failure to control the mind the way he desired. He said that if a man suffers from indigestion because of overeating, he should resort to fasting instead of resorting to carminative mixtures, as not only would fasting relieve him, but would also serve as a reminder for him not to overeat in the future. He used to meditate regularly and observed *Maun Vrat* once every week. He maintained disciplined life and showed compassion towards every form of life and believed in forgiveness to keep him mentally strong and fit (Kant and Bhargava, 2019, Guha 2018).

As mentioned before, for Gandhi, both a healthy body and mind always mattered for the good health of an individual and the society. Gandhi had a unique way of motivating people towards maintaining good health. In doing so he would liken the human body to *Kurukshetra* (a field of conflict) and *Dharmakshetra* (a field of doing one's duty and right action). And for Gandhi, any lethargy in improving one's good health is sin. The body as a *Dharmakshetra*, as Gandhi would suggest, it is the duty of an individual to keep the body in good shape (Gandhi as cited in Gupta & Kant, 2019). Gandhi said the people are in a mad rush today, increasing their wants senselessly, instead of enhancing their self-worth and knowledge. A day will come when they exclaim at what they have been doing (Gandhi, 1968). This is so true in today's fast changing materialistic world. For good health Gandhi proposed ten important practices. They are walking: Be active, stay healthy; Balanced Diet: Key to health; Meditation: To fight daily stress; De-addiction: Avoid alcohol and tobacco; Think positive: Enhance mental strength; Compassion for others: Makes world a healthy place; Forgiveness: Promotes inner peace; Non-violence: Healthy way to sort issues; Early to bed, early to rise: Balancing the body clock and Fasting: To reset your body and promote discipline. Gandhiji followed and advised an eco-friendly approach for the better public health both at the individual and community level. For example; on malaria Gandhi said, 'I will not congratulate you, if you tell me that you have distributed thousand quinine pills, go there with spades and shovels, fill up stagnant pools, see to the drainage, see that their wells are properly dredged and their tank is not contaminated…you must teach them sanitation and hygiene, which alone can prevent malaria' (Gandhi as cited in Dhiman & Valecha, 2019). He always believed that prevention is better than cure (Lindley 2018).

Gandhi and Public Health in India

Gandhi lived in an era when India was faced with problems like poverty, illiteracy, social inequality, untouchability coupled with political instability. The country was crippled with diseases like malaria, filariasis, plague, tuberculosis, leprosy, cholera, malnutrition with poor living conditions resulting in huge morbidity and low life expectancy. The country has moved ahead since then and a lot has happened around science during the last 150 years. We have seen the green revolution, white revolution, IT revolution, and growth of biotechnology with the availability of new molecular diagnostic tools, which has changed the direction of new India. We have been able to eradicate diseases like smallpox, polio, guinea worm, and neonatal tetanus. Prevalence rate of leprosy has come down from 54 per 10,000 in 1869 to 0.66 per 10,000 in the recent past. Treatment of leprosy has changed from Chaulmoogra oil and Dapsone to MDT. The MIP vaccine has also been launched. Similarly, the TB treatment has moved ahead from a sanatorium-based approach to home-based treatment with DOTS. We have been able to control malaria significantly over these years. Treatment has shifted from quinine to ACT, the new line of drug. Deaths due to water-borne diseases have come down from 2391 per one million in 1881to 576 per million in 2016, toilet coverage which was only three percent in 1946 has gone up to 90% in 2019. Life expectancy has increased from 24.6% in 1871 to 68% in 2018. What Gandhiji believed and did during his time may not be as effective today when we have the best of technologies but what he did during that time with limited resources was admirable and equally effective. However, his ideology of cleanliness, physical fitness, mental health, balanced diet, and disciplined lifestyle by avoiding tobacco and alcohol is still relevant in modern times when we are struggling with emerging non-communicable diseases.

As mentioned before, Gandhi always integrated the mind and body as one entity for a healthy life. Hence, he would stress more on the necessity of healers of souls in a society. Accordingly, he would maintain that the presence of multiple hospitals and other medical infrastructures cannot be a good sign of healthy civilization. The less we and others pamper our bodies the better for us and the world (Gandhi, 1927a, b).

Though Gandhi's understandings, ideas, and practices of health hardly find popular mention in our society, yet some ardent followers of Gandhi would still subscribe to his ideas. As the Dalai Lama, arguably the living Gandhi, would reiterate, the strange habits of human beings surprise him like no other living animal on earth. On one hand, the human sacrifices his health in the pursuit of making money and on the other hand sacrifices money to maintain good health. Such a paradox is necessarily a result of the inability of humans to live in the present and the nonacceptance of their death. As the human civilization encounters multiple diseases and struggles to counter the threats, Gandhi's case of simple living, daily exercises, limited diet as required by the body, and nature therapy continue to offer viable solutions to most of the health issues. It is important to mention that what Gandhi preached to others he first experimented on him. His solutions to most of the complex problems were simple but effective. We still need Gandhi and his ideology, rather his philosophy of good health is more relevant in today's fast changing world. As the world is celebrating the 150th birth anniversary of Gandhi and at the same time facing the pandemic of the century, revisiting his ideas, and following them might be a good tribute to one of the greatest souls.

References

Bhargava, B., & Kant, R. (2019). Health File of Mahatma Gandhi: His Experiments with Dietetics and Nature Cure. *Indian Journal of Medical Research, 149*(Supp), S5-S23.

Dietrich, R.F. (2008), David Staller's "Project Shaw". *Shaw The Annual of Bernard Shaw Studies*. Vol 28. Penn State University Press, Pennsylvania: 239–43.

Dhiman, Ramesh and Valecha, Neena (2019). Reducing Malaria using Environment-friendly Approach: A Gandhian Way of Life. *Indian Journal of Medical Research*. 149 (Supp): S95-S103.

Gandhi, M. (1927a). *Young India*. September 19.

Gandhi, M. K. (1927b). *The story of My Experiments with truth*. Navjeevan Publishing House, Ahmedabad.

Gandhi, M. (November 20, 1931). The Moral basis of vegetarianism. Address to the London Vegetarian Society. Available at https://www.mkgandhi.org/ebks/moralbasis_vegetarianism.pdf . Retrieved on May 10, 2021.

Gandhi, M. K. (1968). Mahatma: Life of Gandhi (1869–1948). Sevagram. Available at https://www.mkgandhi.org/sevagram/mad_rush.htm. Retrieved on May 10, 2021.

Guha, R. (May 14, 2016). The Mahatma on Medicine. *The Telegraph*.

Guha, R. (2018). *The year that changed the world (1914–1948)*. Penguin.

Gupta, E. D., & Kant, R. (2019). Gandhian virtues and their relevance to health. *Indian Journal of Medical Research, 149*(Supp), S39-S47.

Just, A. (1903). *Return to Nature* (1st edn., translation by Benedict Lust. New York: B. Lust Publishing.

Kant, R., & Bhargava, B. (2019). Demystifying human diseases. *Indian Journal of Medical Research, 149*(Supp), S25-S37.

Lindley, M. (2018). *Gandhi on Health*. Gandhi Research Foundation.

Nayyar, S. (1944). Medicine for the masses. In *Gandhi: His life and Work*, published on Gandhi's 75th birthday.
Salt, H. S. (1886). *A Plea for Vegetarianism and other Essays*. The Vegetarian Society.
Talwalkar, G. R. (1949). Gandhi and medicine. In *Incidents of Gandhiji's life*. Vora & Co.

Dr Rajni Kant is currently working as Director, ICMR-Regional Medical Research Centre (RMRC), Gorakhpur with additional charge as Scientist 'G' and Head, Division of Research Management, Policy, Planning and Coordination (RMPPC) at ICMR Hqrs, New Delhi.

Part V
Conflict Resolution and Peace

Chapter 12
Peaceful Resolution of Violent Conflicts in India: The Gandhian Way

Anshuman Behera

Abstract This chapter reasons with the Gandhian strategy of non-violent and peaceful conflict resolution in an Indian context. The first part of the chapter provides a brief note on the existing violent conflicts in India: the Maoist conflict, ethnic conflicts in the Northeast, separatism in Kashmir, and religious tensions. The second section engages with the critical aspects of Gandhian ideas for peaceful conflict resolution. Gandhi's ideas like engaging with the conflict parties, early solutions to hostilities, and positive social construction in the post-conflict societies are discussed in detail in this section. The chapter, at the end, argues that the Indian State, following Gandhi, should start engaging with the violent groups operating in different parts of India. Moreover, there should be a political will to resolve these conflicts at the earliest. The issues of violent conflicts should not be put under the carpet. Efforts like initiating negotiation with multiple violent groups hold the key to the successful and peaceful resolution of these conflicts.

Keywords Gandhi · Peaceful conflict resolution · Non-violence · Violent conflicts Negotiation · Maoist conflict

Introduction

It is an irony that the Gandhian approach of peaceful conflict resolution, which played a major role during the freedom struggle against the British colonial rule (read *Satyagraha* along with other practices of Mahatma Gandhi), hardly finds a place in post-independent India's response to violent conflicts. Contrary to the Gandhian approach of peaceful conflict resolution, the Indian state continues to emphasize on counter-violence measures by considering strong military responses to deal with violent conflicts. Through the military involvement against the violent conflicts, the Indian state asserts its monopoly over violence and hardly explores the avenues to engage in negotiation or dialogues with the groups involved in violent movements.

A. Behera (✉)
National Institute of Advanced Studies, Indian Institute of Science Campus, Bengaluru, Karnataka 560012, India
e-mail: anshumanbehera@nias.res.in

© National Institute of Advanced Studies 2022
A. Behera and S. Nayak (eds.), *Gandhi in the Twenty First Century*,
https://doi.org/10.1007/978-981-16-8476-0_12

This approach has brought some success containing the levels of violent activities, but the strife persists.

This paper attempts to explore the Gandhian approach of peaceful conflict resolution and provide an alternative way of engaging with violent conflicts, specifically in the Indian context. Reiterating Gandhi's position on negotiation as key to peaceful resolution of conflicts, the paper argues that in response to the ineffectual counter-violence approach to bring peace, the Indian state should go for negotiations, particularly with the militant groups to explore the possibility of resolving conflicts.

The paper is divided into four major sections. The first section discusses Gandhi's ideas of understanding conflicts within the broad frameworks of Conflict Studies literature. This section also discerns Gandhi's ideas of non-violent and peaceful resolution of conflicts. In the second part of the paper, major violent conflicts in India and responses of successive governments and civil societies to those conflicts in India are deliberated. The third part of the paper expounds on the disparity between the Indian state's response and Gandhi's ideas in dealing with violent conflicts. The last part of the paper offers possible suggestions to the Indian state in dealing with violent conflicts effectively.

Peaceful Conflict Resolution: A Gandhian Approach

Before embarking on the conceptual and theoretical aspects of non-violent and peaceful conflict resolution, it is important to situate Gandhi's ideas with reference to the Indian political context of the early twentieth century. Colonial India, at the beginning of the twentieth century, was witnessing several violent struggles against British rule. These struggles were the outcome of various violent confrontations with the colonial forces to gain independence. It is important to mention that the idea of violent confrontation with the British, to gain freedom, garnered support within India and the Indian diaspora abroad. Some of the significant violent freedom movements against the British Raj such as Subash Chandra Bose-led Indian National Army (INA) and Ghadar Movement had a massive impact. The Ghadar Movement (Puri, 1980) in Punjab was supported by the ethnic Punjabis in California state of the US. The existing literature (Juergensmeyer, 2007) suggests that the boatload of weapons was transported to India by the Punjabi diaspora, living in California, to fight and dislodge the British rule. Similarly, most Indian nationalists during this period believed that the only way to attain freedom against colonial rule was through armed uprising. Under this backdrop of radical and violent sentiments against British rule, Gandhi's take on non-violent resistance and peaceful conflict resolution was revolutionary. It also offered an alternative discourse to fight injustice and colonialism. He stressed upon peaceful means to achieve the desired goals.

There were many early instances when Gandhi openly rejected violent action against injustice. One such was the killing of a British officer, Sir William Curzon Wyllie, on July 1, 1909, by an Indian radical freedom fighter, Madan Lal Dhingra, at the Institute of Imperial Studies, London. William Curzon was the political confidante

12 Peaceful Resolution of Violent Conflicts in India: The Gandhian Way

to the Secretary of State for India, Lord Morley. Madan Lal Dhingra, an Indian student in London, shot five rounds of the bullet (at close range) and killed William Curzon. While the British media declared Dhingra as a murderer, he claimed himself as a freedom fighter. In a move to legitimize his action against William Curzon, Dhingra believed his real judge of this situation were his own 'conscience' and his close associates Vinayak Damodar Savarkar, H K Koregaonkar, and Harnam Singh, who were also advocates of militant nationalism (Datta, 2019), in India House London.

This incident had taken place a few weeks before Gandhi arrived in London to lobby the British Parliament on behalf of South African Indian immigrants (Juergensmeyer, 2007). Critiquing Dhingra's violent action, Gandhi wrote in *Hind Swaraj* that:

> Do you not tremble to think of freeing India by assassination? What we need to do is to sacrifice ourselves. It is a cowardly thought, that of killing others. Whom do you suppose to free by assassination? The millions of India do not desire it. Those who are intoxicated by the wretched modern civilization think these things. Those who will rise to power by murder will certainly not make the nation happy. Those who believe that India has gained by Dhingra's act and other similar acts in India make a serious mistake. Dhingra was a patriot, but his love was blind. He gave his body in a wrong way; its ultimate result can only be mischievous (Gandhi, 2010).

The strong criticism of Dhingra's violent act echoed in Gandhi's rejection of militant nationalism against British rule. Gandhi agreed with the radical nationalists that the British had no place in India but the violent ways to fight colonialism were not subscribed by him. Gandhi feared that if independence were attained through violent means, violence would become a national character (Gandhi, 2001). Moreover, Gandhi also believed that the tactics of terrorism and guerrilla warfare, practised by many fringe groups amongst the radical freedom fighters, could not fight the legitimacy of the mighty state power of the British. Gandhi's rejection of terrorism and guerrilla tactics, in fighting against injustice, carries substantial value in the current scenario both in India and elsewhere. Gandhi's ideas of delegitimizing British rule were fundamentally grounded on the principles of non-violence. Right from criticizing Dhingra's violent act against the British officer, Gandhi maintained his belief in non-violence and peaceful resolution of conflicts all through. Accordingly in the year 1931, Gandhi reasserted, 'I will not purchase my country's freedom at the cost of non-violence' (Nanda, 2002). The deep influence of Gandhi's assertion of non-violent resistance to the violent regimes (read British Colonialism) can be found in the seminal works of Naees (1965). Answering to a problem formulation, can non-violent defense replace military defense, Naees proposes a five-tiered programme:

> First, clarification of national commitment, based on numerous dialogues, use of multiple loyalties, and contact with potential "enemies". In other words, depolarisation and humanisation to counteract mobilisation for violence when governments so decide. Second, international service, "relieving human poverty, suffering, and threats to personal indignity [sic] and integrity"; removing "important causes of conflicts and wars" through "peaceful man-to-man interaction between potential 'enemies'". With "no political 'strings' attached", development in other countries of a positive attitude toward its sponsors is possible; valuable training can also be used in one's own country, and friendly ties are useful should there be conflict. Third, improving our own society, "a non-military defence program would give

us a society far more worth defending", for instance through decentralisation, autonomous decision-making. Fourth, non-military resistance in case of an occupation, combined or not with military defence, also after military defeat. Fifth, research, not assuming we already know all the answers. (Naees in Galtung, 2011).

The foundation of Gandhi's non-violent and peaceful approach, for conflict resolution, begins with an examination of the nature of conflicts. To understand the nature of a conflict, Gandhi focussed largely on its issues than the actors involved. Nonetheless, such a position should not mislead to the idea that Gandhi gives lesser priorities in investigating the actors involved in a conflict. Identifying the stakeholders in a conflict is one of the most critical aspects of meaningful engagement with conflict resolution. Gandhi's primacy of examining the issues substantiates an attempt to engage with larger perspectives in a conflict rather than merely confining it to the individuals involved. Hence, Gandhi's focus is more on the principles that guide a conflict than the personalities. Accordingly, every conflict, as Gandhi reasons, is a contestation on two levels-between persons and between principles (Juergensmeyer, 2021). The primacy of examining the issues helps to understand the values, principles, and demands of the stakeholders in a conflict. Once the values and the demands are examined, identifying the stakeholders becomes the next crucial step. Examining the issues is so critical that there is a need to separate between the real issues and the distorted sentiments. The latter often overshadows the real issues and works as a hindrance towards conflict resolution. The use of violence, in most cases, can be seen as a distorted emotion that often fails to represent real issues. Similarly, identifying the contenders, those who initiate, pursue, and determine the outcome of a conflict is also a tricky affair. In most cases, the perceived involvement of many people does not make them genuine contenders. The very exercise of identifying the contenders should not be confused with excluding any one of them in the process of peaceful negotiation. Here, Gandhi's ideas of engaging with the actors in a conflict begin with accommodation and move to a peaceful resolution. Accordingly, unlike some other positions (Fogg, 1985), Gandhi does not place accommodation and peacefulness as two separate processes.

Understanding Conflict Norms: Gandhian Perspectives

A major intervention with Gandhi's idea of peaceful conflict resolution has been offered by Johan Galtung in his seminal works (Galtung, 1992, 1996; 2008a; b). As Thomas Weber has pointed out in his work (2001), Galtung's intervention is in the form of summarizing Gandhi's conflict norms (Galtung, 1992). The first norm, in this regard, is to enable a good understanding of a conflict in relation to its objectives, issues, stakeholders involved, and the environment in which the conflict operates. What is important in understanding conflict, in this manner, is to have positive intentions of considering it as opportunity to know and understand the positions of the opponents. There is a commonality between Gandhi's position on positive thinking on conflicts and Simmel's work on the associative values of conflict

(Simmel, 1955). The second norm stresses the non-violent aspect of conflict actors' activities. Non-violence can be engaged through two main approaches: principled and pragmatic (Weber, 2003). A principled position of non-violence emphasizes human harmony and rejects coercion and violence morally, whereas a pragmatic approach addresses conflict as 'normal' and holds that rejection of violence is an effective way of challenging power (Weber, 2003).

During a conflict, as Gandhi suggests, the actors need to refrain from violent expressions which include harming or hurting with words or deeds. Moreover, a non-violent way of pursuing conflict would include neither an open nor a secret way of functioning that would allow the conflict actors to non-cooperation with the evil elements. Willingness to sacrifice to the opponent and pursuit of non-polarization are also key elements to warrant non-violent activities of the conflict actors. The third norm is to determine a peaceful result at the end of a conflict. The central idea here is to keep the momentum of non-continuation of the struggle going. As opposed to the continuation of most violent conflicts, especially in the case of India, Gandhi would have suggested ceasing the conflict. Striving towards negotiation and peaceful dialogues amongst the actors of a conflict holds the key to this process. To put an end to the conflict through negotiation process, Gandhi suggests seeking positive social transformation of the conflict actors that involves: the one who initiates the negotiation and the one who agrees to oneself and the opponent. A central aspect for negotiation of a peaceful conflict resolution is to aim for conversion rather than coercion. Contrary to this position of Gandhi, what we witness in India in most cases is, negotiation between the conflict actors often takes place through coercive measures. The ceasefire agreement between militant groups and the Indian state can be seen through the prism of coercion.

Gandhi's puritan approach to conflict resolution, as aptly put by Galtung (1996) promotes better engagement between the conflict actors. To Gandhi, it is the duty of a Satyagrahi to engage in interactions on multiple levels from person-to-person, group-to-group, and society-to-society. And it is only through engagement at multiple levels one can go forward towards integration (fusion). In the concept of Rama Rajya, which Gandhi mentioned explicitly as his desire, there are no borderlines based on gender, caste, race, and nation that the steps towards integration would respect. Here, the whole objective of integration is not necessarily directed against any individual or a community; rather its motive is about containing all forms of violence. This should be understood as an integration of humankind. The process of engagement and the subsequent integration depends on an important aspect of compromise. The significant aspect of compromise must be practised in principle even when all grievances are addressed, and all claims are met. As Gandhi suggests, it is through compromise that the conflict parties come closer to each other and take mutual positions by agreeing to conciliate their tough stances. Another important aspect of Gandhi's ideas on peaceful conflict resolution is the transformation of the societies in a post-resolution period. Resolution of conflict, as Gandhi says, is not the only desired outcome; equally desirable is the positive impact on the conflict parties in the post-resolution scenario. Accordingly, the criterion of conflict impact can be threefold: a new social structure as conflict resolution in the conventional sense, and a higher level of self-purification in all actors, both in the Satyagraha-group and in the adversaries (Galtung, 1996).

In the same way as Galtung, Gandhi's ideas of peaceful conflict resolution have been summarized by Arne Naess. He engages with Gandhi's idealist perspective of individuals and their groups. Highlighting that the interests of the human beings to maximize their interests within larger collectivities drive their behaviour for peaceful coexistence, he underlines the following ideas of Gandhi towards a peaceful conflict resolution: human beings have numerous common interests (Naess, 1974); expressions of violence are anticipated only from the opponents who are against humiliation and provocation directed at them. However, the less a conflict group is likely to resort to violent expressions, the better it understands the position of the other side. A key to initiate a dialogue for conflict resolution is to identify the common and essential interests of both the parties and then it will be possible to establish cooperation. As mentioned before, engagement with the opponent in terms of establishing personal contact should be sought. In that course, one should not be biased and judgmental and one should not exploit the weak position of the opponent. Thus, an element of trust plays an important role. However, an unwillingness to compromise on non-essentials (what Coser terms as distorted emotions) (Coser, 1956) decreases the possibility of peaceful resolution.

Satyagraha and Peaceful Conflict Resolution

For many scholars, Gandhi's idea of peaceful conflict resolution is founded on the concept of Satyagraha. The root meaning of the term, Satyagraha, is 'insistence on truth', hence truth-force. The term Satyagraha has also been likened with 'non-violent resistance', 'non-violent direct action' (Bond, 1988), 'passive resistance' (Gandhi, 1996), and 'militant nonviolence' (Hanigan, 1982). An extensive meaning of the term encompasses 'civil insistence on or tenacity in the pursuit of truth, aimed to penetrate the barriers of prejudice, ill-will, dogmatism, self-righteousness, and selfishness, to reach out to and activate the soul of opponent' (Nimbalkar, 2013). In the context of Conflict Studies, Satyagraha means reaching out to the opponent without prejudices and negativities for a peaceful resolution.

To broaden the discussion on peaceful conflict resolution, one should engage with the three main components of Satyagraha: Truth (Satya), non-violence (ahimsa), and self-suffering (Tapasya). In the discourse of conflict and conflict resolution, Truth is often understood as the right path and leads to justice. In other words, adherence to the right path will yield justice, by addressing the grievances of the adversaries in a fair manner. The aspect of guaranteeing fair treatment of adversaries is the most critical in following the right path-truth. While Truth (Satya) is the ultimate aspect in ensuring justice; ahimsa (non-violence) becomes the way to achieve it (Chander, 1945). Emphasizing on the inseparable connection between truth and non-violence, Gandhi says 'Satyagraha is essentially a weapon of the truthful. A Satyagrahi is pledged to non-violence, and, unless people observe it in thought, word and deed, I cannot offer mass Satyagraha' (Gandhi, 1969). Hence, any attempt on non-violent conflict resolution should offer mutually acceptable conditions without any humiliation or manipulation by the opponent stakeholders. In Gandhi's views, if it fails to impress upon the opponent through peaceful negotiations and dialogues, one can still resolve the conflicts with patience and sympathy (Guha, 1996). The third aspect of the Satyagraha pertaining to conflict resolution is self-suffering-Tapasya which is primarily connected to the moral persuasion of the opponent. A larger meaning of Tapasya implies developing the spirit of detachment and non-attachment. The practice and development of Tapasya also helps one to lead a non-violent life. It is only when one has ceased to be attached to oneself, one can offer non-violent resistance to an aggressor or oppressor (Doctor, 1992). Accordingly, the process of moral persuasion is steered by the necessity to be empathetic to the opponents' issues and grievances. This means there is a need to understand the grievances of the parties involved in a conflict without attributing judgments.

Building upon these three foundational components, Bondurant (1958) has offered a nine-step module in the Satyagraha campaign. The first and foremost step is negotiation and arbitration. It insists on resolving the conflicts through dialogues and engagement with opponents supported by established channels. Efforts, at the very beginning, must minimize the risk of conflict. If the conflict persists, the next steps that follow are direct action, agitation, ultimatum, and self-purification. The sixth step is resistance. Bondurant (1958) offers four major forms of resistance: picketing, dharnas, slow-down strikes, and non-violent forms of general large-scale strikes. Economic boycott and non-cooperation are also critical steps. In this step, the agitating party is advised to peacefully boycott the products that strengthen the economy of the opponent and not to cooperate with the authority. Non-cooperation, for Gandhi, is aimed at the wrong deeds of the oppressor. He stresses that non-cooperation with evil is as much a duty as is cooperation with good (Haksar, 1976). Hence, in a conflict, the opponents should go for non-cooperation solely against wrong values and actions. Similarly, civil disobedience is also an important step that peacefully promotes to disobey the authority of the opponent. Gandhi's ideas on civil disobedience do not offer any scope for anarchical actions. For Gandhi, intelligent understanding, and obligation to follow the laws of a society are the pre-conditions for a satyagrahi to choose civil disobedience. According to Gandhi:

> A Satyagrahi obeys the laws of society intelligently and of his own free will because he considers it to be his sacred duty to do so. It is only when a person has thus obeyed the laws of society scrupulously that he is in a position to judge as to which particular rules are good and just and which unjust and iniquitous. Only then does the right accrue to him of the civil disobedience of certain laws in well-defined circumstances. The last step is assertive *Satyagraha* and parallel government. The main objective here is to establish new sovereignty through delegitimizing the old one. (Gandhi, 1969)

To summarize, Gandhi's ideas of peaceful conflict resolution begin with a positive understanding of the conflict to an extent that it offers an opportunity to understand the opponent. Important components of peaceful engagement, integration, and connection with the opponent at multiple levels hold the key to resolve conflict. Gandhi rules out the scope for mistrust and polarization of conflict parties. Rejecting negative and assertive group identities that lead to polarization is one of the most important contributions of Gandhi. He reiterates that conflict cannot be put under the carpet and must be settled while resolving a conflict through peaceful means. One of Gandhi's most important aspects of conflict resolution is the positive transformation of individuals and the societies involved in it. Aptly put by Joan Bondurant, the main objective of Gandhi's idea of conflict resolution, 'is not to assert positions, but to create possibilities' (Bondurant, 1958). In accordance with his thought, it has been observed that with assertion of positions by conflicting actors, conflicts sustain for a long time.

Based on the above analysis of Gandhi's ideas on peaceful resolution of conflicts, the next section tries to reason out the incongruity between Gandhi's positions and that of the Indian state in responding to the violent conflicts. Prior to the investigation of the discrepancy between the two, some of the major violent conflicts in India are also discussed.

Violent Conflicts in India: A Brief Enquiry

The post-independent India, in its endeavour for state and nation-building, has been able to agree upon a consensus of a democratic, socialist, and sovereign republic state that ensures the fundamental rights of each citizen and respects the regional as well as the national identities. Adherence to a democratic and parliamentary form of governance within the constitutional framework can be seen as a guarantee for equality, individual liberty, and nation-building. However, soon after the promulgation of the constitution, the 'consensus' centered on the idea of the Indian state, as enshrined in the constitution, has been challenged in multiple forms from various platforms. While the assertion of regional identities has initially challenged the nation-building process, the rise of militant groups in many shapes and forms also poses a serious threat to state sovereignty. Since the early 1950s, India has been witnessing several violent conflicts in different parts of the country. The emergence of several violent movements can be seen as conflicts that have disagreements with the consensus on the idea of India. A critical assessment of the major violent conflicts in India is discussed below.

A major conflict in India has been in the form of Maoist violence. The violent political movement waged by the Communist Party of India-Maoist (CPI-Maoist), Maoists in short, claims to have their presence in ten states covering 180 districts of India. Starting from a small village of Naxalbari, known as the Naxalbari movement, in West Bengal in the late 1960s, the Maoist movement has evolved in many shapes and forms over the last fifty years (Behera, 2018a, b). So far as the objectives of the Maoists go, they reject the Indian parliamentary form of democracy and call it a sham. According to the Maoists, a 'semi-colonial and semi-feudal nature' of the Indian state should be fought by a protracted armed struggle to capture power and to herald a 'new democratic order'. The Maoists in their last phase, of nearly six decades of prevalence, have been successful in garnering support from some of the least-privileged sections like the tribal and other marginalized communities, mostly in the Central and the Eastern parts of India. The Maoists have managed to do so by raising the issues of deprivation and dispossession of rights and entitlements of the tribal and other marginalized groups which are perceived by them as major failures in the governance system of the Indian state. The concentrations of the Maoist activities are mostly confined in and around the tribal-dominated areas of Eastern and Central India, a region that has been historically subjected to exploitation, dispossession from their land and resources, and alienation from the state. As mentioned before, the Maoist movement operates against the parliamentary form of governance, 'semi-feudal and semi-colonial nature of the state, deprivation, and dispossession of land rights amongst the marginalized and a faulty development model that produces inequality' (Sharma & Behera, 2014).

A close analysis of the conflict between the Maoists and the Indian state reveals that this has been a protracted competition of two sets of values. The state considers the Maoists as a security threat. This is evident from the fact that the former Prime Minister of India, Manmohan Singh, has termed the Maoists as the single largest internal security threat. Accordingly, the state's narrative of Maoists related to a security threat is a dominant one and it has overshadowed most of the genuine grievances that the local people have since the independence. Hence, the issues of the conflict are about state security versus the rights and survivability of the deprived section of the population. The second set of conflicting values is about the Maoists' outright rejection of the democratic form of governance and the use of violence to fight injustice. It is necessary to mention that the use of violence is a commonality between the Maoists and the Indian state as an important medium to fight injustice and to safeguard state security, respectively. Moreover, identifying the stakeholders in this conflict is slightly complicated. It would be safe to argue that there are many stakeholders than merely the state and the Maoists, as widely perceived. Since the issues of the conflict go beyond the security narrative of the state and the Maoists' objectives of seizing power for the sake of the rights and entitlements of its people, the list of stakeholders is multi-folded. Considering the involvement of several stakeholders with multiple issues, the violent conflict between the Maoists and the Indian state merits a better understanding for resolution.

The issue of identity-induced demands for autonomy/freedom in some parts of India's North-eastern states is another significant conflict. A majority of India's North-eastern states have remained volatile, as multiple armed groups function in these regions for causes specific to their respective states. In most cases, there are instances of multiple armed groups operating in a single state (South Asia Terrorism Portal, 2019) signifying assertion of identities and autonomies at regional, sub-regional, and local levels. Though the agendas for which these armed groups fight for are different in many North-eastern states, what remains common is the violent expression of their demands. The violence is often directed against the Indian state and the state machinery. However, in the last few years, the dynamics of insurgency in the North-eastern states witnesses noticeable changes. Over the last decade, many groups have given into a ceasefire agreement with the state and the union government, but there have been factions amongst the militant groups that continue to carry out violent activities. Apart from the presence of the armed groups against the Indian state, the North-eastern states have also been platforms of intra- and inter-ethnic group conflicts. These conflicts are often led by majoritarian objectives wherein the ethnic groups perceive themselves as minorities and feel insecure against a perceived majority. Following their notion, these ethnic groups seek special status (in most cases demands for territorial arrangement) and justify their demands as a fight against the majority. However, the very demand for the special provision or a separate territory is spearheaded by majoritarian principles (Behera, 2018a, b). Hence, identifying the stakeholders in the ethnic conflicts of the North-eastern states is a difficult task. The rising number of intra-group conflicts involves multiple groups as stakeholders. Therefore, it is safe to put that the conflicts in the North-eastern states have multiple actors (read the ethnic groups) and the state.

The other major violent conflict in India is in the state of Jammu and Kashmir (J&K). The nature of conflict in J&K is multi-layered (Devadas, 2018). On the one hand, there is a demand for autonomy, Azadi, in terms of complete separation from the Indian state as claimed by some constituencies, and on the other hand, is a demand for greater autonomy within the constitutional framework of India as claimed by some others. Secondly, J&K has been a major theatre of terrorists, at least for the last three decades, supported by the state of Pakistan across the border. The conflicts in J&K pose serious threats to India's internal as well as external security. As widely perceived, the J&K conflict has often been seen as a demand for independence from India and/or an attempt to join Pakistan. In the last seventy years, violent activities in several forms have remained a constant feature of the conflict. The main issues of conflicts in J&K are India's sovereignty and integrity, the struggle for separation and autonomy, and Pakistan-sponsored terrorism. Consequently, there are four main actors involved: the Indian state, separatists, people demanding autonomy, and Pakistan.

Yet another major conflict in India is communal tensions amongst the religious groups. Though communal rifts between the Hindus and the Muslims are highlighted the most they also involve other religious groups like the Sikhs and the Christians. The communal tensions in India are often witnessed when the integral links between the structure of the civil societies and the intercommunity links are broken (Varshney, 2002). Post-independent India has witnessed several ugly episodes of communal tensions, in the form of riots, killing thousands of people, and widening the gaps amongst the religious communities. The sustained gap, amongst the religious communities, not only helps to polarize them, but also challenges the very secular ethos of the Indian state. Unlike the West, the distinctiveness of Indian secularism ensures equal status and opportunity to each religious group (Bhargava, 2006). However, despite the constitutional guarantee on religious freedom and equality, the communal tension continues to be a major threat to the idea of India. The main issues of communal conflicts in India are intolerance-induced assertion of religious identity and extreme polarization amongst the religious groups. Apart from the fundamentalists of each religious sect, the civil societies and political parties backing up respective fundamentalist groups are the chief actors in these conflicts.

While the above-mentioned violent conflicts continue to pose challenges, the Indian state has taken several steps to deal effectively with them. One of the major steps to curb violent activities is counter-violent approach with strong military support against the militant groups. In the North-eastern states, J&K, and the Maoist controlled areas, the Indian state has deployed heavy security forces to fight the militant groups. Through this process, the state asserts its monopoly over the use of force. While this approach, as the state claims, has provided results in bringing down the level of violence, the armed conflict in India continues to remain. It is important to observe that, both the cases of resistance by the non-state actors and the responses from the state use violent methods to express their views and to achieve their objectives. One can safely argue that both the action and reaction subscribe to violence alike. Hence, they are far from adhering to a Gandhian position of engagement with conflicts in non-violent ways.

Another crucial response to violent conflicts is the development approach. It is relatively a new approach that has been adopted as recommended by a group of experts under the supervision of the former Planning Commission of India (Bandopadhyay, 2008). The findings of this study suggested that poverty and lack of development, in terms of economic growth and modernity, are some of the major factors leading to violent conflicts. A major criticism of the development approach is while it mostly focuses on the economic and development aspects, it overlooks the facets of emotions, values, and identities that also play major roles in inducing conflicts. However, under this approach, the state has taken up several development initiatives to enhance the living standards of the local population and refrain them from joining violent groups. Despite the initiatives, it has been observed that, in many cases, these developments have been the major sources of conflicts (Behera, 2017). Along with the development approach policies like surrender and rehabilitation of the militants and public perception, management is also being put in place to curb the violent activities.

From the aforementioned responses of the state to deal with violent conflict, it is evident that the state has not been able to creatively engage with the actors of violence. The efforts to resolve the conflict have not been able to yield many results. The Indian state, through its security and development responses, continues to assert its supremacy and monopoly over coercion. Accordingly, the state also demonstrates its unwillingness to engage with the opponents to know their demands and issues. By doing so, the state misses the opportunity to understand the people and their grievances. In the last seven decades of violent conflicts in India, one does not or cannot recall many instances where the state has unconditionally engaged in dialogues and subsequent negotiations with the opponents (read militant groups). Hence, it has failed to create an environment where both parties could spell out their positions and come out with a peaceful resolution. Considering the above analysis, this paper argues, when the responses have not been able to produce many results to resolving violent conflicts, the Gandhian approach of peaceful conflict resolution offers an alternative to engage in and solve these violent conflicts.

Peaceful Resolution of Conflict: A Way Forward

Drawing from the above discussion, it is evident that the Indian state's responses to the violent conflict take a fundamental exit from Gandhi's idea of peaceful resolution. Contrary to the Gandhian approach, the state often uses coercive measures to assert its monopoly over violence, refraining from exploring the possibilities. In cases like communal tensions, it is observed that the state, civil societies, and the political parties often contribute to polarizing the conflict parties which leads to conflict as a never-ending process. It goes against Gandhi's idea that stresses non-polarization as a major step towards conflict resolution. A departure from Gandhi's idea in this regard is the unwillingness of the successive governments to positively engage with the conflicts. Violent conflicts are often understood as a negative happening in society. Hence, they need to be eliminated using force. In this process, the state misses multiple opportunities to know the positions of the opponents. As against the Gandhian ideas, the state often identifies the weak positions of the militant groups and acts against them. What is more worrisome is that most of the violent conflicts in India continue for decades now because of the unwillingness of the state to resolve the conflict.

To put an end to the violent conflicts in a peaceful manner, the Indian state should consider the following policy recommendations. Contrary to the present position, the state should create conditions for dialogue with the opponent groups. As Gandhi suggested, the state machinery should use the established channels, formal and informal, to build communication with the opponents. Once the channels of communication and dialogue are established, the state with the help of the civil societies should offer unconditional negotiations to the armed groups. It is the responsibility of the state, more than any armed group, to initiate the negotiation process. As stated earlier, negotiation must be engaged with the armed groups to understand their positions without any bias, and as Gandhi suggested, there should not be any attempt to humiliate the opponents. The previous negotiations (read the negotiation process between the People's War Group (PWG) and the Andhra Pradesh Government) should not be a reference point as several conditions from both sides eventually lead to the unfortunate fiasco. The Government of the day must trust and prevent from polarizing the groups. It has been observed that polarization, both at the armed group level and the societal level, acts as a single important factor to sustain the conflicts. The state should avoid citing the examples of just a few cases like Tripura where the violence level has come down drastically as success stories. As Gandhi says, resolution of conflict should not be the only desirable objective; transformation of individuals and the societies at the end of a conflict should be more desired. As the existing approaches of the Indian state continue to offer limited results in resolving conflicts, the Gandhian idea of peaceful conflict resolution offers a credible way forward.

References

Bandopadhyay, D. (2008). *Development challenges in extremist affected areas*. New Delhi: Planning Commission Government of India.
Behera, A. (2017). Development as a source of conflict: The Sahukars, displaced people and the maoists in Koraput. *The round Table, 106*(5), 543–556.
Behera, A. (2018a). From Mao to Maoism: the Indian path. In N. Pani & A. Behera (Eds), *Reasoning Indian politics: philosopher politicians to politicians seeking philosophy*. London: Routledge.
Behera, A. (2018). The majoritarian way to democracy: The bodoland conflict in Assam. *Alternatives: Global Local Political, 42*(3), 135–145.
Bhargava, R. (2006). The distinctiveness of Indian secularism. In T. N. Srinivasan (Ed.), *The future of secularism* (pp. 20–53). Oxford University Press.
Bond, D. G. (1988). The nature and meanings of nonviolent direct action: An exploratory study. *Journal of Peace Research., 25*(1), 81–89.
Bondurant, J. V. (1958). *Conquest of violence: The gandhian philosophy of conflict*. University of California Press.
Bondurant, J. V. (1958). *Conquest of violence: The gandhian philosophy of conflict Princeton*. Princeton University Press
Chander, J. P. (1945). *Teachings of Mahatma Gandhi*. Lahore: The Indian Printing Works.
Coser, L. A. (1956). *The functions of social conflict*. The Free Press.
Datta, N. (2019). Juxtaposing two ideas of India. *The Tribune*. Retrieved January 10, 2021, from https://www.tribuneindia.com/news/archive/features/juxtaposing-two-ideas-of-india-839568.
Devadas, D. (2018). *The generation of rage in Kashmir*. Oxford University Press.
Doctor, A. H. (1992). The man in Gandhi Philosophy. *The Indian Journal of Political Science., 53*(2), 152–167.
Fogg, R. W. (1985). Dealing with conflict: A repertoire of creative, peaceful approaches. *Journal of Conflict Resolution., 29*(2), 330–358.
Galtung, J. (1992). *The way is the goal: Gandhi today*. Ahmedabad: Gujarat Vidyapith Peace Research Center.
Galtung, J. (1996). *Peace by peaceful means: Peace and conflict development and civilisation*. PRIO, Sage.
Galtung, J. (2008a). *50 Years: 100 Peace and Conflict Perspectives*. Transcend University Press.
Galtung, J. (2008b). *50 Years: 25 Intellectual Landscapes Explored*. Transcend University Press.
Galtung, J. (2011). Arne Naess, peace and Gandhi. *Inquiry, 54*(1), 31–41.
Gandhi, L. (1996). Concerning violence: The limits and circulations of Gandhian "Ahisma" or passive resistance. *Cultural Critique, 35*, 105–147.
Gandhi, M. K. (1969). *An autobiography or the story of my experiments with truth*. Ahmedabad: Navajivan Mudranalaya.
Gandhi, M. K. (2001). Non-violent resistance (Satyagraha). New York: Dover Publications, INC.
Gandhi, M. (2010). *Hind Swaraj (Centenary Edition)*. Delhi: Rajpal & Sons (p. 56).
Guha, R. (1996). *Subaltern studies III: Writings on South Asian history and society*. Oxford University Press.
Haksar, V. (1976). Rawls and Gandhi on civil disobedience. *Inquiry: An Interdisciplinary Journal of Philosophy, 19*(1–4), 151–192.
Hanigan, J.P. (1982). Militant nonviolence: A spirituality for the pursuit of social justice. *Horizons: The Journal of the College Theology Society, 9*(1), 7–22.
Juergensmeyer, M. (2007). Gandhi vs. Terrorism. *Dædalus*, 30–39.
Juergensmeyer, M. (2021). Global Gandhi. *Social Change, 51*(1), 12–22.
Naess, A. (1965). *Gandhi and the nuclear age*. The Bedminster Press.
Naess, A. (1974). *Gandhi and group conflict: An exploration of Satyagraha*. Universitetsforlaget.
Nanda, B.R. (2002). Gandhi and non-violence: Doctrines of Ahimsa and Satyagraha. *World Affairs: The Journal of International Issues 6*(1), 54–62.

Nimbalkar, N. (2013). An approach to peace: Gandhi on conflict resolution through Satyagraha. *Journal of Natal and Zulu History, 31*(2), 130–138.

Puri, H. K. (1980). Revolutionary organization: A study of the Ghadar movement. *Social Scientist., 9*(2–3), 53–66.

Sharma, S., & Behera, A. (2014). *Militant groups in South Asia.* Institute for Defence Studies and Analyses and Pentagon Press.

Simmel, G. (1955). *Conflict and the web of group affiliation.* The Free Press.

South Asia Terrorism Portal. (2019). *Insurgency in Northeast.* Retrieved October 12, 2019, from Institute for Conflict Management: https://www.satp.org/terrorist-groups/india-insurgencynortheast

Varshney, A. (2002). *Ethnic conflict and civic life: Hindus and Muslims in India.* Yale University Press.

Weber, T. (2001). Gandhian philosophy, conflict resolution theory and practical approaches to negotiation. *Journal of Peace research*, 493–513.

Weber, T. (2003). Nonviolence is who? Gene sharp and Gandhi. *Peace and Change, 28*(2), 250–270.

Anshuman Behera is Associate Professor at the National Institute of Advanced Studies (NIAS), Bengaluru. Dr. Behera writes on internal conflicts in India, Bangladesh, and Nepal and on political processes in South Asia.

Chapter 13
Gandhi's *Satya*: Truth Entails Peace

Venkata Rayudu Posina

Abstract What is Gandhi's *satya*? How does truth entail peace? *Satya* or truth, for Gandhi, is experiential. The experiential truth of Gandhi does not exclude epistemological, metaphysical, or moral facets of truth, but is an unequivocal acknowledgement of the subjective basis of the pursuit of objectivity. In admitting my truth, your truth, our truth, their truth, etc., Gandhi brought into clear focus the reality of I and we—the subjects (or viewpoints) of subjective experiences (views). The totality of these subjective viewpoints, along with their mutual relationships, constitutes an objective frame of reference for reconciling or putting together seemingly irreconcilable perceptions into a unitary whole of mutual understanding and an ever more refined comprehension of reality, thereby engendering peace. Considering the generality of the basic tenet—viewpoint dependence of views—of Gandhi's *satyagraha* and in view of the kinship between positive conception of peace and unity, I put forward '*satyagraha* for science' as a method to address numerous foundational problems in various branches of science centred on unity such as the binding problem in neuroscience.

Keywords Gandhi · *Satya* · *Satyagraha* · Peace · Satyagraha for Science

Introduction

'Traffic light turned red', I alerted the cab driver, lest the driver was unaware of the change in the state-of-affairs of the world out there. I saw a traffic light turning red, which happens to correspond to the traffic light turning red, which, in turn, gave me the licence to treat my individual subjective perception of reality as the objective reality we all are collectively suspended in. This conflation of reality and its models is justified by its undeniable utility in our everyday transactions with reality (cf. things, thoughts, and people). However, it is a philosophical mistake to confuse objective reality with the subjective perception modelling it. The price we pay for this

---

V. R. Posina (✉)
National Institute of Design, 12 HMT Link Road, Bengaluru, Karnataka 560022, India
e-mail: vf29@nid.edu

© National Institute of Advanced Studies 2022
A. Behera and S. Nayak (eds.), *Gandhi in the Twenty First Century*,
https://doi.org/10.1007/978-981-16-8476-0_13

commonplace mistake is discounted self: subtraction of the self in transmuting "I see it *as* red" to 'it *is* red'. Although unmindful of (what Saint Augustine christened) 'the region of unlikeness' we inhabit, this mortal mistake is inconsequential unless, say, I see a circle and you see a rectangle, when we both look at one and the same thing. I claim that 'it is a circle' and you claim that 'it is a rectangle'. One thing cannot be two things. Hence, a problem: what is the truth? Or a conflict: who is right? But first, how do we go about deciding 'what is true' or 'who is right'? It is in this context of resolving differences that we find Gandhi's *satya*—experiential truth—as a proper conception of truth. Here I show how Gandhi's *satya*, in reconciling seemingly incompatible truths, entails peace. In the following, I begin with an explanation of Gandhi's *satya*. Equipped with Gandhi's experiential conceptualization of truth, along with the admission of attendant subjectivity, I substantiate—based on a positive definition of PEACE as a state of unitary wholeness—the claim: truth entails peace. Gandhi's *satyagraha*—holding onto truth—a pathway to peace, in the light of its generality—different views can be united by relating underlying viewpoints—is also a pathway to solve problems of unity such as the binding problem, i.e., the problem of putting together colour and shape into the coloured-shapes populating our everyday experience in consciousness studies.

Before we get to the core of the chapter, a few terminological clarifications are in order. First, I use the word 'viewpoint' not only to denote a location in space from which a person views an object, but also as a stand-in for the self—entire enchilada of selves—autobiographical self, bodily self, cognitive self, conceptual self, ecological self, embodied self, emotional self, empirical self, experiential self, mental self, metaphysical self, moral self, narrative self, physical self, social self, spiritual self, transcendental self, etc. (see Gallagher, 2000). Also, a view (appearance, observation, perception, or subjective experience) is not only a view of an object, but is also [simultaneously] a view from a viewpoint (subject); as such appearances and observations are treated as perceptual experiences of a subject (see Albright, 1994, 2015). Furthermore, one might be able to step out of one's body (Altschuler & Ramachandran, 2007) or forced out (Kandel et al., 2000, p. 489), but not out of one's experience simply because of the primacy of experience (Posina, 2017), with experience subsuming cognition et al. (see Posina et al., 2017).

Gandhi's *Satya*

What is Gandhi's *satya* or truth? How did Gandhi conceptualize TRUTH? In Gandhi's own words, "truth is self-evident" (Gandhi, 1959, p. 10). First, let us ask: what is self-evident to all selves—to each self? That I am in excruciating pain is self-evident in my subjective experience of pounding headache; I need no brain scan to tell me that I am in pain. The sounds I hear, the scenes I see, the thoughts I think, and the emotions I feel are all self-evident in my subjective experience. Of course, there are many truths that are not self-evident. But, if the truth were to be self-evident, then it must be the truth of subjective experience. Thus, in Gandhi's conceptualization, truth is experiential (see also Bilgrami, 2003). Even more importantly, the subject of subjective experiences (or viewpoint of observations) is integral to Gandhi's conception of truth: "It has been my experience that I am always true from my point of view" (Gandhi, 1955, p. 12). This [seemingly] nondescript observation of Gandhi has all the purchasing power we need to show that Gandhi's *satya*—experiential truth—entails peace.

Truth Entails Peace

Let us consider a conflict or disagreement familiar to all students of *Anekantavada* of Jainism, including Gandhi. It is the familiar story of blind men getting to know an elephant. Being blind, they try to figure out what an elephant is like by feeling it with their hands. The one who touched the elephant's ear asserted: elephant is like a plantain leaf, while the one who touched elephant's belly asserted: elephant is like a wall, while the one who touched the elephant's tail asserted: elephant is like a snake. Needless to note, they end up arguing which, not surprisingly, does not bring them any closer to the truth of what an elephant is like. How can we turn this futile argument into a fruitful pursuit of truth?

Gandhi claimed "to be a passionate seeker after Truth" (CWMG, 1958, pp. 230–231). So, let us imagine the blind men (seeking the truth about an elephant) as Gandhis, say: Tall Gandhi, Medium Gandhi, and Short Gandhi. The Tall Gandhi, upon touching the ear of the elephant, would say: I think elephant is like a plantain leaf, while the Medium Gandhi, upon touching the belly of the elephant, would say: I think elephant is like a wall, while the Short Gandhi, upon touching the tail of the elephant, would say: I think elephant is like a snake. In adding 'I think', [every] Gandhi transformed what would have otherwise been branded as subjectivity, which is rather removed from matters of truth and reality, into positional objectivity, with the position being the subject (I) of subjective experiences (see Sen, 1993). The totality of these subjects (Tall Gandhi, Medium Gandhi, and Short Gandhi) constitutes an objective system of coordinates to put together seemingly incompatible pieces of knowledge—plantain leaf, wall, and snake—into a unitary understanding, i.e., the elephant. The operation of putting together, which is a process of resolving arguments or conflicts, can be made more concrete with a simpler example. Consider a cylinder standing on its base; the front-view of which is rectangle, while the top-view is circle. Before we know, we have a conflict—rectangle *vs.* circle—if we discount the viewpoints. Once we incorporate the viewpoints, the two viewpoints together constitute a coordinate system within which we can put together the seemingly incompatible pieces of knowledge into a unitary understanding:

$$\text{Rectangle}_{\text{Front-view}} \text{ AND } \text{Circle}_{\text{Top-view}} = \text{Cylinder}$$

In the present context, it is important to note that the notion of PEACE, engendered by resolving conflicts, is a positive definition of peace characterized by wholeness and unity, where all parts of the whole fit-together somewhat like the parts—eyes, nose, mouth, ears, neck, hands, legs, etc.—of a body fit-together into the body (see Fiala, 2018). Peace, when understood as a unitary whole resulting from putting together all that fits together, which is determined by the totality of viewpoints, is synonymous with truth. By virtue of the reflexivity of entailment relation (Lawvere & Rosebrugh, 2003, p. 196), we conclude truth entails peace, which is in accord with Gandhi's assertion: "Truth is the end" (Gandhi, 1955, p. 37).

Satyagraha for Science

It is interesting to note that Gandhi's truth—subjectivity of the pursuit of objectivity—is reminiscent of the contemporary understanding of scientific practices seeking the unity of sciences, especially James Clerk Maxwell's doctrine-dependent differential visibility of phenomena (Lawvere, 2001) and F. William Lawvere's Functorial Semantics, wherein subjective generalization—abstract theories and concrete models—of objective particulars is determined by doctrines (Lawvere, 2004; see also Lawvere & Rosebrugh, 2003, pp. 14–15, 239–240; Lawvere & Schanuel, 2009, pp. 84–90, 180–182, 309). Here particulars, generals, and doctrines correspond to objects, subjective experiences (views), and subjects (viewpoints), respectively (Posina, 2020).

Oftentimes, parallels or analogies tend to be the basis for the development of methods, models, and theories. For example, in introducing category theory Lawvere and Schanuel (1997, p. xiii) discuss how analogies became methods: "they [categorical ideas] first appeared only as dimly perceived analogies between subjects. Since Eilenberg & MacLane (1945), when the notion of 'category' was first precisely formulated, these analogies have been sharpened and have become explicit ways in which one subject is transformed into another." Along these lines, Lawvere (2002, p. 1) notes: "I noticed the analogy between the triangle inequality and a categorical composition law. The categorical connection is sufficient to suggest a whole system of constructions and theorems appropriate for metric spaces!" Later, Lawvere (2005, p. 1) adds: "Rejecting the complacent description of that identification (of triangle inequality and composition law) as a mere analogy or amusement, its relentless pursuit is continued, revealing convexity and geodesics as concepts having a definite meaning over any closed category."

It is in this spirit, having noticed 'unity' in the positive conception of peace and having recognized the generality of *satyagraha* as a method to bring about peace, i.e., reconcile differences in views by relating the underlying different, in Gandhi's words, "angles of vision" (Gandhi, 1955, p. 64; see also ibid. p. 21; Gandhi, 1968, p. 107, 264, 311; Juergensmeyer, 2007), I put forward '*satyagraha* for science' as a method for pursuing, at various scales, unity in science.

Problems of unity or putting together are ubiquitous in science. For example, Albright et al., (2000, p. S2), upon summing up a century of neuroscience research, conclude: "the issue is whether we can succeed in developing new strategies for combining reductionist and holistic approaches in order to provide a meaningful bridge between molecular mechanism and mental processes: a true molecular biology of cognition." In a similar vein, Carla Shatz, in charting a post-reductionist science, acknowledges: "the challenge now is how to put the molecules back into cells, and the cells back into the [neural] systems, and systems back into [brain] trying to really understand behaviour and perception" (Gershon, 2001). In physics, there are the problems of unifying classical and quantum mechanics and of unifying quantum mechanics and relativity theory.

In mathematics, there is the problem of unifying algebra, arithmetic, calculus, logic, and geometry. Note that these struggles for unification are no idle pursuits: unification allows one "to put the vast storehouse [of bits and pieces of knowledge] in order, and to find the appropriate tool when it is needed, so that the new ideas and methods collected and developed as one goes through life can find their appropriate places as well" (Lawvere & Schanuel, 1997, p. xiii). In fact, "the unification of mathematics is an important strategy for learning, developing, and using mathematics" (Lawvere & Schanuel, 2009, p. 378). The great geometer Charles Ehresmann cautioned: "without some unifying theory, the mathematicians would fatally tend to use divergent, incompatible languages, like the builders of the tower of Babel" (Ehresmann, 1966, p. 4). Ehresmann envisioned a mathematical education that recognizes unifying theory as fundamental: "theory of categories seems to be the most characteristic unifying trend in present day mathematics; for that reason, I think it will soon have to be taught at the university level like other fundamentals as early as linear algebra or topology" (ibid. p. 5). All the more important is the fact that "explicit use of the unity and cohesiveness of mathematics sparks the many particular processes whereby ignorance becomes knowledge" (Lawvere, 1991, p. 2). James Clerk Maxwell's Electromagnetic Field (Maxwell, 1865), in providing a unified account of electricity, magnetism, and light, is a stellar example of the significance of unification. More broadly, "Mathematics is the key for the understanding of the whole Universe, *unifying all human thinking*, from Sciences to Philosophy and Metaphysics. So, the great ideal of Plato and Leibniz, the ideal of Mathematics as the essence of all knowledge, might at last be attained" (Ehresmann, 1966, pp. 6–7, *emphasis mine*; see also Lawvere & Schanuel, 2009, p. 129).

A foundational problem of unification in neuroscience is the binding problem of putting together *qualitatively* different perceptual attributes (e.g., colour, shape) into the unity (coloured-shapes) of our conscious experience (Albright et al., 2000, pp. S36-S37; Brook & Raymont, 2017; Croner & Albright, 1999; Kandel et al., 2013, p. 368, 437, 447; Roskies, 1999). The problem is particularly difficult because we are fluent in putting together quantities (e.g., addition, multiplication), but not so much so in putting together *qualities*. Note that the unification we are seeking is an understanding of the unity of conscious experience: "binding of visual attributes is tantamount to their reaching the perceiver's awareness" (Albright et al., 2000, p. S37). For example, colours and shapes are unified in our conscious experience: every time we see a colour, it is the colour of a shape and every shape we see has a colour. An amusing quail-story in this context is: painters, envious of musicians, who readily produce pleasant sounds (music) without verbal meanings, sought to create visual music, i.e., pure colour devoid of shape. Unfortunately, no matter how and what coloured paint painters splashed on a canvas, it always conveyed some shape to their chagrin, which they deftly labelled abstract painting (see Gage, 1993).

Returning to the problem of unification, the problem of putting together is not limited to visual domain: at the next level, we have the problem of combining *qualitatively* different perceptual modalities—visual, auditory, tactile, taste, and smell—into the unity of consciousness that we all experience (Albright et al., 2000, pp. S36-S37; Brook & Raymont, 2017; Croner & Albright, 1999; Kandel et al., 2013, p. 368, 437, 447; Roskies, 1999). Andrée Ehresmann and her colleagues developed a general mathematical framework: Memory Evolutive Systems (MES), wherein the problem of putting together or binding is modelled as colimit (which is a generalization of the more familiar operation of sum to accommodate putting together of structures along with their mutual relations; Ehresmann & Vanbremeersch, 2007, pp. 49–71). It is fascinating to note that, although MES was developed completely independent of *satyagraha*, the formation of colimit in MES as a solution to the binding problem is reminiscent of putting together different views into a unitary whole, by way of analysing views into views-viewpoints, as we discuss below. In MES, views and their underlying viewpoints are explicitly modelled as co-regulators and their underlying landscapes, with colimit of different partial views, i.e., co-regulators corresponding to different landscapes, resulting in unified conscious experience. Considering the generality of MES, it can be applied to problems of putting together at various scales beginning with atomic physics and going all the way to social conflicts and philosophical differences (Ehresmann, 2012; Ehresmann & Vanbremeersch, 2007, pp. 65–66, 79, 226, 230–231, 283; Ehresmann & Vanbremeersch, 2019).

Let us now examine the problem of putting together in detail. As I eat Tirupati Laddu, I experience the sweet taste, savour the mouth-watering aroma, see the pleasant yellow colour and round shape, feel the smooth indentations of the laddu on my fingertips and its soft granular texture in my mouth, and hear the barely audible sound of chewing not as discrete perceptual attributes suspended in some experiential void, but as a unitary whole. Now, the question is: what does Gandhi's *satyagraha* have to say about how *qualitatively* different vision, audition, touch, taste, and smell can all be put together into a unified conscious experience? Treating different perceptual attributes (e.g., yellow laddu) as different views from their respective viewpoints (eyes), we find that vision is a view from the viewpoint of eyes (or photoreceptors), touch is a view from the viewpoint of skin (mechanoreceptors), smell is a view from the viewpoint of nose (chemoreceptors), etc. (see Albright, 2015, p. 22, 38; Kandel et al., 2013, pp. 449–451). Going by our earlier experience with resolving different views—rectangle *vs.* circle—into the unity of cylinder by relating corresponding viewpoints: front-view and top-view, we realize that first the viewpoints—chemoreceptor, photoreceptor, and mechanoreceptor—need to be related to one another (recollect that it is the relation between front-view and top-view that determined the putting together of rectangle and circle into cylinder). Once we have a space of sensory transducers converting environmental energy, wherein the relations between chemical, light, and mechanical stimuli is specified enough to form an objective frame of reference (as in the case of front-view and top-view), then sights, sounds, smells, and tastes will all fall into place resulting in a unified conscious percept (just as circle and rectangle combined into a circle as soon as we recognized circle as top-view and rectangle as front-view). Constructing a totality of *qualitatively* different types of stimuli (light, chemical, and mechanical) requires conceptualizing quantities with different physical units as categories (universes of discourse) of a Grothendieck-Cantor type of abstraction (Lawvere, 2003).

Admittedly, the programme of research we arrived at by applying the method of Gandhi's *satyagraha* to the binding problem is monumental (application of *satyagraha* was never easy and not meant for selfie-scientists; cf. Geman & Geman, 2016). Fortunately, students of consciousness studies are not all alone in struggling with *qualities*; we are in good company: "the core of mathematical theories is in the variation of quantity in space and in the emergence of *quality* within that" (Lawvere, 2014, p. 3 / 716, *emphasis mine*). Even more fortunately, the basic ingredients that we need—COHESION and QUALITY—have been axiomatized (Lawvere, 2007), which enables us to begin conceptualizing a category of *quality types*, wherein the mutual relations between *qualities* are specified, as a first step towards the objective reference frame of *qualitatively* different physical stimuli (viewpoints) that is needed to put together different perceptual attributes (views) into a unified conscious experience.

Let me now bring back our enlightening elephant. Peter Johnstone (University of Cambridge) named his magnum opus: *Sketches of an Elephant* (Johnstone, 2002). Here the elephant is a mathematical object called topos. One familiar example of topos is the topos of sets, where a set is a collection of elements (Lawvere & Rosebrugh, 2003, pp. 1–2). For example, Fruits = {banana, apple} is a set of two elements: banana and apple. Sets such as the just mentioned Fruits, along with functions between sets (a function f from the set Fruits to a set Colours = {yellow, red} is an assignment of an element in the set Colours to each element in the set Fruits; e.g., f (banana) = yellow and f (apple) = red) form a topos by virtue of the following properties that the category (mathematical universe of discourse) of sets and functions has: 1. There is an empty set { }, 2. There is a single-element set {•}, 3. Sum of sets is a set, 4. Product of sets is a set, 5. Totality of all functions from a set to a set is a set, and 6. There is a two-element truth value set {false, true} (ibid. pp. 111–113; Lawvere & Schanuel, 2009, pp. 13–18, 352–353). Once you abstract out these properties and call it a topos, then you will find that there are other mathematical universes of discourse (categories such as graphs and dynamical systems) that have these properties and hence are toposes. Before long you have one saying "topos is a space", another saying "topos is a theory", yet another saying "topos is a mathematical universe" and there is no stopping them sayings, all of which reminded Johnstone of our enlightening elephant: "topos resembles an elephant in that it is possible to come up with very different descriptions of what topos is, depending on the direction from which one approaches it" (Johnstone, 2002, p. vii; see also Sen, 1980). Application of Gandhi's *satyagraha* immediately suggests forming an objective reference frame of 'directions of approach' (viewpoints) to put together different [incomplete/partial] descriptions (views) into a complete picture of topos. Unfortunately, Johnstone, not having the aid of Gandhi's *satyagraha*, could not get the moral of our enlightening elephant story: "the important thing about the elephant is that 'however you approach it, it is still the same animal'; this book is an attempt to demonstrate that the same is true of topos" (ibid. p. viii). The problem with Johnstone's self-comforting reading is that, however, Johnstone approaches it, it is still the same elephant, *but* depending on the direction Johnstone approaches it, Johnstone may find it to be a snake or a wall or a plantain leaf (as we discussed earlier); it's only by putting together these views by way of taking into account the underlying viewpoints that Johnstone may get to know that there is an elephant.

Concluding Remarks

Gandhi's *satya*, by virtue of being an experiential conceptualization of truth, undid the cardinal sin of cognition: treating subjective models of reality as reality. In doing so, Gandhi paved the way for peace by acknowledging the subjective nature of the pursuit of truth. This acknowledgement constitutes a method for resolving incompatible percepts into a mutually agreeable reality within the objective framework formed of the totality of contending subjects (viewpoints).

In light of the realization that Gandhi's oft-repeated claim: "the only means for the realization of Truth is *ahimsa*" (Gandhi, 1940, p. 615) is an assertion of the ontological determination of epistemology (Posina, 2016), along with the presently discussed Gandhi's experiential conceptualization of truth and the application of Gandhi's *satyagraha* to the foundational problems of unity in neuroscience and mathematics, one cannot help but cease to read the title of Gandhi's autobiography: *My Experiments with Truth* (Gandhi, 1940; here it is worth noting the etymological kinship between experience and experiment, which is planned perception) metaphorically and start recognizing Gandhi as a serious scientist. The genius of Gandhi that flowered in the field of science, in addition to blooming in metaphysical realm and blossoming in political arena, is a middle way paved in his thoughtful synthesis of Hindu absolutism with Jain *anekantavada* (Rao, 2017, p. 40; see also Gardner, 2011, pp. 289–330).

In closing, I address potential criticisms. One immediate criticism is the absence of *purva-paksha* or the contrary point of view. There is no engagement with any of the many well-established theories of truth. Yes, truth, as Gandhi recognized, "is as old as hills" (Gandhi, 1955, p. 7); naturally, there is no dearth of theories of truth. However, my objective here is to bring Gandhi's scientific genius into figural salience—for all to see. Not unlike beauty defined as figure-sans-background, Gandhi's experiential conception of truth needs no background of other theories to stand out. So is the case with peace. While contemporary peacebuilders think of truth as the first step in bringing about lasting peace (Tolbert, 2016), Gandhi's *satyagraha* was aeons ahead in realizing that we need to hold onto truth every step of our way towards peace (Gandhi, 1968). It is this incomparable genius of Gandhi that Einstein celebrates: "Generations to come, it may be, will scarce believe that such a one as this ever in flesh and blood walked upon this Earth" (Einstein, 1950, p. 240).

References

Albright, T. D. (1994). Why do things look as they do? *Trends in Neurosciences, 17*, 175–177.
Albright, T. D. (2015). Perceiving. *Dædalus, 144*, 22–41.
Albright, T. D., Jessell, T. M., Kandel, E. R., & Posner, M. I. (2000). Neural science: A century of progress and the mysteries that remain. *Neuron, 25*, S1–S55.
Altschuler, E. L., & Ramachandran, V. S. (2007). A simple method to stand outside oneself. *Perception, 36*, 632–634.
Bilgrami, A. (2003). Gandhi, the philosopher. *Economic and Political Weekly, 38*, 4159–4165.
Brook, A., Raymont, P. (2017). The unity of consciousness. In E.N. Zalta (ed.), *The stanford encyclopedia of philosophy*. https://plato.stanford.edu/archives/sum2017/entries/consciousness-unity/.
Croner, L. J., & Albright, T. D. (1999). Seeing the big picture: Integration of image cues in the primate visual system. *Neuron, 24*, 777–789.
CWMG. (1958) *Collected works of Mahatma Gandhi (100 volumes) (1958—1994)*, Delhi: Government of India.
Ehresmann, C. (1966). Trends toward unity in mathematics. *Cahiers De Topologie Et Géométrie Différentielle Catégoriques, 8*, 1–7.
Ehresmann, A. C. (2012). MENS, an info-computational model for (neuro-)cognitive systems capable of creativity. *Entropy, 14*, 1703–1716.
Ehresmann, A. C., & Vanbremeersch, J.-P. (2007). *Memory evolutive systems: Hierarchy*. Elsevier Science.
Ehresmann, A., & Vanbremeersch, J.-P. (2019). MES: A mathematical model for the revival of natural philosophy. *Philosophies, 4*, 1–20.
Eilenberg, S., & MacLane, S. (1945). General theory of natural equivalences. *Transactions of the American Mathematical Society, 58*, 231–294.
Einstein, A. (1950). *Out of my later years*. Philosophical Library.
Fiala, A. (2018) Pacifism. In E.N. Zalta (ed.), *The stanford encyclopedia of philosophy*. https://plato.stanford.edu/archives/fall2018/entries/pacifism/.
Gage, J. (1993). *Colour and culture: Practice and meaning from antiquity to abstraction*. University of California Press.
Gallagher, S. (2000). Philosophical conceptions of the self: Implications for cognitive science. *Trends in Cognitive Sciences, 4*, 14–21.
Gandhi, M. K. (1940). *The story of my experiments with truth*. Navajivan Publishing House.
Gandhi, M. K. (1955). *Truth is god*. Navajivan Publishing House.
Gandhi, M. K. (1959). *The message of the gita*. Navajivan Publishing House.
Gandhi, M. K. (1968). *Satyagraha in South Africa*. Navajivan Publishing House.
Gardner, H. (2011). *Creating minds: An anatomy of creativity seen through the lives of Freud, Einstein, Picasso, Stravinsky, Eliot, Graham, and Gandhi*. Basic Books.
Geman, D., & Geman, S. (2016). Science in the age of selfies. *Proceedings of the National Academy of Sciences of the United States of America, 113*, 9384–9387.
Gershon, D. (2001). All systems go for neuroscience. *Nature, 414*, 4–5.
Johnstone, P. (2002). *Sketches of an elephant: A topos theory compendium (3 volumes)*. Clarendon Press.
Juergensmeyer, M. (2007). Gandhi vs. terrorism. *Dædalus, 136*, 30–39.
Kandel, E.R., Schwartz, J.H., Jessell, T.M. (2000). *Principles of Neural Science* (4th ed.). New York: McGraw-Hill.
Kandel, E.R., Schwartz, J.H., Jessell, T.M., Siegelbaum, S.A., Hudspeth, A.J. (2013) *Principles of Neural Science* (5th ed.). New York: McGraw Hill.
Lawvere, F.W. (1991). Some thoughts on the future of category theory. In Carboni, A., Pedicchio, M. C., Rosolini G. (eds.), *Category Theory*. New York: Springer-Verlag.
Lawvere, F.W. (2001). Sketches and platonic ideas. Retrieved May 10, 2020 from https://www.mta.ca/~cat-dist/archive/2001/01-12.

Lawvere, F. W. (2002). Enriched categories in the logic of geometry and analysis. *Reprints in Theory and Applications of Categories, 1*, 1–39.

Lawvere, F. W. (2003). Foundations and applications: Axiomatization and education. *The Bulletin of Symbolic Logic, 9*, 213–224.

Lawvere, F. W. (2004). Functorial semantics of algebraic theories and some algebraic problems in the context of functorial semantics of algebraic theories. *Reprints in Theory and Applications of Categories, 5*, 1–121.

Lawvere, F. W. (2005). Taking categories seriously. *Reprints in Theory and Applications of Categories, 8*, 1–24.

Lawvere, F. W. (2007). Axiomatic cohesion. *Theory and Applications of Categories, 19*, 41–49.

Lawvere, F. W. (2014). Comments on the development of topos theory. *Reprints in Theory and Applications of Categories, 24*, 1–22.

Lawvere, F. W., & Rosebrugh, R. (2003). *Sets for mathematics*. Cambridge University Press.

Lawvere, F.W., & Schanuel, S.H. (1997). *Conceptual mathematics: A first introduction to categories* (1st ed.). Cambridge: Cambridge University Press.

Lawvere, F.W., & Schanuel, S.H. (2009). *Conceptual mathematics: A first introduction to categories* (2nd ed.). Cambridge: Cambridge University Press.

Maxwell, J. C. (1865). A dynamical theory of the electromagnetic field. *Philosophical Transactions of the Royal Society of London, 155*, 459–512.

Posina, V. R. (2016). Truth through nonviolence. *GITAM Journal of Gandhian Studies, 5*, 143–150.

Posina, V. R. (2017). Symbolic conscious experience. *Tattva–Journal of Philosophy, 9*, 1–12.

Posina, V. R. (2020). Hard, harder, and the hardest problem: The society of cognitive selves. *Tattva–Journal of Philosophy, 12*, 75–92.

Posina, V. R., Ghista, D. N., & Roy, S. (2017). Functorial semantics for the advancement of the science of cognition. *Mind & Matter, 15*, 161–184.

Rao, K. R. (2017). *Gandhi's Dharma*. Oxford University Press.

Roskies, A. L. (1999). The binding problem. *Neuron, 24*, 7–9.

Sen, A. (1980). Description as choice. *Oxford Economic Papers, 32*, 353–369.

Sen, A. (1993). Positional objectivity. *Philosophy & Public Affairs, 22*, 126–145.

Tolbert, D. (2016). Truth is the first step towards peace. https://www.ictj.org/news/truth-first-step-peace.

Venkata Rayudu Posina is constructing a category of Reflecting, which is required, in addition to the familiar categories of Being and Becoming, to synthesize ontology and epistemology into which reality is analyzed.

Chapter 14
Dissent and Protest Movements in India: Revisiting Gandhi's Ideas of Peaceful Protest

Ambikesh Kumar Tripathi

Abstract For the last few years, dissents and protests are being seen almost everywhere in the world. Some of them were violent and occupation movements against consumerism, traditional institutions, and capitalism, with little success; while some were peaceful protests against racism, corruption, and the state's policies. Peaceful protests are often characterized as Gandhian movement; but many of such peaceful movement turns violent or disrupted from the notion of Gandhian dissent, for instance, Black Lives Matter movement—a protest against racism—in the US. Many peaceful protests are being organized in the name Gandhian way of dissent across the world without understanding Gandhi's eternal spirit of Satyagraha, and this has led to the flood of critiques against limits of success about it. Scholars of subaltern studies criticize Gandhian Satyagraha as surrender and subordination of poor and oppressed that can never pose real challenges to India's elites. But this is not reality. Gandhi's Satyagraha is based on the purity of soul and theory of persuasion. There is a kind of social construction, not enmity in Gandhian dissents. This research paper attempts to redefine the Gandhian notion of dissent and protest in the twenty-first century. It also analyses some contemporary so-called peaceful movements in India that have been labelled as Gandhian movements—whether they were or not?

Keywords Gandhi · Peaceful protest · Dissent · Satyagraha · Sedition · Non-violent resistance

Introduction

Anthologies on dissent and dissidence are not new; however, one could still comment and reflect on their timing and tonality. Going back to the early-twentieth century, when the choice was between 'a future or no future' (Hobsbawm, 1995) (An eminent Marxist historian from Britain, Eric J. Hobsbawm (1917–2012), having seen the rise of European Fascism in the early-twentieth century summed up the choice of every

---

A. K. Tripathi (✉)
Department of Gandhian and Peace Studies, Mahatma Gandhi Central University (MGCUB), Motihari, Bihar, India

© National Institute of Advanced Studies 2022
A. Behera and S. Nayak (eds.), *Gandhi in the Twenty First Century*,
https://doi.org/10.1007/978-981-16-8476-0_14

thinking individual, and thus his choice of being a Communist, as between 'a world or no world'). George Orwell, a man of the Left, was learning to fragment the Left with capital L into several other lefts. This 'othering' was spatial, ideological, and even dissenting! Orwell, in *Homage to Catalonia* (1938) persistently makes observations that show his gripping disturbance with the Soviet action against Spain, and how in Soviet 'totalitarian certainty' of their worldview, nothing they did, could go wrong. The arrogant coherence of a worldview, which might or might not, accept that there are rival articulations of the world, distinct articulations of social order, regime, and political action, may end up collapsing different categories of dissent and dissidence into activism, crowd action, and sometimes, majoritarianism (Orwell, 1945, 1949). It is important to highlight that Orwell extends the observations of Catalonia in *Animal Farm* (1945), and *Nineteen Eighty-Four* (1949) which are about the dangers of arrogant coherence in worldviews. One led to the Stalinist purge, and the other to dystopian censorship and surveillance. Going back to the anthologies on dissent and their timings, let us gaze on the Indian case. In recent years, we received a flood of essays, compilations, and titles that suggested a celebratory tonality of dissent (Roy, 2020; Thapar, 2020; Vajpeyi, 2017). The implicit and explicit idea in this manifested authorial intent was to suggest that the Indian state was becoming 'intolerant of dissent'. It started with a debate on 'Indian Nationalism', with original contributions on 'what, when and how of Indian nationalism(s)' appearing, while many anthologies were also slated (Thapar et al., 2016; Habib, 2017) The publications on universities as a site of dissent and public action debating nationalism and other categories were also at the foreground at the same time (Nair, 2017; Apoorvananda, 2018). The emphasis on timing is crucial here because dissent has been understood in different ways throughout the long political history of contemporary India, and before. For instance, historians like Romila Thapar would show a lineage of dissent and resistance from the times of Buddha, to date. Of course, they would also accentuate different phases, characteristics, and temporalities of dissent in its long history, but we need to ask why as an operative category and as an instrument of public action, dissent, and peaceful protests become more important in certain times than others? With the advent of political theorizing, at least in the Western school of political thought, in elite Greek intellectual tradition is typically believed that ordinary men are inadequate to rule themselves (Ober, 1998). Therefore, the persistence of Athenian popular rule presented a problem that how to explain a regime's outward success based on the inherent wisdom and robust viability of non-elite citizens' decisions? (Ober, 1998). Are we facing the same problem in modern parliamentary democracy today? It is only pertinent to ask the question because right at the forefront of any organized dissent, which presents itself as a Gandhian peaceful protest, dubbed as *'Grammar of Anarchy'* (phrase used by Dr. B R Ambedkar in the Constituent Assembly in 1949) otherwise, elite intellectuals are omnipresent to make a case for the same. After all, who adjudges a protest as peaceful, or organized? Is it only the public action of the participants at large, or is it something else? Intellectual designs, may be? On the 'Grammar of Anarchy', as rightly articulated by Ambedkar, it is important to revisit his ideas. Bhimrao Ambedkar said in his speech to the Constituent Assembly on November 25, 1949, 'We must forsake revolution's deadly techniques. It entails that civil disobedience, non-cooperation, and satyagraha must be abandoned. There was a plethora of justification for unconstitutional techniques when the constitutional ways were not available for achieving social and economic objectives. There can be no justification for these illegitimate techniques when constitutional methods are open. These tactics are nothing more than the *Grammar of Anarchy*, and the sooner we get rid of them would be better for us' (Ambedkar, 1949).

The Indian Constitution protects freedom of expression, belief, faith, and worship; Article 19(1) ensures freedom of speech and expression, freedom of peaceful assembly and assembly without arms, and freedom to form associations or unions. Do they constitute and define dissent for us? A constitutional limit on dissent, whether we choose to call it a definition, guarantee, or a right, would still not do justice to various forms, contexts, and content of dissent as expressed by people. For instance, the dissent of littérateur might not be the same as those of university students, or farmers at the brink of an agrarian crisis. Dissent regarding gender and cultural diversities might be incompatible. What then really makes the cause of dissenters come together in specific moments of history? Think of May 68. A period of civil unrest which linked universities to the factories. In France, a series occupation protests by students started against consumerism, traditional institutions, and capitalism. The ongoing police repression of demonstrators prompted trade union confederations to urge solidarity strikes, with more than 22% of France's population taking part in the demonstrations (Harman, 1988; Siedman, 2004). Do we have similar instances in the political history of contemporary India? A polity, in which the Gandhian *satyagraha*, and peaceful mass movements, were theorized and tested for the first time, did it reward itself a repetition after the long freedom struggle? India witnessed a range of public outcries and protests over languages, regional configurations, secessionist movements, internal emergency, violent agrarian movements such as Naxalbari, but did these movements, and some of which being dubbed peaceful, rally themselves into a mass movement with class solidarities? As recently as 2016, we witnessed universities, led by Delhi-based Jawaharlal Nehru University (JNU) at the forefront of the student movement. But unlike the meeting of universities and factories in 'May 68' in France, we did not encounter the same in Delhi, 2016.

Non-violent Resistance: When and How?

Non-violent resistance, or more precisely, 'passive resistance' has been a category of critique for long. If we look at Subaltern Studies, the historians collective criticized Gandhi's non-violent leadership of the nationalist movement, claiming that Gandhi constantly attempts to channelize the dissent voices of the poor and oppressed into a non-violent movement that could never be able to pose a real challenge to India's elites (Guha, 1992). In Subaltern historiographic viewpoints, Gandhian notion of dissent is nothing more than a *safety-valve*, that outwards the discontents and anger of oppressed masses through praise and persuasions. It restricts the process of revolutionary restructuring of the society which could have happened and leaves the people at the mercy of the ruler. Gandhi, as Guha (1992) argued, had contempt and fear for the masses, labelling them a violence-prone *mob*. In 1921, Gandhi had railed against what he called *mobocracy*, which he said was undermining the Non-cooperation Movement of that year (Hardiman, 2013). If we expand the breadth of this argument, we find that Subaltern Studies was basically reconfiguring the Rajani Palme Dutt thesis on Gandhi. Dutt has described Gandhian non-violence as 'an apparently innocent humanitarian or expedient term that contained concealed within it, not only the refusal of the final struggle, but also the thwarting of the immediate struggle by the effort to settle the interests of the masses with the interests of the big bourgeoisie and landlords, which were invariably opposed to any decisive mass struggle' (Dutt, 1994). It is interesting to note that Dutt was espousing to the classical Marxist line while explaining the passive resistance, sans considering the realities of mass struggle in a long-time which Gandhi was leading. For instance, consider what Karl Marx had to say about the same. While writing on the bourgeoisie's passive resistance (*passiver Widerstand*) to the demands of the working class in Germany in 1848, Karl Marx has described the 'old state' as 'revolutionary in relation to the conservatives, and conservatives in relation to the revolutionaries' (Marx, 1977).

The Marxist persistence on 'violent revolution' and their deep disgust for 'passive resistance' in the Indian case seems to have changed after the Naxalbari decade (1967–1977) which culminated with the 'internal emergency'. During the Naxalbari decade, the Indian state came down heavily on every attempt to dislodge the public order with contempt and force (Banerjee, 2008). And it led to a churning and intellectual outpouring on why the state, in its nature, deals with passive resistance in deliberation, while dislodges active resistance through force. It has been proposed that passive resistance fosters dialogue, negotiation, and persuasion and does not distance the political allies (Sharp, 1973). Study of Chenoweth and Stephan tells us that 'the literature on non-violent method suggests that it has proven exceedingly effective at a purely pragmatic level all across the world in the twentieth century and beyond. Out of 323 major movements that occurred between 1900 and 2006 that have sought regime change, end of foreign occupation/invasions, etc. Of the 323, the majority in number were violent, while *approximal* 100 were non-violent. The Scholars find in their research the frequency of non-violent movements and their success rates have risen quickly. Contrast to them, violent movements have mostly met with dead ends' (Chenoweth & Stephan, 2011). The question, therefore, would be, could we locate the ongoing protests in India, be at the universities, over parliamentary bills, or simply, in the name of accentuating the right of dissent as a constitutional guarantee, as a shift from 'violent' to 'non-violent' paradigm because of the Gandhian urgency, which was somewhat disregarded and made a cause of derision before?

The Gandhian urgency takes its legitimacy from the history of the nationalist movement. He experimented with many prevalent social assumptions, developing in-depth analyses, comprehensive syntheses, and innovative principles, and rejecting unconvincing and anachronistic ideas. As a reformer, he tackled in a realistic manner the most difficult social evils that had been deeply entrenched in the Indian soil for centuries.This political manoeuvre' means Gandhian way to do politics. Before

Gandhi, the Indian National Congress was limited to some reforms and to get some space in institutions ruled by the Britishers. Gandhian urgency turned this limitation into an approach of movement with greater demands, i.e. the party becoming a movement. This transmutation of 'elitist' into 'mass' which Gandhi brought into life still lives on through what Partha Chatterjee a distinction between 'civil society', which is elite-led and organized, and 'political society', less formalized, unwieldy (Chatterjee, 2003). Chatterjee (1984) has argued that Gandhi makes a fundamental moral critique of civil society. Gandhi, one could argue, critique, not of the moral individual but of the avaricious bourgeois individual. He does not collapse the individual in the community. Rather, the genuine and abstract principles of religion or morality are universal, but they are not always self-evident or could be scientifically or theoretically proved beyond all doubt. Nor is it always found in our scriptures. Gandhi writes, 'the question occurs as to what to do with the Smritis that contain texts... that are repugnant to the moral sense. I have already stated that everything printed in the name of scriptures should not have to be accepted as God's message or inspired words' (Gandhi in Chatterjee, 1984). Chatterjee says, 'truth, according to Gandhi, did not lie in history, and science does not have special access to it. Truth was moral: it is unified, immutable, and transcending... It could only be found in one's own life experience, in the unwavering practise of moral living. It could never be properly described in terms of rational theoretical discourse; lyrical and poetic manifestation could be the only authentic way of expression to it' (Chatterjee, 1984).

The point, then, one could be making is how far the civil society and political society engage and involve themselves in a dialogue while dissenting. And why do they come together being one when there is a Gandhian urgency regarding the protest. Does the idea that for a protest to be successful has gone to the grassroots of democracy, or not? And whether the protests of all kinds feel a pressure of state's contempt for disorder, and thus, shape their protest as peaceful?

Gandhi's Vocabulary

As a practical idealist, if we can call him that, Gandhi acknowledged and accepted the fact that he needed to act through the instruments available in the society at that time. In his initial struggles in South Africa and India, Gandhi first tried to fight injustice through appeals, negotiations, and persuasions with government leaders; presented petitions to legislatures; took legal actions in courts; writes in the mass media, and therefore, mobilizes the public organizations within the existing system of politics and the boundaries of laws. He soon realized that the existing tools and techniques were ineffectual in addressing injustice. He also concluded that the system of laws was unjust and immoral. What then? Whenever the traditional channels for change become ineffectual in a political system, only two outcomes are possible. Either the challenge of change dries up and dies down, or the advocates of change historically speaking, abandon the political system and resort to violent attacks on the system causing deaths and destruction in the name of revolution. For Gandhi only those who is truth seeker can be nonviolent and a nonviolent could be Satyagrahi and ultimately disobedient towards unjust-laws. Gandhi's analysis rejected both options of non-action and violence; his creative genius invented the third option, *Satyagraha—Satya* (Truth) and *Aagrah* (Force), i.e. extra-constitutional means to raise the voice against injustice, which is combined of non-violence and dynamism, without the destruction of the system and without the perpetuation of violence.

The requirement, almost a mandatory condition, of non-violence and passive resistance in Gandhian satyagraha is a strategy at its core. Analysing the nature of social forces, Gandhi correctly concluded that direct non-violent action against an unjust political system cannot be carried out by a handful of elites. When revolutionaries are few, they are tempted to become clandestine and to use violence and terror to become effective. The mass movements, by their nature, cannot rely on the use of violence because of two reasons. In forming the class solidarity, mass movements welcome peasants, students, women, working class, and an array of class allies who are people at large. They cannot be guided through the modus-operandi of 'professional revolutionaries' and have different social and cultural commitments in their everyday. Moreover, they cannot continue with a movement for a very long time. They've to return to their quotidian senses to take care of what they might consider 'normalcy'. Therefore, though as a generalization, but quite provocatively and convincingly, Bipan Chandra, in *The Long-Term Dynamics* offers an almost mathematical equation of S-T-S (Struggle-Truce-Struggle) for the Gandhian mass movements. It essentially argues that the Gandhian mass movement utilized a breathing space of 'truce' to expand on its mass base for the next phase of the movement, while also putting the gains of the last movement to use. This led Gandhi to continuously expand on the mass base of his movements. It always added on new class allies. For instance, believing in the equality of sexes, Gandhi welcomed the women of India in the political space. The earlier cases of women's participation were mostly limited to social and educational reforms, with lone voices from Marathi and Bengali social spaces making echoes. However, Gandhian mass movements welcomed women on a great scale in terms of political viability. In short, Gandhism transformed millions of frustrated, unhappy, and angry people into satyagrahis, non-violent revolutionaries seeking truth and justice. However, it is crucial to analyse, that satyagraha as a strategy works with which kind of state, and in what measures? It is because satyagraha as a concept is closely related to its clone-nemesis which Gandhi called *Duragraha* (read perversity).

Gandhi was operational under a colonial state, a semi-democratic state with a limited franchise in which 'apolitical' gradually was transmuting into 'political' under the tutelage of politics of association and then mass movement. The Gramscian notion of hegemony was applied in the Indian context by Bipan Chandra and Bhagwan Josh. The state, according to Gramsci, is a blend of coercion and hegemony (Gramsci, 1998). As long as a ruling class is capable of moral and political leadership, it enjoys hegemony by achieving the consent of the masses. Chandra (1993) describes the British state as semi-hegemonic and legal authoritarian, based on the fact that the colonial authority relied greatly on the Indian people's acquiescence in their control on the two notions: (1) that the foreign rulers were benevolent and just, (2) that the colonial rulers were invincible.

The basic thesis of the Gandhian strategy was an engagement of political action against the colonial state. This strategy was rooted in the central premise that no state could rule over the individuals without their consent. Burrowes writes, 'Gandhi's struggle in India was based on his observation that illegitimate control can only succeed in certain circumstances' (Burrowes, 1996). And many political commentators and historians have relied on this thesis to expound on the Gandhian mass movement as an exercise in persistently testing and questioning the colonial state's legitimacy. However, there is a problem of overestimation here. Such commentators have hardly considered the conception of collaborators of the state. Even under the colonial state, some 1.8 lakh British personnel (including women and children) ruling some 36 crore Indians cannot be explained without taking the role, functions, and responsibilities of collaborators of the state, who acted in unison to state's law and 'rule of law' in whatever measure it was available to Indians. This point finds an extension in contemporary India in which Gandhi returned to his afterlife as a messiah of protest movements. Even though various protest movements have continuously challenged the legitimacy of the state, a large class of collaborators has stood with the 'rule of law' as the state sees it fit. Collaborators might not always be a category of abuse. People, even in the majority, may choose to be within the realms of the state, and not challenge it, because for them their consent makes it legitimate. In the Gandhian case, barring the well-made distinctions he outlined between satyagraha and *duragraha*, his methods were much abused in a parliamentary democracy in which institutions are lively, functioning, and sensitive. Mostly, it seems that political society, along with civil society, has many times used and abused satyagraha to create a deliberate use of disorder to forge a political bargain. For instance, a bunch of people stopping a railway train marking a chakka jam or band is a common scene in Indian political life. Most of them would claim to be satyagrahis and peaceful protestors. But are they so? Consider an extract on the recent NRC-CAA controversy, which could be quoted at length here, 'One of the CAA-NRC movement's slogans, '*Don't be silent, don't be violent*,' is a simple English translation of Gandhi's main campaigning method, satyagraha. The CAA dissenters face an old challenge: how to build a powerful mass movement without giving a trigger-happy regime the pretext of violent disorder. Gandhi spent his adult life refining his response to that question. In Contemporary resistance movements in South Africa and the United States, Gandhi's methods were studied and adopted with varying degrees of success, but his influence was explicitly acknowledged. On the other hand, 'Gandhi is missing in his own's country, which he had contributed to build, where his experiments in civil disobedience would be expected to be an obvious source of inspiration' (Kesavan, 2021). Gandhi is thoroughly out from contemporary social and political dissent movements in regards to theory as well as in praxis; he has remained only in lip services of the so-called activists.

The commentator while evoking Gandhi and satyagraha never indulges in the analysis of the nature of the state. Is the Indian state today the same semi-democratic, legal authoritarian system, with the limited franchise where people have no refuse but to adopt extra-constitutional methods to push their demand? And have they succeeded in broadening the mass base of their movements like Gandhi did? Moreover, have they truly adhered to the principles of non-violence, which let us say, the long-on-going framer protestors displayed on the Republic Day in 2021? What do we make of these connections where movements of all kinds are dubbed as Gandhian, in the end, in the hope to let them remain non-violent so that they could deal with the state for a successful resolution? Another commentator wrote, 'Gandhi's non-violent approaches are still praised by individuals who want to effect change without resorting to violence. Many people think of Gandhi as a spiritual man who strove to strike a balance in the realm of both- *idea* and *action*, yet he had a dissident mind both as a thinker and as a practitioner. When we speak to Gandhi as a dissident mind, we are referring to him as a non-conformist who lived and thought differently than other people. Gandhi, as a non-conformist, had a strong drive to succeed. In other words, he possessed the character of greatness as a dissident intellect' (Jahanbegloo, 2020).

And the point of analysis of the state and political system goes missing. At some point of time, one starts wondering whether this omission is deliberate, and the key elite intellectuals still scratch their heads on the problem we have started with. The problem of 'how to explain the apparent success of a regime "irrationally" based on the inherent wisdom and practical efficacy of decisions made by non-elite citizens?' In a democratic political system with the universal adult franchise, why do different political persuasions who have ridiculed the Gandhian mass movement and passive resistance are trying hard to evoke peaceful protests on the streets and not let the debates proceed in the elected parliament? The key to understanding this fallacy is to keep our gaze fixed on the state in which Gandhi functioned and operated as a key strategist of a nationalist movement and keep going back to the political historiography of the movement by the key intellectual movements which evoke Gandhi now, tirelessly.

Farmer's Protest: A Case in Point

The ongoing farmer's protest at the Singhu border has been described as '*transcending the barriers of religion, race, class, and wealth*' and 'concerning far more than any agricultural policy' (Kaur, 2021). There have been attempts to locate the contemporary farmer's protest on the lines of a long resistance against global capitalism, authoritarianism, and even a challenge to the 'populist hegemony of the Right in India' (Gudavarthy, 2021). However, with a movement which is still unfolding with some mentionable timeline signifiers, could it be adjudged for causing a cleavage in what was just a year ago was analysed by the commentators as 'producing an optic of conflict between '*economic elites*' and '*cultural subalterns*' (Ibid). Who is who in this conflict and the movement, anyway? The protesting farmers, majorly from Punjab, Haryana, and western Uttar Pradesh are supposedly the most prosperous in their economic category. Are they farming elites, cultural subalterns, or are they peasantry, which Gandhi mobilized in the past? We cannot be sure! As the event unfolds between the site of protest, public meeting, and organized marches on the one side, and news headlines, and quick turns in scholarly commentaries, on the other, the operative categories of protest seem to have been lost in the foreground. The protest started with dissatisfaction with three agricultural legislations, and as people kept joining it, so did the issues take on an additive proportionality. A Gandhian perspective would require shaping a dialogue with the protesting farmers straightaway, and asking them, are they seeking an acceptance of their demand by the Government of India, or are they organising some 'Occupy Movement' to challenge the global capitalism?

Peasants were not supposed to be political, in the first place. Arguably, they were in an 'apolitical' category. Their consciousness, or the idea of being a 'class for itself' has been described as 'vague', suggesting that, 'this hazy consciousness of 'peasantness' as a subset of subalternity, poverty, exploitation, and oppression has no geographical boundaries because it is based on peasants' mutual recognition of the similarity of their relationships to nature, production, and non-peasants' (Hobsbawm, 1973). Peasants had to undergo the transformation of industrial labour and urban unions to be politically organized, and then, become 'clearly' political. It is important to mention here that the debates on peasant and industrial labour are extensive and have been discussed with geographical and political nuances. Going back to those debates, here, is beyond the scope of this paper. Subaltern Studies, responding and critiquing to the earlier Marxist position, basing itself on the Maoist premises, and the 'Southern Question' as described by Antonia Gramsci argued that Indian peasant was 'political' and had a 'subaltern consciousness' right now it started resisting the colonial state and never allowed it to present itself as a hegemonic power; it remained only dominant (Guha, 1997). And then, enters Gandhi. As discussed above, the Gandhian emphasis on non-violence and passive resistance with peasants as the core of mass movement allowed it to call any violent ruptures as 'mobocracy'. Peasants in the accidental and uncontrolled reaction of 'Chauri Chaura', in a moment, became the 'mob' from Satyagrahis (Amin, 2006). Ranajit Guha described this usage of 'mobocracy' by Gandhi as 'an ugly word greased with loathing, a sign of craving for control and its frustration, [that] is lifted directly out of the lexicon of elitist usage' (Guha, 1993). The idea being that the Working Class, Proletariat, Peasants, Subaltern, and finally, and recently, Multitude in the lineage of a romantic search for the revolutionary class may swiftly oscillate between 'people' (read subjects or citizens) and 'mob' based on their method of political mobilization. As scholars have observed, 'In the long romantic search of a revolutionary class, Hardt and Negri's 'Multitude' is the latest. 'From the working class to the multitude, the conditions and functionalities of these classes have multiplied and muscled through the theorization of intellectual elites, and sometimes, by the revolutionaries themselves' (Negri & Hardt, 2004). The moment of violence decisively prejudges whether the drivers of a protest would be called 'people' or 'mob'! A brief detour is warranted here. On 25 August 2017, rife rioting in northern India began after Gurmeet Ram Rahim, patron of a Dera in Haryana was convicted of rape. The riots, firstly, broke out in Panchkula and were quickly spread to other parts of Haryana, Punjab, western Uttar Pradesh, and the national capital region of Delhi. At least 41 people were killed, many of them in Panchkula, where 32 people were allegedly killed by police gunfire. The rioters in this case could be identified as peasants, working class, or citizens, among other. However, most contemporary commentators identified them as 'mobs' in the news analysis. They were called out as 'anarchist' with a leading national daily suggesting. Indeed, mob violence is difficult to control without resorting to excessive force, but the government appeared to rely only on the sect's followers' good judgement in this situation (The Hindu, 2017). The historiographic and theoretical question which stays with us is this. How do we decide whether a class of people, in their acts of political action and mobilization, are showing themselves as 'crowd', 'mob' or 'citizens'? (Rudé, 1964, 1980).

It brings us to our point-in-case. The protesting farmers on January 26, 2021, in their tractor rally to the Red Fort, were identifying themselves as, what? Were they up to break the 'Right-wing hegemony' or offered subaltern resistance to global capitalism, as some commentators have suggested? A political commentator in one of the popular news websites evoked Gramsci, that great Italian theorist and activist, arguing that a democratic state can only remain democratic if it can elicit voluntary consent to its policies through reasoned persuasion.; he called this 'hegemony' (Raina, 2021); and, when it fails to do so, as a last resort, it uses coercive measures, such as engineering violence to discredit anyone who opposes its authority (Ibid). The commentator was writing a eulogy for the farmers' tractor rally on the Republic Day, even going far as to call it, 'A Republic Day Like No Other: Not the State but "We the People" Will Take Centre-stage' (Ibid). Next day, after the rally turned violent, right at the Red Fort, the same news space got weary and busy analysing the reasons for violence and finding the identities of the perpetrators (Kumar, 2021). Another national daily which has been cited above calling protestors in the Dera case as mob, in the case of farmers' protest suggested, 'the anarchy and mindless violence unleashed on the nation's capital by a section of protesting farmers on Republic Day were reprehensible' (The Hindu, 2021).

The reasons for the point-in-case are simple and may be summed up here in three pointers. The consensus over the efficacy and significance of peaceful protests and passive resistance is complete, concise, and coherent. The analyses of tactical and strategical vantage points of any movements and protests would defect the moment violent ruptures are identified. Secondly, the constitutional limits of dissent, despite offering a lot to shape and nurture it, limit the causalities of anarchy and disorder. And, lastly, the intellectual elites may have their reasonings to define the nature of a protest, but their lexicon might not always have sufficient vocabulary and categories to do so. The Gandhian urgency of any protest and movement in a parliamentary democracy is bound by a limit of non-violence. It was true for the colonial state; it remains so for the post-colonial continuums. In fact, the nature of both these states shares a consensus over the efficacy of non-violence, and their contempt for violence. The 'political society' which at many times is shaped and defined by 'Crowds in History' might not always choose an organized passive resistance to raise its concerns, but the 'civil society' for sure would distance itself from any organized or spontaneous violence due to statist compulsions. Gandhi, both as a method and action, necessarily reiterates this point.

References

Amin, S. (2006). *Event, memory, metaphor: Chauri chaura, 1920–1922*. Delhi: Penguin.
Apoorvananda (Ed.). (2018). *The idea of university*. Delhi: Context.
Banerjee, S. (2008). *In the wake of Naxalbari*. New Delhi: Shishu Sahitya Samsad Pvt. Limited.
Burrowes, R. J. (1996). *The strategy of nonviolent defense—A Gandhian approach*. Albany State University of New York Press.
Chandra, B. (1993). *Indian national movement—The long dynamics* (p. 18). New Delhi: Vikas Publishing House Pvt. Ltd.
Chatterji, P. (1984). Gandhi and the critique of civil society. In R. Guha (ed.), *Subaltern studies III*. Delhi: Oxford University Press.
Chatterji, P. (2003). *The politics of the governed: Reflections on popular politics in most of the world*. Delhi: Permanent Black.
Chenoweth, E., & Stephan, M. J. (2011). *Why civil resistance works: The strategic logic nonviolent conflict*. New York: Columbia University Press.
Dutt, R. P. (1994). *India To-Day* (pp. 307–308). New Delhi: People's Publishing House.
George O. (2021). *Nineteen Eighty-Four* (Edited with an introduction and Notes by John Bowen). Oxford: Oxford University Press.
Gramsci, A. (1998). *Selections from the prison notebooks* (p. 12). Chennai: Orient Longman. (Reprint), p. 12.
Gudavarthy, A. (2018). *India after Modi: Populism and the right*. Delhi: Bloomsbury.
Gudavarthy, A. (2021, 20 February). Populism and rhetoric amidst farmers' protest in India, E-International relations. Retrieved April 23, 2021, from https://www.e-ir.info/2021/02/20/opinion-populism-and-rhetoric-amidst-the-farmers-protest-in-india/.
Guha, R. (1992). *In 'discipline and mobilize' subaltern studies* (Vol. VII). Delhi: Oxford University Press.
Guha, R. (1993). Discipline and mobilize. In P. Chatterjee & G. Pandey (Eds.), *Subaltern studies VII: Writings on south asian history and society* (pp. 69–120). New Delhi: Oxford University Press.
Guha, R. (1997). *Dominance without hegemony history and power in colonial India*. Harvard University Press.
Habib, S. I. (Ed.). (2017). *Indian nationalism: The essential writings*. Delhi: Aleph Book Co.
Hardiman, D. (2013). Towards a history of non-violent resistance. *Economic and Political Weekly, 48*(23), 41–48. Retrieved August 24, 2021, from http://www.jstor.org/stable/23527210.
Harman, C. (1988). *The fire last time: 1968 and after*. London: Bookmarks.
Hobsbawm, E. (1973). Peasants and politics. *The Journal of Peasant Studies, 1*(1), 3–22.
Hobsbawm, E. J. (1995). *Age of extremes: The short twentieth century, 1914–1991*. London: Abacus.
Rudé, G. (1964). *The crowd in history. A study of popular disturbances in France and England, 1730–1848*. New York: Wiley.
Rudé, G. (1980). *Also, ideology and popular protest*. New York: Lawrence & Wishart.
Sharp, G. (1973). *Politics of non-violent action, Part 3: The dynamics of non-violent action* (pp. 594–810). Boston: Porter Sargent.
Siedman, M. (2004). *The imaginary revolution: Parisian students and workers in 1968*. Berghahn.
Thapar, R. (2020). *Voice of dissent: An essay*. Delhi: Seagull Books.
Thapar, R., et al. (2016). *On nationalism*. Delhi: Aleph Book Co.
Jahanbegloo, R. (January 30, 2020). Gandhi, the Dissident. *The Hindu*. Retrieved January 13, 2021, from https://www.thehindu.com/opinion/op-ed/gandhi-the-dissident/article30686019.ece.

Kaur, S. (February 17, 2021). India's farmers are protesting authoritarianism disguised as capitalism. Sounds familiar?' *NBC News*. Retrieved April 23, 2021, from https://www.nbcnews.com/think/opinion/india-s-farmers-are-protesting-authoritarianism-disguised-capitalism-sound-familiar-ncna1258028.

Kesavan, M. (June 24, 2021). Missing Gandhi. *The Telegraph*. Retrieved June 25, 2021, from https://www.telegraphindia.com/opinion/mahatma-gandhi-political-mobilzation-should-be-a-lesson-for-future-protests-and-dissent/cid/1736956.

Kumar, R. (2021). Here's what really happened during the republic day tractor rally. *The Wire*, January 27, 2021. Retrieved May 10, 2021, from https://thewire.in/agriculture/farmers-republic-day-tractor-march-eyewitness-account.

Marx, K. (1977). The bourgeoisie and the counter-revolution, Neue Rheinische Zeitung, 15 December 1848, in Karl Marx and Frederick Engels, Collected Works, vol. 8, 1848–1849. London: Lawrence and Wishart.

Nair, J., et al. (2017). *What the nation really need to know: The JNU nationalism lectures*. Delhi: Harper Collins.

Negri, A., & Hardt, M. (2004). *Multitude: War and democracy in the age of empire*. New York: Penguin.

Ober, J. (1998). *Political dissent in democratic Athens*. Princeton University Press.

Orwell, G. (1945). *Animal farm: A fairy story*. London: Secker and Warburg.

Raina, B. (2021). A Republic Day like no other: Not the State but 'we the people' will take centrestage. *The Wire*. January 26, 2021. Retrieved May 10, 2021, from https://thewire.in/rights/republic-day-2021-we-the-people-centrestage-farmers-tractor-rally.

Roy, A. (2020). *Azadi: Freedom, fascism, fiction*. Delhi: Penguin.

The Hindu. (2017, 27 August). Anarchy in Panchkula: Gurmeet Ram Rahim Singh's Conviction. Retrieved May 10, 2021, from https://www.thehindu.com/opinion/editorial/anarchy-in-panchkula/article19571267.ece.

The Hindu. (2021, 28 January). A wrong turn: On Republic Day violence. Retrieved on May 10, 2021, from https://www.thehindu.com/opinion/editorial/a-wrong-turn-the-hindu-editorial-on-violence-at-farmers-republic-day-tractor-rally/article33679024.ece.

Vajpeyi, A. (2017). *India dissents: 3000 years of difference, doubt, and argument*. Delhi: Speaking Tiger.

Dr. Ambikesh Kumar Tripathi is an Assistant Professor in the Department of Gandhian and Peace Studies and Coordinator of Centre for Gandhian Research at Mahatma Gandhi Central University (MGCUB), Motihari, Bihar.

Chapter 15
Mahatma Gandhi: Architect of Non-violent Conflict Resolution

Pascal Alan Nazareth

Abstract In this chapter, Gandhi as an 'architect of non-violent conflict resolution' is discussed. While Gandhi's ideas of *Ahmisa* (Non-violence) and *Satyagraha* were found to be discussed in popular discourses, the use of Gandhian ideas to resolve internal conflicts in many countries outside India. This chapter begins with engaging with the concepts of Soul force and truth force and their influence in the peaceful resolution of conflicts globally. This chapter attempts to revisit the non-violent conflict resolution strategy advocated by Gandhi. In the process of doing so, the first part of the chapter highlights the philosophy behind Gandhi's strong belief in *Satyagraha* in resolving violent conflicts. The second part of the paper highlights the influence and effectiveness of Gandhi's own experience with non-violent conflict resolution and the role of Gandhian principles globally. The third section of the paper offers the need for revisiting Gandhi in peacefully resolving the conflicts in twenty-first century.

Keywords Mahatma Gandhi · Conflict resolution · Non-violence · Soul force · *Satyagraha*

Introduction

Arguably, or it goes without any argument, Mahatma Gandhi pioneered the idea of the non-violent way of resolving conflicts. Gandhi's idea of *Satyagraha* offers a simple, non-antagonistic, yet very effective way forward to deal with violent conflicts in a peaceful manner. The power of *soul force,* as it has been a popular concept in outside India, has been instrumental in more than one way to fight violence and injustice and has come out victorious in terms of liberating the weak and subsequently empowering them. While there is hardly any major work, scholarly and otherwise, that contests Gandhi's non-violent conflict resolution methods; the strategies adopted to deal with the violent conflicts do not really follow the Gandhian Path. This paper is an attempt to revisit the non-violent conflict resolution strategy advocated by Gandhi. In the

P. A. Nazareth (✉)
Former Indian Diplomat, Bengaluru, India

© National Institute of Advanced Studies 2022
A. Behera and S. Nayak (eds.), *Gandhi in the Twenty First Century*,
https://doi.org/10.1007/978-981-16-8476-0_15

process of doing so, the first part of the paper highlights the philosophy behind Gandhi's strong belief in *Satyagraha* in resolving violent conflicts. The second part of the paper highlights the influence and effectiveness of Gandhi's own experience with non-violent conflict resolution and the role of Gandhian principles globally. The third section of the paper offers the need for revisiting Gandhi in peacefully resolving the conflicts in twenty-first century.

Gandhi's ideas on non-violent conflict resolution are based on the concept of *Satyagraha*. In this context, the pursuit of attainment of peace can be articulated around three important aspects: truth, non-violence, and justice. An important step towards non-violence in a conflictual situation could be through not aiming for the seizure of power, rather the engagement should be towards the transformation of relationship between the conflicting parties. The engagement of two parties without antagonizing the relationship would work towards attaining peace and subsequently ensuring justice. The crux of Gandhi's ideas for peaceful and non-violent conflict resolution can be traced through the following articulation of his ideas.

At the centre of Gandhi's ideas of non-violent conflict resolution is *Satya*, the truth. For him, *Satya* can hardly be destroyed as it holds the world and in nutshell, holding on to *Satya* is the doctrine of *Satyagraha* (Gandhi, 1968). Accordingly, it is only through holding on to the truth which implies justice, peace can be achieved (Gandhi, 2012). While articulating the process of achieving peace through holding on to the truth, Gandhi reflects on an important issue of power. Linking power to the God, Gandhi highlights it as a living force that pervades everything. However, contrary to the popular understanding of power which often connotes a negative meaning, Gandhi articulates power through 'soul force' which connotes the living law of life (Gandhi as cited in Nazareth, 2011). Power, as law of love, can be applied with 'scientific precision' to resolve conflicts and thereby establish peace. The consent of the people to be governed, for Gandhi, is a critical aspect of any government. It is only through the consent of the people, directly or indirectly, the governments derive power. Hence, consent is a sign of a dialogical process that should not be undermined by the power holder (Gandhi as cited in Swaminathan and Patel, 1988). Contrary to the violent revolutions, the objectives of Gandhi's non-violent struggle aren't guided by the objectives of seizing complete power. Rather, the non-violent struggle aims at arriving at mutually acceptable agreements (Weber, 2001). In this process, issues like defeating or humiliating the opponent, which often lead to conflicts, are absent. Gandhi's ideas of non-violent struggle through understanding the positions of opponents make efforts in transforming relationships through a peaceful transfer of power (Gandhi as cited in Thomas Merton, 2007). For Gandhi, several conflicts and misunderstandings will disappear only if the opponents make efforts to understand each other's positions (Gandhi, 2009). With this brief introduction on peaceful and non-violent resolution of conflicts, the following section highlights Gandhi's experience in this regard.

Gandhi's Experience with Peaceful Conflict Resolution

The first major conflict issue Gandhi faced was *racialism* because of which he was thrown out of the first-class carriage he was seated in at Pietermaritzburg Station in South Africa, despite having a first-class ticket and not causing any disturbance to a fellow passenger. When this happened, he was initially tempted to return to India but recalled Lord Krishna's injunction in the Bhagwat Gita that when faced with injustice and evil, one's bounden duty is to confront it irrespective of success or failure. Being deeply imbued with Jainism's *Ahimsa Paramo Dharma* ethical values he was aware that he had to do this non-violently. From Christ's 'Sermon on the Mount' exhortation that 'Blessed are those who are persecuted because of righteousness' he was conscious that this would entail self-suffering. His *Satyagraha* conflict resolution strategy, which he conceived at this time and publicly enunciated on September 11, 1906, emanated from these spiritual inspirations. The prime requirements for its practice were a deep faith in the firm commitment to truth, love, and non-violence. It also required identification of the root causes of every conflict before undertaking to confront it.

Richard Attenborough's 'Gandhi' film clearly show's where and how Gandhi enunciated his *Satyagraha* strategy and launched it by burning his supporters' racial identity passes as their protest the unjust humiliating racial laws of South Africa. It also shows their subsequent imprisonment suffering for this 'crime' as also their final triumph. What it does not show is the amazing transformation in the relationship between General Smuts and Gandhi. The former had inflicted much humiliation and suffering on Gandhi yet in taking leave of him on the eve of his departure for India, Gandhi presented him with a pair of slippers he had himself made while in prison. The general preserved them and some years later paid Gandhi the following glowing tribute:

> Gandhi was one of the great men of my time and my acquaintance with him over a period of 30 years has only deepened my high respect for him. I always found him ready to discuss in a reasonable and fair-minded manner and always searching for a solution along peaceful lines. Gandhi has left behind a name almost unequalled in the world today. He is an outstanding leader of men (Smuts, 2019).

The Attenborough film also shows how effectively Gandhi handled the conflict between the indigo farmers of Champaran and their British landlords and between the Indian people and their colonial masters over the unjust Salt Law. Both these conflicts were settled with mutual satisfaction and without animosity despite the injustices and sufferings inflicted by the British on the Indians. When Independence was granted, both sides parted as friends and India joined the British Commonwealth as an equal partner. It also requested Lord Mountbatten, the British Viceroy, to take the charge of its Governor General until its Constitution was drafted and adopted and it emerged as a sovereign republic. Writing on Gandhi's contribution to India's freedom struggle through non-violent means, Arnold Toynbee, a British historian, wrote that 'Gandhi was as much a benefactor of Britain as of his own country. He made it impossible for us to go on ruling India but at the same time made it possible for us to abdicate without rancour and without dishonour' (Arnold Toynbee in Nanda, 2010).

The radical transformation which Gandhi's *Satyagraha* strategy brought about in India is also noteworthy. Almost overnight, a minimally democratic, highly caste ridden, feudal, women and untouchables oppressed India changed the form of governance to a constitutional democracy ending the age-old discriminatory practices based on various social and gendered divisions. The new India adopted the universal adult franchise with an objective to ensure equality, empowering the disadvantaged sections, and moreover, creating spaces for democratic values both socially and politically.

Gandhi's *Satyagraha:* A Global Phenomenon

The extent to which Gandhi's *Satyagraha* (known in the US and other foreign countries as *Soul Force*) strategy has transformed the global scenario is seen in the following facts: When India attained Independence and was admitted to the UN, it was its 37th member. Today it has 192 members. Nearly all these 155 new UN member countries are former European colonies. Most of them attained their independence through 'soul force' struggles, aided by India's strenuous decolonization efforts at the UN.

The US had fought a four year-long civil war to abolish slavery and preserve its unity. It lost more of its soldiers in this war (mainly because of lack of medical care for the wounded) than in the two World Wars. Yet the political and social status of the former slaves remained largely unchanged until one intrepid middle aged, Gandhi inspired a woman named Rosa Parks (Kohl, 1991), who resisted to give up her seat to a white co-passenger on a Montgomery City bus on December 1, 1955, as she was then legally required to do. She was penalized for this 'crime' with a fine and imprisonment. But the year-long boycott of the Montgomery City buses which that city's blacks, which was conceived led by another Gandhi inspired, recently ordained, a 24-year-old black pastor named Martin Luther King initially bankrupted the mentioned bus company and subsequently led to the US Supreme Court banning racial discrimination in all public services and places all over the US. The crowning glory of this national movement to end racial discrimination in the US, which Rosa Parks triggered and Martin Luther King had led for 13 years until his assassination in 1968, was the entry of president (from a black community) in the White House in January 2008. For over 50 years now, Rosa Parks has been hailed as the 'Mother of the American Freedom Movement'. When she died in 2005 at age 92, her body was placed in the 'Rotunda' in Washington for public tribute and a statue of hers now adorns its Statuary of America's most renowned leaders.

In South Africa, its many centuries of racial discrimination and many decades of Apartheid were finally ended with a 5 year, arduous 'soul force' in Port Elizabeth led by its black youth leaders (Marable, 1998). When this happened, Colonel Laurent

Du Plessis, former Chief of Military Intelligence of South Africa's Eastern Cape province declared (as seen in the *'Force More Powerful' film* titled *'Freedom in our Lifetime'*), the *'armed struggle came to nothing.... It was the people's mass action, the economic boycotts and international pressure, that brought about the change. The boycotts were very effective. Not to buy is not a crime. What do you do with people who do not buy? You cannot shoot all of them. De Klerk had no option but to take the action he did'*. The action that President F. W. De Klerk took when he succeeded P.W. Botha (who resigned in 1989) was to lift the ban on Black political parties, free Nelson Mandela, and negotiate a new constitution with him based on universal adult franchise and hold South Africa's first free elections in 1994. The ANC won an overwhelming victory and Mandela became the President. From being Africa's pariah state, South Africa suddenly emerged as its most admired nation and Mandela as the symbol of its indomitable will for freedom. However, the real heroes of its freedom struggle were 27-year-old, Port Elizabeth youth organizer Mkhuseli Jack, and his collaborators Tango Lamani, Mike Xego, and Janet Cherry.

Also, in the 1980s, the Marcos dictatorship, in the Philippines, was ended with a 'soul force' struggle led by the brave Mrs. Corazon Aquino, widow of assassinated senator Benigno Aquino, who had contested against President Marcos in an earlier election. Her struggle, which was supported by the Catholic church and millions of Filipinos was hailed as the ERDA (Peoples Power) Revolution, as she defeated Ferdinand Marcos in the 1986 presidential election to become the President of the Philippines (1986–1992). It is important to mention that she was Asia's first woman head of state.

During the same period, all Eastern Europe's Communist dictatorships, including that of the Soviet Union were ended with 'soul force' struggles. These commenced in Poland. This one, known as 'Solidarność' was led for almost ten years by a Gdansk shipyard worker named Lech Walesa. Awarded with the prestigious Nobel Prize in 1983, he was also elected as the President of Poland in 1990. The 'soul force struggle' in Czechoslovakia, known as the 'Velvet Revolution' was led by its reputed dramatist Vaclav Havel. He was elected president of Czechoslovakia in 1989 and of the Czech Republic in 1993. He has described 'soul force' as 'Power of the Powerless'.

In March 1990, the 17-year Augusto Pinochet military dictatorship in Chile was ended with a similar 'soul force' struggle which was fought mainly with silent street marches and television messages of 'Chile Si, Pinochet No' (Chile Yes, Pinochet No).

Perhaps the most unusual of these momentous struggles is that of Evo Morales (Webber, 2010), a minimally educated Aymara (indigenous Bolivian) cocoa, farmer who led a march in 2003 from the small provincial town of Cochabamba to La Paz, Bolivia's capital. He had only about 50 other marchers with him when he started, but when he reached La Paz, their number had swelled to almost 10,000. Their demand was simple. Raise the royalty on Bolivia's natural gas exports from 15 to 50% and utilize this additional revenue for providing education, housing, and medical facilities to the Bolivian people, particularly its indigenous communities. The govt. then in office rejected this demand and in the ensuing turmoil had to demit office. The next govt. initially resisted this demand but thereafter was constrained to accept it. This greatly enhanced Evo Morales's popularity and enabled him to win the 2006 presidential election and become Bolivia's first Aymara president since its conquest by Spain 500 years earlier. He is still in that high office and has done much to ameliorate the political and social status and living conditions of his fellow Aymara people.

Until 1947, almost all the world map was in five colours: pink for British, Green for French, Yellow for Portuguese, blue for Italians, and brown for Belgians. The world map is now free of all these colours. There has never been a more radical transformation of global political geography as between 1947 (when India attained independence) and 1997 (when the last British Colony was returned to China). But the trigger for this incredible transformation was gestated in 1894, at Pietermaritzburg in South Africa, when a 24-year-old, three piece suited Indian barrister was thrown out of a first-class carriage because of the colour of his skin and was transformed from a timid young man into a fearless *Soul Force Warrior* determined to confront racialism and all other such social evils and the conflicts they engender with Truth, love, and non-violence.

Conclusion

The world in twenty-first century is witnessing several violent conflicts in different forms and shades. While the countries faced with violent conflicts experiment with multiple strategies to deal with these violent conflicts; a simple, yet well-tested *Satyagraha* strategy somehow goes untried. The politics of antagonism and binary could be the sole factor behind the political leaders not showing enough courage to adopt *Satyagraha* and effectively deal with the violent conflicts in a peaceful manner. As we experience more such conflicts, it is important to fall back on Gandhi's ideas. In conclusion, I would like to highlight three of the innumerable tributes that have been to Gandhi as the architect of non-violent conflict resolution.

One can safely argue that people will continue to turn to Gandhi for peaceful resolutions whenever they face violent episodes: be it religious riots, military occupation, ethnic conflicts, internal instabilities, or any other forms of hostilities. King (1999), corroborates such a position in her book on Gandhi and Martin Luther King Jr. According to Mary E. King, Gandhi pioneered in fighting multiple forms of militant struggles: colonialism, casteism, racism, economic exploitation, religious and ethnic supremacy, for people's democracy, and for peaceful social and political transformations. Hence, the relevance of Gandhi and his ideas will not die down unless conflicts cease to exist.

A pioneer of peace, Gandhi experimented with 'war without violence' (Sharp, 2005). Though some thinkers might find the ideas and works of Gandhi towards non-violent conflict resolution not adequate in every circumstance, but they all agree to the point that his ideas represented historic significance to the ethical values in socio-political interactions. Gandhi's ideas showed the way out for peaceful yet effective resistance to oppression and injustice. Having discussed Gandhi's ideas on non-violent resolution of conflicts and their relevance in contemporary society, I would like to conclude the paper with the words of Ralph Bultjens (1984) on Gandhi:

> The fragility of modern civilization is exposed by the frighteningly ineffective way in which our world approaches conflict resolution….This somewhat pessimistic reading of history is challenged by one major exception, Mahatma Gandhi's application of policies and techniques of non-violence in India. Gandhi's success both redeems human nature from the inevitability of its historical experience and suggests the viability of non-violence in modern situations.

References

Gandhi, M. K. (1968). *Satyagraha in South Africa, Part II, Chapter 16 on "Women in Jail"* (p. 323). Navjivan Press.
Gandhi, M. (2007). *In Thomas Merton. Gandhi on non-violence* (p. 40). New Directions Publishing.
Gandhi, M. K. (1988). The theory and practice of passive resistance. In K. Swaminathan, & C. N. Patel (Eds.), *A Gandhi Reader* (p. 21). Hyderabad: Orient Longman.
Gandhi, M. K. (2009). Non-violent resistance. In R. J. Pennock, & J. W. Chapman (Eds.), *Political and legal obligation* (pp. 193–194). New Brunswick: Aldine Transaction.
Gandhi, M. K. (2012). *Non-violent resistance: Satyagraha*. Dover Publications Inc.
King, M. E. (1999). *Mahatma Gandhi and Martin Luther King Jr.—The power of non-violent action*. Paris: UNESCO.
Kohl, H. (1991). The politics of children's literature: The story of Rosa Parks and the Montgomery Bus Boycott. *Journal of Education, 173*(1), 35–50.
Marable, M. (1998). *Black leadership*. Columbia University Press.
Nanda, B. R. (2010). *Gandhi and his Critics*. Oxford University Press.
Nazareth Pascal Alan. (2011). Fathoming the sources and significance of Swami Vivekananda's humanism and universalism. *Quest-the Journal of UGC-ASC Nainital, 5*(2), 173–178.
Sharp, G. (2005). *Waging nonviolent struggle: 20th Century practice and 21st century potential*. Porters Sargent Publishers.
Smuts, J. C. *Tribute to Mahatma Gandhi*. Retrieved September 15, 2019, from https://gandhiashramsabarmati.org/en/the-mahatma/tributes.html#sliderid-29-30.
Webber, J. R. (2010). Carlos Mesa, Evo Morales, and a Divided Bolivia (2003–2005). *Latin American Perspectives, 37*(3), 51–70.
Weber, T. (2001). Gandhian philosophy, conflict resolution theory and practical approaches to negotiation. *Journal of Peace Research, 38*(4), 493–513.

Pascal Alan Nazareth is a former Indian Diplomat served in India's diplomatic and consular missions in Tokyo, Rangoon, Lima, London, Chicago, and New York and as India's High Commissioner to Ghana and Ambassador to Liberia, Togo, Burkina Faso, Egypt, Mexico, Guatemala and El Salvador

CPSIA information can be obtained
at www.ICGtesting.com
Printed in the USA
BVHW041755160223
658686BV00009B/183

9 789811 684784